Caroline Sanderson and later worked in publishing before becoming a freelance writer and books journalist. She compiles monthly non-fiction previews for *The Bookseller* magazine where she is Associate Editor. She is also programme director of Stroud Book Festival and a Royal Literary Fund Writing for Life Fellow, supporting writing skills within the NHS. In 2024, she was appointed Honorary President of the Society of Indexers. The author of six non-fiction books, Sanderson is married with two twenty-something children, and lives in the Gloucestershire Cotswolds in a house with too few bookshelves. Music was her first love, and will quite possibly be her last.

BY THE SAME AUTHOR

Pick Your Brains: Greece
A Rambling Fancy: In the Footsteps of Jane Austen
Kiss Chase and Conkers: The Games We Played
Someone Like Adele
Jane Austen: The Life of a Literary Titan

LISTEN WITH FATHER

How I Learned to Love Classical Music

Caroline Sanderson

unbound

First published in 2025

Unbound
An imprint of Boundless Publishing Group
c/o Max Accountants, Ketton Suite, The King Centre,
Main Road, Barleythorpe, Rutland, LE15 7WD
www.unbound.com
All rights reserved

© Caroline Sanderson, 2025

The right of Caroline Sanderson to be identified as the author
of this work has been asserted in accordance with Section 77 of the Copyright,
Designs and Patents Act, 1988. No part of this publication may be copied,
reproduced, stored in a retrieval system, or transmitted, in any form
or by any means without the prior permission of the publisher, nor be
otherwise circulated in any form of binding or cover other than that in
which it is published and without a similar condition being imposed
on the subsequent purchaser.

While every effort has been made to trace the owners of copyright material reproduced
herein, the publisher would like to apologise for any omissions and will be pleased to
incorporate missing acknowledgements in any further editions.

Typeset by Jouve (UK), Milton Keynes

A CIP record for this book is available from the British Library

ISBN 978-1-78965-205-5 (paperback)
ISBN 978-1-78965-206-2 (ebook)

Printed in Great Britain by Clays Ltd, Elcograf S.p.A.

1 3 5 7 9 8 6 4 2

In memoriam
Peter Darrell Sanderson
1934–2013

And for my mother, Margaret Sanderson

Music is as powerful as it gets. It is love made liquid.

Bella Bathurst, *Sound: A Story of Hearing Lost and Found* (2017)

Contents

Overture   1

1. The Effect of Mozart   5
   Piano Concerto No. 22 in E-flat major, K. 482
2. The Rite of Stravinsky   37
   The Firebird Suite, Petrushka and The Rite of Spring
3. The Feelings of Ferrier   67
   'Blow the Wind Southerly' (traditional)
4. The Love of Brahms   97
   Symphony No. 4 in E minor
5. The Serendipities of Schumann   121
   Kinderszenen, Robert Schumann and Piano Concerto in A minor, Clara Schumann
6. The Swan Songs of Sibelius   157
   Symphonies No. 5 in E-flat major, No. 6 in D minor and No. 7 in C major
7. The Consolations of Chopin   193
   Études, Opus 10
8. The Soul of Strauss   221
   Ein Heldenleben

Coda	243
Acknowledgements	253
Bibliography	255
Recordings	259
Notes	263
Supporters	271
In Memoriam	275

Overture

It's a bright Sunday morning. Here I come, four years old, walking down the stairs at home. Across the parquet floor of the hall I can see the door to the dining room is ajar. Music flows from behind it and, so it feels, right at me. I step forward and into its embrace. I listen. Then I tiptoe to the door and push it open so I can see my daddy's blue reel-to-reel tape recorder in the corner of the room. I love watching the spinning reels of this machine, marvelling at the way the tape unwinds from the fast-moving left-hand one, while winding up much more slowly on the right-hand one. But today it is the music that has my full attention.

Daddy is sitting at the dining table, his dark wavy hair flopping across his forehead as he frowns at his weekend paperwork. He looks up at the interruption, and then smiles when he realises that I, too, am listening to his music. It is Mozart's Piano Concerto No. 22 in E-flat major, he tells me – the third movement, the Rondo. I quickly forget the name and number of the piece. But to the day Daddy dies, I remember the Rondo.

Forty-six years later, I am driving up the M5 motorway. It's a fine April morning, and Dad has been dead for two and a half years. The sun warms the right side of my face to a blush as I drive north, the baby alps of the Malvern Hills filling the western horizon.

My car stereo is playing the Rondo of Mozart's Piano Concerto No. 22 in E-flat major. It's a CD I took on impulse from Dad's collection soon after he died. The soloist is Alfred Brendel, playing with the orchestra of the Academy of St Martin in the Fields, conducted by Sir Neville Marriner. It's unusual for me to listen to classical music in the car: I generally cue my vintage iPod up with some Lucinda Williams or Nanci Griffith, or another of the rootsy Americana singers I love. But for some reason I am listening to this piece again today, and I turn the volume up loud like some baroque boy racer.

The music scours through me as I drive; it is as if a chemical is being streamed through my nervous system. I badly want to pull over with the sting of it, but I can't.

Dad is suddenly next to me again. He isn't alive, but the music brings him back from wherever he now is, as nothing else has done since cancer took him away while I kept vigil by his bedside. As I sob, it is as if grief is peeling off me in shreds, like skin does after sunburn.

Then, as my tears subside, I begin to notice how the music gives tone to my mourning. I feel its pulse as it resounds in my head, and then the way it earths me as the notes glide away. Somehow this short but long-remembered piece by Mozart has opened up the way to a more significant kind of remembrance, which I have so far failed to pave a path to.

And so I make a resolution: I will choose eight pieces of music Dad loved – one for each decade of his life – and listen to them with great care and attention. To try to work out what it was he so appreciated about classical music, as I should have done while he was alive. It will be my requiem. And my thanksgiving for the ordinary, decent man who was my father.

Chapter 1

The Effect of Mozart

Piano Concerto No. 22 in E-flat major, K. 482

Mozart. The golden boy, the archangel, the Sachertorte of composers. How daunting it feels to start my act of remembrance with his crème de la crème compositions. But why begin anywhere else?

For the next few weeks, I play the Alfred Brendel recording of Piano Concerto No. 22 whenever I'm alone in the car. Before long, I can hear the piece without crying, but with this new composure comes a realisation that I have no idea how to listen to it. I love letting the prettiness of the piece sweep over me, and the newly soothing way it reminds me of Dad, but what exactly it was I found so arresting about it as a four-year-old I can no longer tell. I've mislaid the acuity of my child's ear somewhere along the way.

Once he'd witnessed me mesmerised by Mozart, Dad made many gentle attempts over the next four decades to persuade me to share his love of classical music. He'd call me into the dining room where I'd watch, fascinated, as he took out a wheel of music and put it on the reel-to-reel, threading the tape across to the take-up spool. Then some other Mozart or perhaps some Schubert would start playing as I sat fidgeting, not quite sure what I was supposed to be listening for. Later, when he had a car with a cassette-tape player, Dad would sometimes take me with him when he sloped off to the pub for a swift pint before Sunday lunch. As we drove to The Greyhound, or the Olde Lancaster Inn (where I later worked behind the bar) – pubs in nearby villages, carefully selected by Dad for their lack of piped pop music – there'd be a music quiz where I had to guess the composer. Could I tell the difference between early Beethoven and Mozart? Tchaikovsky from Prokofiev? Spot a piece by the oh-so-prolific Haydn, who wrote over a hundred symphonies? Mostly I couldn't. But through these games, Dad hoped, I think, to nurture a passion for classical music equal to his own. Perhaps I'd even grow up with a gift for it, become an instrumentalist. At the very least I would be a daughter with whom he could always discuss music.

There were lots of inducements to become that daughter. A piano at home, lessons for almost a decade. My piano teacher, Mrs Adams – a kind and patient family friend – taught me not to sag at the elbows as I played, and to recite catchy mnemonics for remembering the notes on the stave, and the order of sharps and flats: Every Good Boy Deserves Favour; All Cows Eat Grass; Father Charles Goes Down And Ends Battle (Battle Ends And Down Goes Father Charles). Eventually, despite my lack of both discipline and enthusiasm, I progressed to Grade 7. I could play competently enough, and, yes, I even learned to play some pieces by Mozart. Looking through a pile of my old music books, I come across the Menuet in C by Mozart's father Leopold, which I had to play for my Grade 1 exam. A note on the page tells me that the piece comes from a manuscript book which Leopold gave to his son on Mozart's seventh birthday in 1763. Sitting down at my own piano now – the one I hardly ever play – I discover that my hands still remember how to play this simple menuet, and I marvel at the neural pathway that I have just cleared of the dust of ages.

I had clarinet lessons for a while, too. Given a choice of instruments to learn at secondary school, I opted for the clarinet because I liked the way it sounded in the role of the Cat in Prokofiev's *Peter and the Wolf*, a piece Dad played to me early on. Like so many children before me, I enjoyed the way each character in the story was represented by a different instrument: the trilling flute as the Bird, the honking oboe as the Duck and the growling French horn for the fearsome Wolf. It was the first time I remember really hearing the differences between the way various instruments of the orchestra sounded. How does a bassoon sound? Why, like the voice of a grandfather.

Unfortunately I conceived an instant, adolescent dislike of my clarinet teacher, Mr Walker, who grew sterner by the week at my failure to practise. The sterner he grew, the more scared and reluctant I was to play. I recoiled from his thick glasses and his coarse, combover hair. I hated the way the clarinet reeds splintered into my tongue when they split, and I never seemed to have the right amount of spit needed to play properly. Too little and my mouth was too parched to find the notes; too much and my condensed breath ran down through the instrument to drip on the floor from the bell. Not even a trip with Dad to Leicester's De Montfort Hall to hear Jack Brymer play Mozart's Clarinet Concerto could spark any dedication. The self-taught Brymer, the son of a South Shields builder and one of the twentieth century's most acclaimed clarinettists, had a musical epiphany at the age of four far more revolutionary than my own when he picked up his father's clarinet from the mantelpiece and began to play.

The trouble was that by now a different genre of music had taken hold of me, and it was all the fault of the girl next door. By then we'd moved to a larger, new-build house in a cul-de-sac in the same village. Three years older than me, my neighbour Louise exuded glamour. She had long brown hair, freckles, pink flares and her own record player. A few years later, as a young adult in the 1980s, she would devote herself to the noble task of nursing young men dying from AIDS-related illnesses. In the early 1970s, this selfless quality was honed through her general tolerance of my needy, daily ringing of the doorbell, asking if I could come in and 'play'. Holed up in her bedroom over the double garage which housed her chain-smoking mother's duck-billed Citroën DS, we listened to David Bowie, T-Rex and Slade, and soon I was as hooked on pop as Louise's mother was on her Player's Navy Cut. Any emotions Mozart might once have stirred went into orbit with Major Tom. From then on, I watched *Top of the Pops* religiously, Dad harrumphing behind the *Leicester Mercury* throughout. While Mum – if pushed – would admit to a penchant for Elvis, never once did I hear Dad concede that pop music could be anything but 'a racket'. Gilbert and Sullivan was as close as he got to 'easy listening'. I, in turn, thought my dad was embarrassingly conservative. It would be years before I realised just how varied his musical tastes were.

Meanwhile, I was nurturing a passion for a different genre of music. Once in possession of my own (second-hand) record player, I soon cast aside the children's classics LPs that my parents had bought me (highlights: Jon Pertwee singing

'Widecombe Fair' and June Whitfield singing 'Puff the Magic Dragon') and started collecting my own records. I remember the intense excitement of buying my first singles with a birthday Boots token while on holiday in Newquay. As first record purchases go, Blondie's 'Hanging on the Telephone' and Ian Dury and the Blockheads' 'Hit Me With Your Rhythm Stick', I still think, were pretty cool. I also loved the Boomtown Rats, and once gave a talk about them in a school music lesson. Mrs Needham, our long-suffering music teacher, who struggled week in, week out to gain our attention, had asked us all to select a musical subject to research and present, perhaps hoping beyond hope that someone would choose a topic as edifying as the piano concertos of Mozart. Instead, I treated her to a litany of enthusiastically presented but banal facts culled from *Smash Hits* magazine about Bob Geldof, Johnnie Fingers, Pete Briquette et al.

A year or two later, my friend Alison introduced me to the Beatles and my taste went retro overnight. I borrowed *Rubber Soul* and *Revolver* from her and played them over and over again. In December 1981, feeling very pleased with my gift idea, I sent away by mail order for Alison's Christmas present: a Beatles poster. On the morning it arrived in the post, I went into the kitchen, tube in hand, to show the poster to Mum. 'Haven't you heard?' she said. 'John Lennon's been shot.' I remember Dad sighing through the lengthy coverage of Lennon's murder on the news that night.

Would Dad too have come to appreciate pop music if he had heard David Bowie when he was seven? Hard to imagine. He was serious-minded and not one for fleeting fashions, either in dress or in cultural pursuits. He often told me that the reason he felt pop music was inferior was because it didn't endure. Pop-music fans were too fickle about what they liked, he said, with most songs all the rage for a week or two at most before disappearing without trace. That's how he saw it. I hated him saying this, but at the time I couldn't come up with any counter-argument. Now, of course, I know he was wrong. I've listened to many albums throughout my adult life: *Blue* (Joni Mitchell), *The River* (Bruce Springsteen), *Tapestry* (Carole King), *Rumours* (Fleetwood Mac) that will stay with me always. But at the time I didn't care enough to try and persuade Dad to see things any other way.

Unlike me, Dad hadn't grown up with classical music streaming through the house. His father ran a dental practice in a Leicestershire coal-mining town, and there was little time or yearning for culture. I never knew my paternal grandparents; they were late Victorians and already in their forties by the time Dad was born in 1934 – an almost certainly unplanned brother for a sister ten years older than him. Mum, who'd met Dad as a teenager on the school bus, tells me his family home was plain and austere and lacking in any 'soft, artistic corners'. For a while Dad had violin and then cello lessons, but he didn't really stick at them, and, given the lack of encouragement, it was hardly surprising. One day, Mum was at the house with Nellie, her future mother-in-law, when Dad returned home, cycling into the yard with a cello strapped to his back. 'What's our Peter gone and got himself now?' his mother exclaimed, shaking her head.

But then, in the sixth form at Ashby-de-la-Zouch Boys' Grammar School, Dad joined the lunchtime Musical Society. I find out more about it from back issues of the school magazine, *The Ashbeian*, from the late 1940s/early 1950s, found among Dad's papers when he died. Mr Ellison, who ran the society, would give classical music recitals on his 'Pam' electric gramophone for the assembled boys to listen to and then discuss. A programme of after-school talks and recitals was also staged: on 11 November 1946, for example, Mr Bellamy spoke on 'The Orchestra in the XVIIIth Century'. It's difficult to imagine similar music-appreciation classes pulling in a lunchtime crowd of teenagers now, but they kindled in Dad an early love of classical music that was to sustain him for life.

At Cambridge University he had a portable record player, which he lugged from Coalville and back again every vacation. Mum remembers how often the records had to be turned over, including a recording of Mozart's Symphony No. 36 – aka the 'Linz' Symphony – conducted by Bruno Walter, which was spread over six discs. Hearing this, I realise I am a technological bridge between the generation which accepted such an interruption and the one which seamlessly streams hours of music directly into their ears. I once told my son – in jest – to 'change the record' and was met with utter incomprehension. After they got married in 1956, my parents saved up for (wonder of wonders) an auto-changing record player that would mechanically flip the disc for you. This was succeeded by a heavy-duty tape recorder – the one I remember as a four-year-old – and reels of pieces recorded from the radio via microphone, followed by various cassette players, and then ultimately, a stacked stereo sound system and CDs.

By the time he died, Dad's CD collection spanned numerous eras and styles, from Purcell to William Walton. But he was always devoted to Mozart, and to the late piano concertos in particular. I grew up in the certain knowledge that Wolfgang Amadeus Mozart was a great composer without ever really understanding why, except that Dad liked him best. Still, attentive, bookish child that I was, I picked up a few facts here and there. My favourite TV programme in the 1970s was *Blue Peter*, which I watched devotedly after school each Monday and Thursday. With an early longing for overseas travel unfulfilled by our annual, childhood summer holidays on chilly East Anglian beaches, I particularly loved a spin-off series called *Blue Peter Special Assignment*, in which presenter Valerie Singleton visited various European cities. In the final episode of the first series, the destination was Vienna, and the programme included a potted account of Mozart's life. I remember being greatly impressed by two facts. Firstly, that Mozart had proposed marriage to the future Marie Antoinette (I already knew what had later happened to her), and, secondly, that he had been buried in an unknown location in a pauper's grave. This 'fact' I later discovered, was untrue, but the idea that you could be both very famous and very poor made a lasting impression.

I also read about Mozart in one of my many Ladybird books. Unsurprisingly, given its target readership, *Lives of the Great Composers Book 1* by Ian Woodward, which also included Bach and Beethoven, concentrated on Mozart's achievements as a child prodigy during the several grand musical tours of Europe he went on with his father Leopold and his elder sister Nannerl, who — not that you'd have known it from my Ladybird — was a talented musician in her own right. I retrieve the book from a box in Mum's loft and read it again. One picture by stalwart Ladybird illustrator Martin Aitchison shows the teenage Mozart by candlelight, quill poised over manuscript pages, sitting in pensive attitude by a window, with St Peter's Basilica in Rome and a starry sky behind him. 'The fourteen-year-old Mozart writes from memory the entire score of an oratorio he has heard only once,' reads the caption.

A few pages later there is a dramatic image of the adult Mozart being kicked down the steps of the Ducal Palace in Salzburg, where he had been working as court organist. Down the steps with him flies a violin, with all but one of its strings broken, along with fluttering pages of music. 'The Archbishop at Salzburg was jealous of Mozart's vast popularity. After a violent quarrel, the Archbishop's friend, the Count of Arco, kicked him out and Mozart left Salzburg for good.'

I absorbed more Mozart mythology a few years later from Miloš Forman's 1984 film version of Peter Shaffer's play *Amadeus*, which I saw when I was a student. It stars F. Murray Abraham as Antonio Salieri, Mozart's jealous rival, and Tom Hulce, whose portrayal of Mozart as a brilliant but spendthrift, and slightly unhinged, overgrown child has determined how many people have come to think of him. When Dad eventually saw *Amadeus* on TV, in his resolutely rational way he disliked it, finding it fanciful and overdramatised. He also baulked at Tom Hulce's American accent.

Despite Dad's dislike of it, it is partly thanks to *Amadeus* that Mozart's biography is the most widely known of any classical composer. I watch *Amadeus* ('Everything You've Heard is True') on DVD again for the first time in more than thirty years. I smile at the blurb on the box, 'The Man . . . The Music . . . The Madness . . . The Murder . . . The Motion Picture', because, just like the sensational tone of newspaper headlines that he was always complaining about, I know it would have irritated Dad immensely. But, watching it again so many years later, I'm as enthralled by *Amadeus* as I was the first time I saw it. Not least by F. Murray Abraham's electrifying performance and the way in which the film plays on the notion that Mozart's genius was God-given.

At the time when Piano Concerto No. 22 was written in 1785, Mozart was married, living in Vienna, his reputation at its height. His compositions, especially his operas, were wildly popular with the public, and for a short time he was raking it in. In his 2016 biography, John Suchet suggests that Mozart's income in the mid-1780s would have been the equivalent of more than £100,000 a year today. Flushed with success, he moved to a lavish new apartment at a prestigious address by St Stephen's Cathedral in 1784. He bought a new piano, clothes, shoes, a carriage, a billiard table. For a while, all of Vienna paid court. In a letter to his daughter Nannerl in 1785, Leopold Mozart writes that the celebrated fellow Austrian composer Joseph Haydn – something of a mentor to Mozart – had told him: 'I tell you before God, and as an honest man, that your son is the greatest composer I know, either personally or by reputation: he has taste and moreover the greatest possible knowledge of the science of composition.'[1]

But Mozart was never able to cement his reputation. Despite the income from commissions and his subscription concerts – for which audiences were invited to sign up in advance in order to hear his latest compositions – his lavish spending and increasing debts meant he still depended on private tuition: the young Beethoven was briefly a pupil. Even his appointment as imperial royal court composer in 1787 brought only a paltry salary. And as the 1780s drew to a close, the fickle musical tastes of the Viennese were changing, and Mozart's concerts were no longer as popular. To compound her husband's increasing ill health, his wife Constanze was often unwell postpartum (she gave birth to six children during their nine-year marriage, only two of whom survived infancy), and the medical bills further drained their resources.

Mozart could have devoted his time only to the commissions that would pay the bills. But composing whatever he felt moved to compose was a compulsion that never waned. During his ten years in Vienna between 1781 and 1791, Mozart created the majority of his most celebrated and revered works. Even as his health was failing in 1791, he wrote *The Magic Flute* ('the most joyful, optimistic, exuberant opera he ever composed', as Suchet calls it), [2] and his jaunty Clarinet Concerto in A major, the piece Dad took me to hear Jack Brymer play. Despite his crushing debts and chronic ill health, Mozart was still creating beautiful, life-enhancing music until the very end of his life. But will a keener insight into Mozart the man help me to a greater appreciation of his music? I feel myself taking refuge in reading round the subject because I'm scared of being an inadequate listener. My lifelong love of books means that I find it hard to shake the habit of looking for the keys to life's mysteries in someone else's words rather than by trusting my own sensibility.

A summer trip to Mozart's birthplace of Salzburg provides me with another form of distraction from my quest to listen better, albeit a relevant and delightful one. There I do everything a Mozart tourist is supposed to do. I have my photograph taken in front of Mozart's pen-in-hand statue in the Mozartplatz. I hoof up Kapuzinerberg on Stefan-Zweig-Weg in pouring rain to view the Mozart monument there. Unveiled in 1877 to mark the first Salzburg Mozart Festival, it bears the inscription 'Jung Gross. Spät Erkannt. Nie Erreict', which I clumsily translate as: 'Great From Young. Belatedly Recognised. Still Unparalleled'. I take tea and tuck into a pricey Schwarzwälder Kirschtorte on the first-floor balcony at Café Tomaselli, a favourite hangout of Mozart's despite its then proprietor, whom he once described as 'a patron of burning coffee soup, of rotten lemonade, of almond milk without almonds and of strawberry ice cream full of ice lumps'. And I stand awed amid the Baroque wedding-cake grandeur of Salzburg Cathedral, where in its softly gleaming font with copper lion pedestals, Mozart was baptised, and as a young adult served as the cathedral organist.

I also visit Salzburg's two Mozart museums: Mozarts Geburtshaus – his birthplace – on the thronging central pedestrian street that is Getreidegasse, and the Mozart Wohnhaus, the larger house in the Makartplatz to which the family moved in 1773. The Geburtshaus, its façade an unmissable canary yellow, is Salzburg's most visited museum. Inside, it's possible with a little imagination to take yourself back to the eighteenth century and the five-room living space occupied by the Mozarts, including the living room, which is now full of portraits, the small kitchen to which tea, coffee and ice cream were fetched in from the Café Tomaselli, and the room where Mozart was born – das Geburtszimmer. As I'm peering reverently into a glass case containing the printed music of six violin sonatas written in London in 1764 by the eight-year-old Mozart and dedicated to the British Queen Charlotte, a teenage fellow visitor starts hollering from the open window to a friend in the street below. I feel a bit peeved at this unruly behaviour in such a sacrosanct setting, but then wonder if the adolescent Mozart once did the same.

In the Wohnhaus, six of Mozart's original pianos are on display, including the concert piano he had in 1782. I stare at it for a while, pondering whether this might be the instrument on which he played Piano Concerto No. 22. The largest room in the Wohnhaus is the Dancing Master's Hall, which the

Mozarts used for music making, and also to display the various keyboard instruments Leopold sold on commission for instrument makers from outside of Salzburg. The Hall also hosted card games and bolt-shooting contests: turns out the Mozarts were mad keen on indoor shooting, firing at targets with air rifles.

The final room of the Wohnhaus is devoted to Mozart's now global celebrity, and the commercial uses for which his fame and name have been appropriated. Constanze, portrayed in *Amadeus* as a bit of a flibbertigibbet, actually proved expert in promoting her husband's legacy after his death. The cult of Mozart took off in the early nineteenth century, when the composer's allegedly 'tragic' life corresponded to the Romantic idea of the unappreciated genius who dies young. Now there are Mozart sausages, and Mozart shirts, and a Lufthansa 'Europe from €99' advert featuring the famous, posthumous portrait of Mozart in white wig and red brocade jacket by Barbara Krafft, contemporarily doctored with sunglasses and the slogan 'My God, Austria is so Cheap These Days'. A sign informs me that the Mozart brand is worth €5 billion to Austria annually. And, indeed, shops all over town are bursting at the seams with Mozart merchandise, including the ubiquitous Mozartkugeln or Mozart Balls, made of marzipan, nougat, pistachio and dark chocolate. It's staggering, and not a little ironic when you think of how Mozart struggled to make money in his own lifetime. Still, I'm not so upset that I hold back from popping into Café Konditorei Fürst and buying myself a bag of the original chocolates invented by Paul Fürst in 1890. After disputes with rival manufacturers, these small balls of deliciousness are now the only ones allowed the designation 'Original Salzburger Mozartkugeln'.

The Mozart museums also provide illuminating context about Mozart's life, both in Salzburg and in Vienna. In Salzburg, the Mozarts were a middle-class, bourgeois family in a bourgeois town that was prosperous from the profits of salt mining, farming and forestry. When Mozart was growing up, the Hapsburg state of Salzburg was still governed by an archbishop prince, elected by the cathedral chapter, but who acted like an absolute monarch. As a young man, Mozart chafed against the strictures of being in the service of the then incumbent, Archbishop Hieronymus von Colloredo. While today's Salzburg is chock-full of tourists from all over the world, in Mozart's time it was by all accounts a stifling, provincial place whose people were, Mozart felt, incapable of appreciating his creative talent. 'I swear by my honour that I can't stand Salzburg and its inhabitants. I mean the native Salzburgians. I find their language – their manners – quite insufferable,' he once wrote to his father, forgetting perhaps that he too was a native Salzburger.[3] It's difficult to avoid an impression of arrogance here, of someone completely convinced of their own superiority.

And this was also a young man whose mind had been irrevocably broadened by travel from an early age as his father flaunted his son's talent around Europe. According to an exhibit in the Geburtshaus, Mozart embarked on seventeen different journeys during his life, spending a total of ten years, two months and two days travelling. It's an astonishing amount when you consider his short lifespan. Once Mozart had departed for Vienna in 1781, he returned to Salzburg only once. Vienna – fast becoming an economic powerhouse since the accession of Enlightenment Holy Roman Emperor Joseph II – was a city of far greater promise for an ambitious composer, and full of wealthy – and cultured – potential patrons.

I spend long moments in the museums staring at portraits of Mozart. It's strange, this compulsion to eyeball the famous, as if it will provide a greater understanding of what drove them. 'Is talent like that written on the face?' asks Salieri early in *Amadeus*, as he searches the room for a glimpse of the composer he has heard so much about, only to find him canoodling with Constanze in the next room.[4] And here in Salzburg is Mozart, depicted by Johann Nepomuk della Croce in 1780/1, dressed in a red coat and white wig, and seated next to Nannerl at the keyboard not long before he left for Vienna for good. Here's a glossy chocolate-box portrait of Mozart aged eight, painted in gala dress by Pietro Antonio Lorenzoni. But it is two depictions of Mozart when older which I find most compelling. There's an unfinished portrait in oils painted in 1782 or 1783 by Joseph Lange, who was married to Constanze's sister Aloysia. Beneath a bush of mousy hair, Mozart's face is angled down and contemplative. Here, he is soberly dressed and serious, even troubled. Nannerl is said to have found this by far the best likeness of her brother.

I'm most taken of all, however, with a silverpoint drawing by Doris Stock, made in Dresden in 1789 and possibly the last portrait of Mozart drawn from life. Mozart is shown sideways on, frankly a plain and mousy-looking man with a distinct cast of worry and weariness around the eyes. This Mozart bears no resemblance to the exuberant dandy of *Amadeus*. Reminiscing a year after his death, Nannerl described her brother as 'small, thin, and pale in colour, and entirely lacking any pretention as to physiognomy and bodily appearance'.[5]

The same evening, I go to a recital in the intimate surroundings of the Romanesque crypt of the abbey church of St Peter. Its beautiful cemetery is the last resting place of both Nannerl

Mozart and, as it happens, of the aforementioned confectioner, Paul Fürst. In the underground room with rough granite pillars and a tiled floor made atmospheric by tealights dotted around, we sit on wooden benches around an August Förster grand piano placed on a thick oriental rug. I listen spellbound while Vivianne Cheng, a young American pianist, plays three Mozart pieces: the Fantasia in D minor (K. 397); the Piano Sonata No. 1 in C major (K. 279), composed in 1774 when Mozart was eighteen; and the Piano Sonata No. 8 in A minor (K. 310), composed in Paris in 1778, around the time of his mother's death.

Cheng is physically expressive in her performance, her torso swaying and bowing. I'm struck by how the tones she unleashes from a single instrument completely fill the tight, windowless space. Whatever miscellaneous emotional baggage we have brought into this room as listeners we are compelled to put to one side for the duration of the music as it seizes the train of our thoughts. Cheng's playing of the Fantasia makes a particularly strong impression on me. Left unfinished at Mozart's death, and later completed by another hand, I find it has an anxious quality, sometimes racing away, sometimes pondering and brooding. This makes sense later when I look up the musical definition of a fantasia and discover that it is a free-form composition with a sense of improvisation about it – a sort of creative holiday from the dictates of more set musical forms. As I walk out into the balmy summer night to catch a train back to the guesthouse where I am staying, just over the nearby border in Germany, I hold an imaginary conversation with Dad in my head. What did he think of the pianist? Wasn't the intimate setting perfect? Had he found the wooden benches a bit hard to sit on after a while?

Shortly after I return home from my trip, I'm commissioned to interview South Korean-born violinist Min Kym about her book *Gone*, an account of her life both before and after her 'soulmate violin' – a 1696 Stradivarius – was stolen from her while she sat in a café at Euston station. The interview is a fascinating close encounter with a much more recent child prodigy. Kym was born in South Korea and began playing the violin at the age of six, after her family moved to the UK. The rapidity of her progress was extraordinary. She passed Grade 2 after eight weeks and, a month later, Grade 4 with the highest mark in the country. At seven, she became the youngest ever pupil at the Purcell School of Music, and her family began to make sacrifices in order to support her career. 'Already it was being made very clear to me what they thought I was, what they thought I'd become,' she writes in *Gone*. With the obedience and conformity traditionally expected of a Korean child, Kym followed the path that was being laid out for her. But occasionally, as her violin increasingly did her talking for her, a warning note of trouble ahead would sound. 'I would hear the words "child prodigy" said of me all the time, and sometimes I used to ponder: what does that mean? I was aware that it was causing a sort of distance,' she tells me.

At the age of eleven, Kym won her first major international competition and, despite pangs for 'a normality that was denied me', her teenage years, like those of Mozart before her, brought increasing amounts of foreign travel as she gave recitals around the world. 'Min the violinist getting ahead . . . Min the person going nowhere,' she writes of this time in *Gone*, when a starry career as a solo performer and recording artist beckoned. Ironically, it was only after her violin was stolen that she began to find some sense of self. 'The violin was a crutch. It was the thing that supported me, and yet once it was gone, I realised that I'd almost built my life on sand,' Kym told me, with devastating insight. 'Eventually I discovered a voice which the violin had completely taken over. This supressed, repressed person came out.' In *Gone*, Kym asserts that a child prodigy is only 'a means to another's end'. While we marvel at the talents of such prodigies, we aren't very comfortable with them, suspecting pushy, scheming parents and a deficiency of love. We find it difficult to believe that rounded, fulfilled adults can result from such an early and ostentatious display of extreme talent. The traditional tales of Mozart's apparent early genius are compelling, but also encourage us to think of him as an otherworldly social misfit.

Almost never is Mozart portrayed as a diligent composer who grafted at his craft, working his stockings off in order to be so supremely talented and prolific. But surely he was: Ludwig von Köchel's 1862 catalogue, still the standard reference, runs to more than 600 works: symphonies, sonatas, concertos, chamber music, church music, twenty-two operas, a final requiem. Perhaps it does better justice to the composer to imagine that the engine which powered his 'genius' – that word from which Mozart has to be surgically removed – was built through his relentless childhood touring of the courts of Europe, and of learning early lessons about different traditions of music – English, German, French, Italian – in the process. But then later, once freed from Leopold's care as well as his control and his exhortations to make the most of his talent, Mozart did struggle to cope alone in the adult world, where the business realities of making his way and living as a freelance composer eluded him completely. As *Amadeus* hints, perhaps Mozart wasn't, 'genius' aside, very smart.

And yet Mozart's name is now inextricably associated with the theory that exposure to classical music, especially ante- and postnatally, as infant brains develop, can make your baby smarter.[6] The term 'Mozart Effect' was first coined in 1993 and derived from a scientific study conducted by three researchers at the Center for the Neurobiology of Learning and Memory at the University of California. The study involved thirty-six college students who were given three sets of standard IQ spatial-reasoning tasks. One group completed the tasks after listening for ten minutes to Mozart's Sonata for Two Pianos in D major; the second group after ten minutes of a relaxation tape with exercises designed to lower blood pressure; and the third after sitting in silence for ten minutes. The students who had listened to Mozart achieved the highest scores. In a letter to the leading scientific journal *Nature* in October 1993, the researchers emphasised the limitations of the study, describing the enhancing effect of the music as 'temporal'.[7] They were also careful not to attribute the effect to a quality found only in Mozart's music. 'Because we used only one musical sample of one composer, various other compositions and musical styles should also be examined. We predict that music lacking complexity, or which is repetitive may interfere with, rather than enhance abstract reasoning.'

But who cares about academic caveats when a study's findings can be fashioned into the kind of sensational headline which so used to irritate Dad. 'Can it be that the music of Mozart is not only exalting but can also improve intelligence?' trumpeted an article entitled 'Mozart's Notes Make Good Brain Food' in the *International Herald Tribune*, published only two days after the cautious University of California study was released.[8] Though follow-up experiments by the researchers showed that listening to the same Mozart sonata as before improved only the students' spatial-temporal reasoning and not overall brain function (and improved it only temporarily at that), the embryonic genie was out of the bottle. Incredibly, despite the fact that none of the research had involved babies or young children, crèches all over America began playing classical music to their charges and the state of Georgia presented every newborn baby with a free classical CD.[9]

In 1996, Don Campbell, a US classical musician and former music critic, trademarked the term 'The Mozart Effect', created a thrusting brand on the back of it, and made a fortune. Visit www.mozarteffect.com and you'll find books, CDs and other resources galore, designed to harness music as a 'powerful catalyst for healing, creativity and development'. In *The Mozart Effect*, his best-known book, Campbell draws on 'medicine, Eastern wisdom and the latest research on learning and creativity' to reveal how exposure to sound, music and other forms of vibrations can have a lifelong effect on health, learning and behaviour. It's difficult to argue with the idea that music can have therapeutic powers. But it's much more difficult to find any evidence that the Mozart 'Effect' is in any way particular to the music of Mozart.

I look up some definitions of 'spatial-temporal reasoning', the one kind of brain activity, according to some evidence, that listening to classical music might benefit. It is, I read, 'the cognitive ability to picture a spatial pattern and understand how items or pieces can fit into that space. Those with a gift for this kind of reasoning can often visualise how things fit together, step-by-step, and how they can be manipulated into different patterns.' 'Musical talent,' I further discover, is one of the most widely acknowledged uses of spatial-temporal reasoning. Those with this kind of talent can not only picture notes on a page, they can visualise how music for several different instruments will fit together. Individuals who write music often visualise notes as a large puzzle, fitting different fractions of notes and rests together to create a whole piece of music. For some, this takes years of study, while others have extremely advanced musical spatial-temporal reasoning.[10]

Mozart fitted the 'extremely advanced' definition perfectly. And Dad is also interesting in this respect. While seemingly not much cop at playing either the violin or the cello, Dad flexed his own well-developed spatial-temporal reasoning skills in a different pursuit. From his early teens he was an accomplished self-taught chess player, whose exploits regularly hit the local headlines. I have a scrapbook of newspaper cuttings from the *Leicester Mercury*, lovingly pasted in from the late 1940s onwards by my grandmother Nellie: '14-year-old Ashby Boy in Chess Final'; 'Sanderson in Chess Final Again'; and even 'Chess Starlet', a headline which conjures up sparkly frocks and dancing shoes rather than the flannel suits and Brylcreemed hair in which Dad is pictured at that time. In early 1949, at the age of fourteen, Dad won his first Leicestershire Junior County Champion title and took home the fetching Silver Knight trophy. He retained the title for the next two years, his clinching match in 1951 reported under the headline 'You Could Have Heard a Pawn Drop'. In 1952 he won it again, and in April the same year was joint winner of the British Boys' Chess Championship in a three-way tie at the annual tournament in Hastings. A play-off to decide a single winner was mooted, but in the end the three young men sportingly agreed to share the trophy and display it on their respective family sideboards for four months each.

That autumn, Dad went up to Sidney Sussex College, Cambridge, on an exhibition scholarship to read mathematics. By November, he was playing for Cambridge University's chess team and was awarded his Half Blue a few months later. In January 1954, Cambridge University Chess Club, of which Dad was by now secretary, played host to two visiting Russian grandmasters, David Bronstein and Vladimir Alatortsev, in a display of simultaneous chess. After Dad died and I was collecting stories for my funeral tribute, Ray, his close university friend and fellow chess player, told me how close Dad had come to beating Alatortsev. The rattled grandmaster, said Ray, unsportingly responded to this show of tactical strength by a student upstart by standing right in front of Dad, impatiently rushing him into his next moves. In the face of Soviet aggression, Dad let the position slip into a drawn ending. Alartortsev drew five out of seventeen matches, but lost none. The missed opportunity to beat a Russian grandmaster rankled with Dad for years afterwards.

Among Dad's personal papers after he died, Mum and I found a sort of personal CV where, in his methodical way, he had recorded notable dates: births, deaths, marriages, his dates of employment, and a few achievements. These included the fact that, while at Cambridge, Dad was ranked among the twenty-five best players in the UK. He continued to play chess after he graduated, winning the Leicestershire County Championship four times in 1957, 1960, 1966 and 1981. That final time, I remember how proud I was of him, and of the trophy, displayed in our house for a whole year. Chess is the centrepiece for one of my most abiding memories of Dad, in which he sits with a small wooden travel chess set on his lap, his fingers clicking the pieces repeatedly back and forth as he tries to work out the forward permutations of a particular position. How he could remember where the pieces had been was a continual source of wonder to me.

Let's assume that there is some kind of Mozart effect, at least on spatial-temporal reasoning skills. Dad's talent for chess was established in his early teens and blossomed throughout his late teens and twenties, at a time when he had started listening seriously to classical music. Did one enhance and nurture the other? It's a tantalising thought. I start to rue the fact that I may have passed up the chance to enhance my own spatial-temporal reasoning by allowing my own classical music listening to tail off completely after a promising early start. I never have been much good at chess.

I now have no way of knowing which pianist and which orchestra were on the recording of Piano Concerto No. 22 I heard when I was four, for the reel-to-reel tape recorder and the reels themselves were long ago disposed of by Dad after he converted to cassette tapes, and then to CDs. I find numerous different recordings of Mozart's piano concertos in his CD collection, particularly of those numbered 20 to 27. In all, Mozart composed twenty-three original concertos for piano and orchestra. His first four concertos were reworkings of music by other composers and then, when he was seventeen, he composed his first wholly original such piece, Piano Concerto No. 5 in D major.

Written a month before his thirtieth birthday, Piano Concerto No. 22 was the third piano concerto Mozart had composed that year. As *Amadeus* shows us, Mozart, as a virtuoso pianist himself, could offer audiences the novelty of hearing a composer play his own compositions, and charge them a handsome fee for the privilege at the subscription concerts he regularly staged. At one of the earliest public performances of No. 22, which took place in late December 1785 (so perhaps not al fresco, as shown in *Amadeus* the film), the piece was so well received that Mozart played the whole of the second movement – the nine-and-a-half-minute Andante – as an encore. This was – as his father recorded in a letter – 'a rather unusual occurrence'.[11]

Though I'm listening to the concerto several times a week, I'm still preparing myself for the moment when I really 'listen' to it once again. I want to be ready, but still feel incapable of hearing all but a fraction of the things such a piece might have to say to me. In search of some advice on what to listen for, I look up the opinions of a few music critics, but this proves both tantalising and intimidating, and makes me feel even more unequal to the task. The reviews are so pronouncing and grand. In *The Concerto: A Listener's Guide*, for example, Michael Steinberg, a musicologist and former music critic of the *Boston Globe*, describes No. 22 as both 'grand and gentle', 'lavishly endowed with lyric themes', and 'a feast of gentle wit'. Meanwhile in *1001 Classical Recordings You Must Hear Before You Die*, contributor Max Loppart highlights the concerto's 'immaculate craftsmanship, astonishingly inventive formal handling, keyboard mastery and the indelible imprint of Mozart's theatrical imagination'. In his *Mozart Piano Concertos*, Philip Radcliffe opines that 'the most notable characteristic of this concerto is a kind of luxuriant leisureliness'. And I'm completely bamboozled by a dismissive comment about No. 22 by über-critic Eric Blom in his 1935 book on Mozart: 'This work is many people's favourite among the piano concertos – until they hear one of the others.'

None of the 'others' will ever mean to me what No. 22 does. But I'm painfully aware that classical music experts use a different language that I can stutter only a few words of. I have next to no knowledge of music theory, having forgotten most of what I did once learn for my Grade 5 Theory exam. It's so early in this journey still, and I feel barely more equipped to listen to Mozart than I was as a four-year-old. In fact, I'm less equipped, for then I had a father and some kind of guide, and now I have neither. My head is full of all the things I have found out about Mozart the man, and I worry that I will now listen to his music with a fact-cluttered brain and all emotion spent, and as a consequence hear nothing very much. I think back to the Geburtshaus in Salzburg, where there is an acoustic room, empty of everything but high-backed wooden seating where you can simply sit and listen to Mozart's music. And that is exactly what I need to do now – empty my mind of all else, and simply listen again. But I still feel daunted.

I cling onto a cue I've taken from John Suchet's Preface to his biography of Mozart, in which he refers to him as 'surely the happiest composer who ever lived. Listening to Mozart's music induces a sense of well-being, a feeling that all is well with the world . . . if a human being can create such beauty, then there will always be hope for humanity.'[12] *Huh*, I think, with little faith. I've retuned all my radios from Radio 4 to Radio 3, partly because the news about humanity is so depressing these days. But a sense of well-being – here at least is something I can listen for.

I line up Dad's two recordings of Piano Concerto No. 22. There's the Alfred Brendel one I've been listening to for months, and a second one I have found among the stacks of Dad's CDs which are still piled up in my parents' dining room. Dated 1959, it features Hungarian-born pianist Annie Fischer, with the Philharmonia Orchestra, conducted by Wolfgang Sawallisch. I've never heard of Fischer, so I look her up, and immediately love the sound of her. A Hungarian Jewish pianist, nicknamed 'Ashtray' Annie for having a cigarette in her mouth at all times except when at the keyboard, she too was something of a child prodigy. She made her public debut in Budapest at the age of ten, and won the first International Liszt Piano Competition in 1933 at the age of nineteen. Her 1995 obituary in the *New York Times* headlines the 'elegance' of her Mozart performances, explaining that because she disliked making recordings, the few that are available are prized by collectors.[13] Discerning of Dad to have this one, then. I know he'll have bought it because of its three-star recommendation in his musical bible, *The Penguin Guide to Recorded Classical Music*. It's a book whose pages Dad was still avidly scouring shortly before he died. The editors praise Fischer's 'gentle, limpid' touch and the 'intimate' manner of her playing.

I take out the Fischer CD, and every day for a week I listen to it hard. Not in the car, not as background music when engaged in some domestic task, and not when writing at my desk. Rather, I try to listen as I have never listened before, in the kind of meditative mode I attempt every morning while doing yoga, trying to shut out everything else and inviting the notes into a cleared mind. I'm sure Dad never listened to music while lying on the floor in Savasana pose. But it's my way of trying to get it right inside me.

The first movement of Piano Concerto No. 22 is an Allegro.

Lively and fast, that is. It jerks you to attention with a woodwind-fanfare blast of a beginning, the orchestra making its presence felt with little preamble. The early stars are the woodwind instruments: the flutes and clarinets, which I spot partly because I've read that Mozart makes a notably big fuss of the clarinet in this concerto. There's an orchestral introduction of over two minutes before the piano makes its entrance, which heightens the anticipation. The piano part begins with an impressive solo of half a minute, which roves right across the keyboard and through the octaves, in an effortless way which, I know even from my own clumsy attempts at playing, requires enormous dexterity. The ensuing conversation between piano and orchestra – in my childish way it's how I think of it – is jaunty and engaging. After four minutes or so, the piano takes the piece into the minor key for a spell – a transition I can at least recognise from my playing days – making the mood more intimate. The whole movement feels like a curious mixture of something extrovert that is happening centre stage, and a more intimate narrative that is going on in the wings. Halfway through, the orchestra repeats its opening fanfare, and the woodwind duets with the piano for a while. Then, as the movement approaches its climax, the orchestra evokes an increasing sense of grandeur before the cadenza.

Cadenza? I didn't have a clue about cadenzas. I discover they are the improvised passages in concertos which allow the soloist to show off her or his virtuosity at will, while using fragments from the piece that is written. The original score for Piano Concerto No. 22 would have been blank at this point, but at its first performance, Mozart would have debuted his own cadenza. The idea of improvising grandly like this is a concept both magnificent and terrifying to a plodding, page-chained piano player like myself, although I learn that performers do have a choice of improvising, or playing a previously set-down cadenza. In his recording with the Academy of St Martin in the Fields, Alfred Brendel plays his own sweetly engaging interpretation. Fischer plays a showier, fiendishly difficult-sounding cadenza by Johann Hummel, an Austrian composer and virtuoso pianist, who was Mozart's pupil for a time. It involves great sweeps up the piano, finished with short high trills, and then thrusting sections with both major and minor passages, alternating with delicate tinkling sections. The orchestra returns for the final thirty seconds of the thirteen-minute movement to end it with as much fanfare as it begins. It's an exhilarating opening to the concerto, and already I have the thrilling sense of listening to something familiar as if for the first time.

Next the Andante. Which means 'at a walking pace', as I remember my piano teacher telling me many times when I was rushing ahead with a piece. But the plaintive, rather mournful quality of the opening string section suggests the walking pace of someone deep in reflection, slowing every so often as their thoughts concentrate, and then quickening again as the emotion discharges a little. The beginning of the piano solo after one and three-quarter minutes gives me goose bumps: Fischer's playing is so expressive, even though this section doesn't 'sound' too difficult to play. After three and a half minutes, the woodwind takes up the story, with the clarinets prominent again, and the piano returns more forcefully halfway through the movement, as if needing to reassert itself. The orchestra responds in kind, whereupon the piano part quietens again, replying with enchanting expression, backed here and there by sweet strings. It could be sentimental but it isn't. Rather, it is extraordinarily moving, without leaving any sense whatsoever of one's emotions being manipulated.

Given that the Andante is the movement Mozart played as an encore for the concerto's first ever audience, I'm struck by what a curiously reflective choice it is for an encore: not at all the triumphant piece you imagine a composer basking in acclaim might play. But it is achingly beautiful: a reprise to send you out into a late eighteenth-century December night in thoughtful, introspective mood, pulling your rich cloak around you a little tighter, and feeling yourself irrevocably changed in some mysterious way.

The third and final movement, the Rondo – defined as a piece with a recurring leading theme, I learn – has the piano immediately sallying forth with the simple tripping melody which first thrilled my ear almost half a century ago. An alternating theme is swiftly taken up by the star clarinets, backed by the rest of the woodwind. Fischer's glittery deftness as she trills and glides across the keys, even when playing more forcefully, is a sweet delight. At times she plays so quietly that I strain to hear, and this in itself is seductive. My long-beloved signature melody returns again and again, each time a little more twirly and elaborate. There is a short final cadenza – the CD sleeve notes do not say whose it is – before the finale, which sounds as if it was deliberately composed so as to have a trick false ending, designed to trip up the inattentive listener.

Annie Fischer's performance both presses down on my heart and leaves me smiling. I search online for film of her performing and find some black-and-white footage in which she plays the Allegro in a live performance, conducted by the same Wolfgang Sawallisch. Perhaps it's even the recording I've been listening to. The diminutive Fischer cuts an elegant figure in full-length checked chiffon, her dark hair pulled into a bun. Her chair appears to be pushed well back and at a slight angle, as if she prefers to perform on the edge of her seat and a little off-centre. Her playing is physically expressive and jaunty: rocking to and fro, she lifts her hands high up off the keys with great flourishes as she completes a section. It's somehow in the ebullient, almost cheeky style of how I imagine Mozart himself might have played the concerto on that December night in 1785.

After listening to the Fischer recording twice a day for a week, I play the Alfred Brendel recording again, and although this is the one that originally made me cry, I now find it less transporting. Fischer's perky lightness of touch, the shimmery quality to her expressive playing transports me in a way that Brendel's more direct and assertive interpretation does not. One day, when feeling low, I listen to Fischer playing the Andante and find myself thinking about Dad when he was dying: diminished, in pain, and too ill even to listen to the music he loved. The effect is almost unbearable, and yet there is nothing in the music which you could pinpoint as an explicit, deliberate tug on the emotions. And then, when I listen to Fischer playing the final movement I loved as a child, the music grounds and comforts me, reminding me that life is a complex counterpoint of emotions, where joy daily duets with sadness.

Yet, whoever is playing, I marvel at the way the concerto evokes such a strong sense of harmony and completeness, looping away on gorgeous, reflective diversions but then bringing us back to earth so satisfyingly. Perhaps this is one of the symptoms of listening to a 'classical' piece. When I buy a new album of popular music, as I do at least every month, I play it daily for the first few weeks until I've had my fill of it. Then it usually slips from my mind for months until I feel the urge to play it again. My reaction to Piano Concerto No. 22 is different: it's a piece I could hear weekly without needing to change the record. But I find it astonishingly difficult to write about with any clarity. It wriggles out of every attempt. It's as if I'm doing a clunky piece of primary-school writing, and showing off adjectives because I've just learned them, rather than finding the right word to express what I really want to say. I worry that this says something about the limitations of my ability to listen, and even my ability to write. But perhaps it also says something important about the genius of Mozart, and the things his music succeeds in expressing where words fail.

No wonder so many of those spellbound by Mozart's music have chosen to hear the divine in it. 'God was singing through this little man to all the world,' says Salieri in Peter Schaffer's *Amadeus*, in a state of wonder even as he plots Mozart's downfall. And yet there's also something entirely unpretentious about Mozart's music: a lightness that is present even when it is busy plucking at the strings of your heart. Though I've still to find a music critic who writes about Mozart in a way that I can get my head round, I come across a quote by Konrad Wolff, a German pianist and author, which encapsulates the simple delight of listening to Mozart's formidably complex music. 'His music speaks of God, of moral values,' he writes, 'but it can also be used to suggest the ringing of wine glasses, or of sleigh bells.'[14] Two more resonant sounds it is hard to imagine.

So ends my first classical music review. It feels primitive; a faltering attempt at a cadenza of my own. But it's a start. And I'm now more alive to the lasting miracle which is Mozart's music. I am learning to marvel at the sheer complexity of just this one piano concerto, albeit from an amateurish distance. How could it have taken me so long to get around to listening to it again even halfway properly? And why did I not do it with Dad while I still could? It is always later than we think.

Now, after at least half a lifetime, Piano Concerto No. 22 in E-flat major (K. 482) is starting to feel like my theme tune again. I'm an agnostic, but listening to this piece puts me into a state of sprightly grace. It's not a still or reverential way of being, but one that is alive, dynamic and optimistic, in the spirit of a four-year-old child tripping down a staircase. It's a strange reaction to a piece of music which never fails to make sharp my bereavement. But it's also a piece which gives me a quiet conviction that Dad still lingers with me somewhere among the bars of the music.

Chapter 2

The Rite of Stravinsky

The Firebird Suite, Petrushka and The Rite of Spring

Stravinsky returns to me one day in December while driving across the Severn Bridge. I'm on my way back from a work meeting in Wales and his short *Symphonies of Wind Instruments* of 1920 is playing on the radio. The gappy, discordant blasts of woodwind and brass are as dazzling as the low winter sun in my wing mirror. I am awestruck by the music's otherworldly quality, but also by its arresting modernity which seems to chime perfectly with the visuals of my journey: the frosted landscape and the square, soaring towers of the suspension bridge. A memory kindles of Dad talking to me about Stravinsky when I was very small. I remember that I loved the composer's name when Dad said it out loud: shivering at the exotic Russian sound of it and how it felt in my mouth when I spoke it to myself.

The Firebird Suite was the first Stravinsky piece Dad played to me. I was immediately captivated by its fiery, infernal tunes, but I also found its stormy drama – so different from the lulling piano tunes of Mozart – a little scary. Still, I enjoyed trying to spot the bits of music which denoted the Firebird herself: I could almost see her glowing. In my memory, it was another piece I happened to overhear Dad playing on his tape recorder. But now I wonder whether he had chosen to play it deliberately, to broaden the interest I had shown in Mozart. Whichever, it was an inspired choice of music to play to a young child.

Igor Stravinsky (1882–1971) once said of his own childhood that it was a 'period of waiting for the moment when I could send everyone and everything connected with it to hell'.[1] Born into a prosperous St Petersburg family, he surprised his parents at the age of two by humming from memory a folk tune he had heard. Both his parents were musicians; his father was the principal bass singer at the famous Mariinsky Theatre, and a well-known artist of the day. But he was no Leopold Mozart with musical ambitions for his son, and ordered Igor to pursue a legal career despite his early talent for music. Still, from the age of seven or eight, the young Igor was taken regularly to the Mariinsky Theatre, where he sat in the family box decorated with winged cupids. And there he fell in love with ballet, and with the music of Russian composer Pyotr Tchaikovsky whom he once glimpsed in person in the theatre foyer, a sighting which Stravinsky later described as one of his 'most treasured memories'.[2] Also formative were the summers Stravinsky spent at the family's country estate outside St Petersburg, where he saw and heard the peasant dances he would later incorporate into his own music.

After his father's death in 1902, Stravinsky, who had begun to compose piano pieces instead of studying statutes, abandoned the law. He was taken on as a pupil by the renowned Russian composer and orchestrator Nikolai Rimsky-Korsakov. Often inspired by fairy and folktales, few of Rimsky-Korsakov's works are now widely known, with the exception of his orchestral suite *Scheherazade*, a haunting piece with an exquisite violin solo which Dad also loved and tried out on me. In the act of listening with father once more, I'm beginning to recollect just how much music Dad played to me throughout my childhood, whether I bothered to listen properly or not. This tenacity, as he pitted himself against my new pop idols, makes me sad, and it also makes me smile.

In 1905 Stravinsky composed his first symphony, and continued to develop rapidly as a composer under Rimsky-Korsakov's tuition until his mentor died in 1908. The grieving Stravinsky wrote a funeral piece for the memorial concert. A few months later, two more Stravinsky pieces, *Scherzo Fantastique* and *Fireworks*, received their first performances in St Petersburg. In the audience was an extraordinary mover and shaker of a man who would provide Stravinsky with the stage that would bring him worldwide fame.

When he first encountered Stravinsky's work, Sergei Diaghilev was already a celebrated impresario, an audacious promotor of the arts and the founder of new avant-garde dance company Ballets Russes, whose stars were the dancer Vaslav Nijinsky, choreographer Michel Fokine and designer Léon Bakst. Diaghilev was on the lookout for composing talent to add to this glittering line-up and, on the strength of hearing Stravinsky's early compositions, asked him to orchestrate some Chopin pieces for a ballet he was producing. He was so pleased with the result that he commissioned a full score from the young composer for the second Paris season of the Ballets Russes, which also included a performance of a ballet for Rimsky-Korsakov's *Scheherazade*.

In an autobiography published in 1936, Stravinsky writes

that ballet was then looked down upon by 'serious musicians' and in the intellectual circles of the day. 'They considered this form of art as an inferior one.'[3] Nevertheless, *L'Oiseau de feu – The Firebird*, Stravinsky's new ballet score inspired by a Russian folktale and first performed at the Paris Opéra on 25 June 1910, was a hit with both critics and public, and brought its composer instant fame. Stravinsky was also fully involved in its staging and attended every rehearsal, and reports that he, Diaghilev and Nijinksy 'generally ended the day with a fine dinner, washed down with a good claret'.[4] Nijinsky did not dance in the first production of *The Firebird*, but Anna Pavlova, the famous Russian ballerina of meringue-dessert fame did. However, Stravinsky writes of his disappointment that Pavlova, 'with her slim, angular figure', was not cast as the Firebird, the role going instead to another prima ballerina, Tamara Karsavina.[5]

I find a performance of *The Firebird* on YouTube by the Mariinsky Ballet company – then still known as the Kirov – in Paris to celebrate the legacy of Nijinksy. Featuring the original Fokine choreography, it stars Russian ballerina Diana Vishneva in the title role, flashing across the stage in a red feather tutu and hairpiece. It's a delicious spectacle, and very Russian in flavour. Then, from Dad's CD collection, I dig out a recording of *The Firebird Suite* played by the Cincinnati Symphony Orchestra, conducted by Paavo Järvi. It's not the original 1910 version of Stravinsky's piece, but a slightly later, extended version from 1919. I download it to my iPod, remembering how I listened to it with Dad when I was five or six, goose bumps rising (again), an image of the Firebird seared into my mind. Listening to it now, however, it doesn't have quite the same visceral effect. Not yet, anyway.

And then, one dark Monday in January, I play *The Firebird Suite* through my headphones while walking to the station to catch an early London train. And, magically, unexpectedly, Stravinsky's music transforms my routine route into a walk of wonder. The low and growly beginning to the piece reels me slowly into a hyperaware, even spooked state in the winter morning darkness and the presence of the Firebird lurks in the trees all around me. When a cyclist shoots past, his red dynamo rear light flashing, I start, and the hair on the back of my neck stands up, because I am convinced that the Firebird is upon me. Safely on the train, I listen again and, as dawn breaks over the Wiltshire downs, something elemental invades this most ordinary of mornings, through the anarchic topsy-turviness of the music, with its frantic xylophones, jarring trombones and jangling triangles. While I frequently play music without consciously listening to it, Stravinsky makes terrible background music. If you half listen to it while doing something else, it rebels in the hearing, jerking you to attention. And it has the power to make the most humdrum of settings course with mystery and magic. By the time I arrive in London, I have decided that what every morning commute needs is the wake-up call of orchestrated triangles.

On the same Cincinnati Symphony Orchestra CD is a recording of Stravinsky's next composition for the Ballets Russes, *Petrushka*. Dad played this piece to me, too, and I loved its folky, jaunty tunes the first time I heard them. Stravinsky's original piece for orchestra included a leading role for the piano, playing the title part of Petrushka (the Russian equivalent of the French Pierrot, or the British Punch). Full of themes from traditional folk tunes, and influences from Italian commedia dell'arte, *Petrushka* tells the story of a puppet made of straw and sawdust, but with the human capacity to love.

Premiered at the Théâtre du Châtelet in Paris on 13 June 1911 with Nijinsky dancing the title role, *Petrushka* – or *Petrouchka* in the original French – was another triumph for the Ballets Russes, and for Stravinsky, whose circle now included Maurice Ravel, Erik Satie, Jean Cocteau and Pablo Picasso. Another friend, fellow composer Claude Debussy, was particularly struck by the music at the point when the Showman first appears and brings his puppets to life. 'There is in it, a kind of sonorous magic, a mysterious transformation of mechanical souls which become human by a spell of which, until now, you seem to be the unique inventor'.[6] Stravinsky always insisted that it is not Petrushka's ghost which appears at the end of the ballet, but a living being with human passions who has been enslaved by evil magic.

There are some striking photographs of various ballet dancers in the role of Petrushka in a book my mum received as an eighteenth birthday present from Dad – then her boyfriend – in 1952. Called *Baron at the Ballet*, it pairs the sumptuous ballet photography of Baron – the professional name of Sterling Henry Nahum – with commentaries by Arnold L. Haskell. When I was a child, I spent hours looking at this book, and its companion volume, *Baron Encore*, poring over the extravagant, ethereal dresses of the ballerinas. Haskell writes of *Petrushka* that it 'remains the greatest of all dramatic ballets, one that is so Russian in spirit that only a Russian company can interpret it'. Yet I watch *Petrushka* online, performed by New York's Joffrey Ballet, with Rudolf Nureyev in the title role. Though the spectacle is both colourful and touching, the way that painted puppets are made to play out a burlesque version of very human passions is also grotesque and disturbing.

Still, I'm pretty sure that Dad loved the music without much bothering about the ballet. So I put the puppets from my mind, resolving to get to grips with the music properly. I read through the sleeve notes from Dad's CD and discover that the human characters in both ballet scores (Prince Ivan, the princesses, the crowds at the Shrovetide Fair) are represented by diatonic motifs, while the supernatural ones (for example, the Firebird) are interpreted by chromatic motifs. I remember playing chromatic scales when I was learning the piano, a fast-fingers exercise where all twelve notes of the scale, both black and white, are played quickly in sequence. Slowly, by listening to both pieces again, and with a bit of background reading, I unravel what this means in terms of *Petrushka*, and in the process discover something about why Stravinsky still sounds so fresh and striking more than a century later.

In the late nineteenth century, certain composers who preceded Stravinsky – Wagner and Mahler, and Beethoven before them – had already shaken up the accepted sound of harmony by introducing more chromatic sequences into their works. The effect is unsettling to the ear because it renders the music less consistently 'tuneful'. But by employing the then revolutionary technique of placing notes from the seven-note diatonic scale (the Do-Re-Me-Fa-So-La-Ti basis of almost all classical music up to that point) against the twelve-note chromatic scale, Stravinsky forced the listener to deal with music that effectively pitches two contrasting sound systems into battle. The dissonance that results launches us into a sort of hinterland between the real world and somewhere more mystical. The effect is deliberately disorientating, and I start to understand why listening to *The Firebird* on a dark winter morning was so spooky.

A renowned example of this is the so-called 'Petrushka chord', which represents the puppet's insults. 'I had in mind a distinct picture of a puppet, suddenly endowed with life, exasperating the patience of the orchestra with diabolical cascades of arpeggio. The orchestra in turn retaliates with menacing trumpet blasts. The outcome is a terrific noise which reaches its climax and ends in the sorrowful and querulous collapse of the poor puppet,' wrote Stravinsky in his autobiography.[7]

I listen to *Petrushka* over and over again, trying to hear the changes and the contrasts and the colour. For days on end the piece becomes my earworm: looping manically through my head every morning when I wake up. But listening in this concentrated way is hard, and the music still baffles me a little.

Hear Me Out is the multi-talented Scottish writer Armando Iannucci's account of his love affair with classical music, which began at the age of thirteen when he heard *The Planets* by Gustav Holst. Despite his years of listening, Iannucci still finds it hard, too. 'Maybe it's because we have a limitless supply of artistic content thrown at us online now, we've forgotten how to make time and room for just one thing, and one thing alone,' he writes. I'm trying hard, but often get distracted and realise that the music I am supposed to be concentrating on has washed over me without really registering. All too frequently, I find myself putting on something Dad would have hated instead: some purging funk and soul on Saturday-night radio, or the feisty pop songs of Taylor Swift, which my own daughter has taught me to love.

Iannucci mostly likes Stravinsky's music, but not always.

Early on in his book he challenges the reader to try and listen to more than two minutes of the composer's *Les Noces* 'without wanting to ram something with a hammer'. I've heard nothing in Stravinsky to make me want to do anything so extreme. But while I loved both *The Firebird* and *Petrushka* the first time I heard them more than forty years ago, appreciating the music properly seems to require a more grown-up application than I have yet acquired. Still, when I do manage to concentrate, I'm entranced by Stravinsky's melodies, and how they manage to be both bracing and alluring at the same time. I love being kept on my toes by his unpredictable tunes, which constantly pinch you alert, even when you've heard them many times. And as I keep listening, I start to notice something capering about his music. Before I know it, images from the *Tom and Jerry* cartoons are spooling through my head.

At first, this is both hilarious and wonderfully appropriate because my serious, cerebral Dad also loved cartoons. The woolly Shaun the Sheep soft toy I bought him because he loved that Aardman series still sits on a low stool in my parents' living room. And when I was a child, Dad and I watched *Tom and Jerry* together almost every weekend. Spike the bulldog (memorable catchphrase: 'Dat's my boy') was Dad's favourite character, but he only appeared in selected episodes. Otherwise, Dad had a strong preference for the 1950s and 1960s version of Tom the cat, whose goofy grey demeanour he always referred to as 'the proper Tom'. But whichever tomcat was on screen, the cavorting soundtracks were unmistakable. Now I find them morphing in my mind into the percussive anarchy of Stravinsky's early ballet pieces, but I'm concerned in case I'm making a trivial, mashed-up connection that would horrify any serious music critic. But then I read something else that Armando Iannucci says and feel reprieved: 'We normally think of Stravinsky as serious, but it was after hearing the Symphony in C that I started seeing him as someone who plays with music,' he writes. So that's it. It's the playfulness I'm hearing.

And there's another reason why Stravinsky and cartoons are so intertwined in my head. When I was seven or eight, Dad took me to the cinema to see Walt Disney's *Fantasia*. It was unusual for Dad to take me to the cinema. In what seemed a Disney-dominated era, it was Mum who took my younger brother and me to see *Cinderella*, *Sleeping Beauty* and *The Jungle Book* for the first time.

Yet, Dad was definitely a film buff. He had both a cine camera, and a cine projector, slightly exotic items in an ordinary Middle England 1970s household. At my annual birthday parties, after we had played pass the parcel, and Kim's Game, and gobbled down sausages on sticks and jelly from flowery paper plates, all the kids assembled in the living room, curtains thrillingly drawn during the daylight hours, for the grand finale: a cartoon film show. Dad had managed to locate a shop on the far side of town which rented out Disney films on cine reel, and this became my annual birthday treat. In our era of cheap DVD stockpiles, this tradition now feels sepia-tinted and quaint, and when I tell my own children about my childhood parties I feel as if I am turning the clock back to a distant era. I used to wonder whether I was romanticising the sense of excitement I always felt, until a chance meeting with Rachel, a childhood friend from that time. Unprompted, she told me that her abiding memory of our friendship remains Dad's cartoon film shows which gave my parties the kind of kudos that parents now spend a fortune to acquire.

Fantasia was first released in 1940 and consists of eight animated segments set to classical music, arranged by English conductor Leopold Stokowski. Regarded by many as Walt Disney's masterpiece, *Fantasia* 'predicted the modern music video', movie-review site Rotten Tomatoes says, calling the film 'a relentlessly inventive blend of the classics with phantasmagorical images'.[8] The classical soundtrack explains why Dad wanted to be the one who took me to see *Fantasia*. He probably hoped the cartoons would persuade me to listen to some proper music at last, music that might sink my burgeoning new obsession with *Top of the Pops*. But I remember my initial disappointment when I realised *Fantasia* wasn't a conventional story like the other Disney films I had seen with Mum.

I watch the film again for the first time in over forty years, and it separates out some of the segments which had morphed together in my memory into a jumbled sequence of fauns, blooming flowers, pirouetting elephants in tutus, and monks. Other parts I had entirely forgotten, including the blue silhouetted opening sequence in which the musicians of the Philadelphia orchestra take to the stage, followed by the figure of Stokowski. To the opening bars of Bach's Toccata and Fugue in D minor, coloured lights spotlight his back view as he conducts. There are action scenes of sections of the orchestra, which in turn give way to abstract animated representations of the ebb and flow of the music. I imagine I found these opening bits quite boring as I sat fidgeting in my seat, and with no sign of any Disney cartoon characters, I was probably already worrying that I was in for two dull hours. Little did I suspect what a lasting impression the film would make.

I imagine I was reeled in a little by the next segment, which features fluttering pastel lights of Tinkerbell-precursor fairies, hallucinogenic dancing toadstools, twirling flowers, flirtatious fish with long eyelashes leaving trails of bubbles, swirling autumn leaves, and bizarre, Cossack-dancing thistles performing to the music of Tchaikovsky's *Nutcracker Suite*. And then comes one of my still vivid memories of the film: its famous cartoon retelling of *The Sorcerer's Apprentice*, in which the familiar figure of Mickey Mouse struggles up flights of steps with constantly overflowing buckets while his master the sorcerer is out. Until, that is, he manages to enchant a broom to do the work for him. How sinister I remember finding the growing army of faceless bucket carriers who keep inexorably transporting water despite the rising flood tide, to the score of Paul Dukas's symphonic piece of 1897, based on a poem by Goethe. I watched with a sense of rising dread that Mickey was fathoms deep in trouble when the sorcerer got home: I, who hated my parents being cross with me.

But it is the next section of *Fantasia* which stuck in my mind for years afterwards. After a short pause in which tubular bells are heaved, clanging, into the orchestra, comes *The Rite of Spring* by Igor Stravinsky. Deems Taylor, the film's morning-suited narrator, introduces this section as a 'pageant', written 'by science, not art', and telling the story of life on earth 'in keeping with Stravinsky's original intention, which was to express primitive life'.[9] The cartoon, the narrator tells us, 'gives a coldly accurate reproduction' of what science thinks went on during the first few billion years of this planet's existence, beginning with those 'tiny little white or green blobs of nothing in particular which lived under the water'.

From the existential opening moment when the voiceover instructed me to 'imagine yourself out in space, billions and billions of years ago, looking down on this lonely, tormented little planet, spinning through an empty sea of nothingness', I was a child riveted. Watching this sequence again, I still find it thrilling as we pan from a view of our galaxy from afar to the tempestuous surface of the earth in its infancy, with its riot of eruptions and roiling, boiling lakes of molten lava and volcanoes blown sky-high with Krakatoa-like violence. There are over six long minutes of fire and brimstone before the inferno is eventually extinguished by the great rainstorms which created the seas.

Then life on earth begins with wriggling, single-celled organisms, which give way to jellies, anemones and plankton, fish and cephalopods. And then come the dinosaurs, whose on-screen conquest of the earth, before expiring en masse, is also among my most abiding memories of *Fantasia*. By that time I was, like many young children, already fascinated by dinosaurs, including the ones pictured on my set of Brooke Bond tea cards, which I studied carefully, marvelling at how a brontosaurus could get to be so very massive while only ever eating mouthfuls of swampy weeds, and petrifying myself about what it would be like to come face to face with a Tyrannosaurus rex. Both species are among the parade of dinosaurs which appear in *Fantasia*, with the T-rex cast to type as the most feared killer.

But even this terrible creature paled beside the true horror of *Fantasia*: its volcanoes. Why volcanoes frightened me so at that time I cannot imagine. But molten lava regularly scorched through my dreams, and in my worst nightmares infant volcanoes burst through the soil in the front garden just below my bedroom window, spewing fiery fountains which melted the glass and incinerated the walls. *Blue Peter*, which had shown a film about the birth of Surtsey, a volcanic island which, terrifyingly, rose right out of the sea off Iceland in the early 1960s, might have been to blame. But now, watching *Fantasia* again, I realise that the origin of my childhood dread was surely that cinema visit with Dad, and those extended sequences of orange Technicolor lava, spewing and surging. With its tumultuous earthquakes and tectonic shifts, and a total eclipse of the sun, this part of the film sowed existential dread into my impressionable young mind. And while the Technicolor animated images were probably the chief cause, I'm convinced that the explosive musical qualities of the opening part of *The Rite of Spring*, which accompanies them, must also have played their part. So it's no surprise when I discover that many of those who heard the first performance of Stravinsky's ballet score also went home in a disturbed state.

Stravinsky wrote *The Rite of Spring* – *Le Sacre du Printemps* – for the 1913 Paris season of Diaghilev's Ballets Russes, with choreography by Nijinsky. The disturbing signature idea behind it first came to him in a 'fleeting vision' while he was working on the final pages of the score for *The Firebird*: 'I saw in my imagination a solemn pagan rite; sage elders, seated in a circle, watched a young girl dance herself to death.' Diaghilev was enchanted by the idea, but Stravinsky, sensing that its composition would be 'a long and difficult task', decided to 'refresh himself' by working on *Petrushka* first instead.[10] After the 1911 Ballets Russes season in Paris, Stravinsky returned to his country estate at Ustyluh, a town now in western Ukraine, to begin work on *The Rite of Spring* in earnest. In composing it, he was inspired by folk tunes, primarily Lithuanian ones, and by his memories of the violent coming of the Russian spring, which, he later recalled, 'seemed to begin in an hour and was like the whole earth cracking. That was the most wonderful event of every year of my childhood.'[11]

The Rite of Spring is subtitled 'scenes of pagan Russia in two parts'. The first part, 'The Adoration of the Earth', begins with the awakening of nature after the long winter, followed by a series of ritual dances – some of them highly frenetic – by the women and men of various Slavonic tribes. It climaxes with a frenzied 'Dance of the Earth'. Part II, 'The Sacrifice', takes place at dawn. From among the young women of the tribe a sacrificial victim is selected to ensure the future fertility of the earth, and the tribal elders gather to witness her final 'Sacrificial Dance', the subject of Stravinsky's sudden, strange original vision of the rite.

While Stravinsky was working on music, first at Ustyluh, and then in Switzerland, Diaghilev had decided to use the new ballet as an opportunity to turn his star dancer and lover Nijinksy into a choreographer. This plan filled Stravinsky with deep misgivings. In his 1936 autobiography he writes, '... notwithstanding our friendliness and my great admiration for his talent as dancer and mime ... [Nijinsky's] ignorance of the most elementary notions of music was flagrant'.[12] Just as he had feared, the production process proved a nightmare. Nijinksy demanded an impossibly high number of rehearsals, and while Stravinsky tried to teach him the rudiments of music, he proved incapable of retaining any of it. Recalling the heavy and stormy atmosphere in the rehearsal room, the composer writes that 'it was evident that the poor boy had been saddled with a task beyond his capacity'.[13]

The Rite of Spring received a famously riotous reception at its première at the Théâtre des Champs-Élysées on 29 May 1913. While some of those present embraced its revolutionary sound and crazy choreography, large sections of the bourgeois and conventional audience expressed outrage at what was being presented to them in the name of art. 'This, surely, was not ballet, but a display of unrestrained and uncensored primitive emotion. The costumes were coarse and rustic, the dancers' moves were ugly; the music was unmistakably lewd,' writes art historian Sue Roe, imagining this stormy reaction in her book *In Montparnasse*.[14]

The writer Gertrude Stein, who was in the audience, recorded the scene in her book *The Autobiography of Alice B. Toklas*: 'We could hear nothing ... one literally could not, through the whole performance, hear the sound of the music.'[15] The artist Marcel Duchamp, who was also present, remarked that the performance of the audience made more of an impression on him than that of the dancers. 'I left the auditorium at the first bars of the prelude, which had at once evoked derisive laughter. I was disgusted,' Stravinsky writes in his autobiography. He headed to the wings of the theatre, where he found Diaghilev flicking the house lights on and off in a vain attempt to restore order, and Nijinsky standing on a chair, shouting out directions to the dancers, who could not hear the orchestra over the din of the audience. 'I had to hold Nijinksy by his clothes, for he was furious and ready to dash on stage at any moment and create a scandal.'[16]

Stravinsky praises Nijinsky's 'unsurpassed rendering' of the role of Petrushka.[17] But he is scathing about his first foray as a choreographer, perhaps holding him responsible for the extreme first-night reaction to *The Rite of Spring*: 'What the choreography expressed was a very laboured and barren effort rather than a plastic realisation flowing simply and naturally from what the music demanded. How far it all was from what I had desired!'[18]

Nijinsky's choreography is indeed bonkers. Online, I watch a recreation of his version of *The Rite of Spring* by the Mariinsky Ballet, performed on the centenary of the first performance at the original venue, the Théâtre des Champs-Élysées.[19] It is such a bizarre mélange of stomping, leaping and punching the air, slapping the earth, incontinent prancing and jigging and zombie-like pacing. The agitating effect this chaotic and weirdly impersonal spectacle had on an audience more used to the dainty, seamless choreography of *Swan Lake* is perhaps not surprising. But the volcanic dissonance of Stravinsky's score must have been equally disturbing, just as it was to me as a small child. Giacomo Puccini, the Italian composer of operas such as *La Bohème* and *Tosca*, who also attended the first performance of *The Rite of Spring*, remarked that it was the 'work of a madman'.[20] 'Listening to this mad music over a century on, I find it's lost none of its raw power,' Clemency Burton-Hill writes of the piece in her book *Year of Wonder*.

By a strange, unplanned serendipity, I find myself trying to get to grips with *The Rite of Spring* just as spring is trying to arrive, not in the uneventful way that is usual for the English climate, but with a turbulence that could be straight out of Stravinsky's childhood. Just as the daffodils in the garden are budding, winter reprises with a vengeance, leaving snow in high drifts against the garden walls and the roads impassable. Though the snow melts a couple of days later, disappearing as quickly as it arrived, the sudden hike in temperatures makes it easier to think of the arrival of spring as Stravinsky did: a violent event which makes the very earth crack open after months of being buried under a deadening layer of snow.

There isn't a recording of *The Rite of Spring* in Dad's CD collection, so I turn to his *Penguin Guide to Compact Discs & DVDs* (2003/4 edition; the spine is cracked with use) for advice about which one to buy. Dad has pencil-starred a Columbia Symphony Orchestra recording of 1960, conducted by Stravinsky himself, and underlined the words, 'This is a CD that should be in every basic collection.' 'It has never been surpassed as an interpretation of this seminal 20th-century score,' reads the review. So I order it. When my CD arrives, I try and wipe any vision of Nijinksy's anarchic choreography from my mind, as I listen over and over again to the score for *The Rite of Spring*. From the opening plaintive bassoon solo which announces the beginning of Stravinsky's 'cracking of the earth' and the debut of spring, the music – without the ballet – penetrates to a deeper place in my imagination. I no longer picture a T-rex eviscerating a stegosaurus, or even a trickle of lava. Instead, I am enthralled by the drama of the music alone – the rapid changes of tempo, of pitch, of volume. It sounds like the circus, like a medieval pageant, a runaway train, a runaway brass band, a belly dance, a blizzard, a slow orgasm, a T-rex in a china shop, driving through a forest on a very dark night, an LSD trip, a shoot-out in a Wild West saloon . . . and a matter of life and death. It sounds like everything – and nothing on earth. It's unsettling, seductive, alienating, hypnotic, bracing and alluring all at once. But I still don't really understand what makes the music able to do all this.

A few more clues come from a BBC Radio 4 programme on Stravinsky, presented by music journalist Ivan Hewett. It's part of a series called *All in a Chord*, which investigates the idea that harmony is a reflection of history.[21] The furore that *The Rite of Spring* première provoked was, the programme argues, in large part due to the frantic dissonant chord which occurs early on in the piece to signify young pagan men beating the earth in order to encourage it to be fruitful. The sense of agitation provoked by the sound and rhythm of the chord also mirrors the historical tension and disquiet in the air in 1913, the year of its first performance, and a year before the outbreak of the First World War, the programme explains. It was a time when Germany was rearming, and both Britain and Germany were building battleships galore. Conflict in the Paris auditorium in 1913 would soon give way to conflict on the field of battle. 'The dissonances in the piece come out of the dissonances in world politics.'[22] Surely a piece for our times, too.

Two constituent chords only a semitone apart and played together produce the dissonant 'Rite of Spring' chord in question. Though close together on the piano, these two chords are miles apart harmonically, and sound 'wrong' when played together. But they also give a 'tremendously energetic scrunch, like dropping the crockery all at once'.[23] This sense of two elements pulling in different directions also reflects the contrast between the primitive earth myths related in the ballet, and the birth of the modern world. Poet T. S. Eliot was among the first to recognise this after hearing a performance of *The Rite of Spring* in London. It seemed to transform, he said, 'the rhythm of the steppes into the scream of the motor horn, the rattle of machinery, the grind of wheels, the beating of iron and steel, the roar of the underground railway, and the other barbaric cries of modern life; and to transform these despairing noises into music'.[24] Eliot was responding to something inhuman in the music, which I think explains why it works so well with the tectonic sequences of lava and lizards in *Fantasia*.

I smile when I read that the American composer and conductor Leonard Bernstein referred to *The Rite of Spring* as 'prehistoric jazz'.[25]

I sit down at the piano and play the two chords. As I pound the keys, the discordant noise jolts up a nervous physical energy in me, and I start picturing the spewing lava from *Fantasia* all over again. It's tremendous fun. But I shouldn't be having fun. I'm still concerned that I'm doing this complex and revered music an injustice. I find myself pining a little for the graceful, resolving melodies of the Mozart piano concerto, which feel so complete in themselves, and which cleanse my head of any sense of music as soundtrack.

Even though it still sounds filmic, even cartoonish sometimes, perhaps this is partly because so many later composers for film were influenced by Stravinsky's music, including John Williams. But, equally, Stravinsky's music never sounds to me as if it needs images to go with it. The marvellous tunes in *The Firebird Suite* and *Petrushka* were sufficient to make an impression on me as a child without me once seeing the ballets for which they were written. The music doesn't need to be paired with anything, even the magical and mysterious stories it was originally written to accompany. The pictures are already there, enshrined in the music.

My dawning understanding of how the music paints such pictures feels like listening progress. But I want to subject Stravinsky to the test of hearing his music live, with no visual distractions other than the presence of an orchestra. The London Philharmonic Orchestra season entitled 'Stravinsky's Journey' at the Royal Festival Hall includes a performance of *The Rite of Spring*. I treat myself to a seat in the front stalls in the hope of experiencing something of the same shock of the new as that Paris audience almost 105 years ago.

An hour before the concert starts, I go to a free in-conversation session with the conductor, Juanjo Mena. The talk is popular and the stalls are almost three-quarters full. Mena speaks eloquently of the difficulties *The Rite of Spring* presents for a conductor, due to its rhythmic complexity and the sheer mass of orchestral sound. When the audience is invited to ask questions, a man pipes up to tell an anecdote about watching Leonard Bernstein conduct *The Rite of Spring* at Croydon's Fairfield Halls during the 1960s. He remembers that Bernstein made the trumpet players start playing with the bells of their instruments between their knees, and then as the piece progressed, gradually raise them until they were pointing straight at the audience. 'I felt pushed back by a wall of sound,' the man recalls.

As I take my seat for the concert, I find myself longing for Dad to be here with me. We would have started the evening with a drink from the bar and chatted about the atmosphere, other concerts he had been to and enjoyed, and what he heard when he listened to Stravinsky. I feel a restlessness, too, from walking through the streets of London and across the river to the South Bank, feeling a hint of spring in the air all the while.

The atmosphere in the concert hall is almost festive as the orchestra takes to the stage. At a time when an unpleasant debate is raging post-Brexit about foreign workers, and who is allowed to stay and who will have to go, the London Philharmonic Orchestra, like most big orchestras around the world, is blatantly multi-national and multi-ethnic. The conductor, Juanjo Mena, is Basque Spanish; the leader of the orchestra, Kevin Lin, Korean American. Sitting four rows back from the front, I have a tremendous close-up view of the large double-bass section. I make a study of the variety of black shoes being worn by the instrumentalists: mirror-shiny brogues, killer heels, black slingbacks with diamanté buckles. It's a Wednesday night in February, but nevertheless a proper classical concert brings a sense of occasion to midweek: white ties and tailcoats, cocktail frocks of net and lace.

Tonight's programme consists of seasonal pieces with a French theme by some of Stravinsky's friends and contemporaries, before *The Rite of Spring*, which is the finale. We hear Debussy's *Printemps*, a symphonic suite, followed by Maurice Ravel's Piano Concerto for the Left Hand, with Benedetto Lupo as soloist. Commissioned by Paul Wittgenstein, a brother of the philosopher Ludwig, who lost his right arm in the First World War, the piece is foot-tappingly jazzy, with the same energy and curly-wurliness I have been hearing in Stravinsky.

Mena, a grand presence in a grey suit with a Nehru collar is such a jaunty and expressive performer that his baton seems redundant, almost disappearing at times into his large fist. I am more used to folk and rock concerts, with their consistent amplification, so am struck by the variations in volume and tone. The mere act of sitting and listening suddenly feels like a wonderful ability to have. I think of my recent interview with writer Bella Bathurst. Within a few short months when she was in her late twenties, Bathurst lost 80 per cent of her hearing. She spent the next twelve years in denial of this hearing loss before pioneering surgery corrected the problem. Her book *Sound: Stories of Hearing Lost and Found* is a rousing testimony to listening, something precious that we should cherish and exercise more appreciatively. In the final pages of her book, she recalls the experience of going to a concert by the Berliner Philharmoniker six weeks after her hearing had been restored. 'It was the first true music I'd heard in more than a decade and I promise you, I absolutely promise, that if you should ever have cause to question the power of music or its capacity to reset the very cells of you, then try going deaf and then getting your hearing back after twelve years,' she writes.

The second half of the concert begins with a rarely played piece by Yorkshire-born composer Frederick Delius (1862–1934), his *Idylle de Printemps*, written a year after he moved permanently to France in his mid-twenties. It is one of his earliest surviving orchestral works, and provides a steadying apéritif before the fireworks of *The Rite of Spring*. Then it's time. Extra reinforcements in all sections of the orchestra are brought on stage. Mena holds out an arm, and the eerie, opening bassoon solo begins, played at 'lento tempo rubato', literally 'slow, robbed time'. This means, I have discovered, that the passage can be dwelt upon, with a slight speeding up and slowing down that is at the will of the soloist.

Heard live, the beautiful sound jungle of Stravinsky's piece is mesmerising to the ear. But the sheer physicality of the orchestra is also riveting. The waves of movement as the musicians bow and bend over their instruments give the orchestra a beautiful visual harmony. With the most emphatic blasts of brass and woodwind, conductor Juanjo Mena's feet leave the ground completely. The leader of the orchestra's pizzicato passages are electrifying to watch. We are not just listening to a piece of music. We are watching a human drama which makes the idea of watching a ballet at the same time feel superfluous. I look around at my fellow audience members. Many, like me, are leaning well forward, their bodies tensed in a stage of hyper-alertness. And so many of them are young, soaking all this up at an age when I barely gave classical music a thought. Stravinsky's music demands a total performance, and a total performance is what we are given. At the end, the applause is rapturous.

Despite the prevailing hostility with which the first performance of *The Rite of Spring* was received, Stravinsky quickly overcame his early notoriety to embark on a long and extraordinarily varied composing career, which brought him worldwide, pop-star level fame. Exiled from his native land following the outbreak of the First World War and the Russian Revolution (he did not return to Russia until 1962), Stravinsky settled first in Switzerland, and then in France, before the outbreak of the Second World War in 1939 led him to leave Europe for the United States, where he was to live permanently. A year later, Disney's *Fantasia* was released. Stravinsky was subsequently courted by the flourishing US film industry and in 1960 was inducted into Hollywood's Walk of Fame. He partied with Cole Porter, slept with Coco Chanel, hung out with the likes of Fred Astaire, Alfred Hitchcock, Greta Garbo and Sergei Rachmaninoff. As Richard Bratby puts in his programme notes for the London Philharmonic Orchestra concert, 'Stravinsky had a gift for putting himself wherever the cultural action was.'

Armando Iannucci writes that Stravinsky's contemporary, Sergei Prokofiev, jealous of all the attention his fellow Russian began to get after *The Rite of Spring*, tried to turn his Second Symphony into 'music of iron and steel that would get him noticed'. The result is a piece Iannucci dubs 'one of the ugliest pieces of music I've come across . . . a deliberate grinding clank of industrial noise that shows no sign of letting up'. It turns out that Stravinsky was a champion exponent of treading the fine line between shocking us with discord and captivating us with melody. Perhaps that's why his music — more often than that of any other twentieth-century composer — is said to epitomise that most creative and yet destructive of centuries.

To the end, Stravinsky's career as a composer was a travelling show, just as Mozart's was two centuries before. He spoke French, German and English as well as Russian. He worked almost every day until the end of his life in April 1971, his ambition always to 'earn every penny that my art would enable me to extract'.[26] Well into his seventh decade, he began each day with Hungarian calisthenics, including walking on his hands. And he was a renowned hypochondriac, walking four miles almost every day on round trips to consult his Los Angeles doctor. Perhaps a man who had lost both his first wife and his eldest daughter to tuberculosis in the late 1930s can be forgiven such an indulgence. Stravinsky was, to the end, records his *New York Times* obituary, 'a fountain of wit and acidulously put wisdom'. And yet for all his worldly sophistication, he remained restless at night, always needing a light on outside his bedroom. For that was how he slept as a boy in St Petersburg.[27]

In the last decade of his life, this man born into the political turbulence of late nineteenth-century Russia had engaged with the politics of the later twentieth century, too. Visiting South Africa in 1962, two years after the Sharpeville Massacre, when the police turned their guns on protesters, and at a time of violent turmoil, Stravinsky insisted on conducting a concert for a Black audience, in defiance of the apartheid laws of that time. In a moving BBC World Service documentary, Michael Dingaan, a South African chorister and conductor, explains that when Stravinsky arrived in South Africa to conduct the all-white symphony orchestra of state broadcaster SABC, he initially seemed reluctant to upset his hosts.[28] In a press conference at the tour's outset, he denies having given any thought to the fact that he would be performing only for white audiences. 'I don't understand these questions,' he said, while protesters outside held up placards reading: 'Music is black and white notes.' Then, asked if he would like to appear before mixed audiences, Stravinsky found the perfect riposte. 'I like to appear before human beings. That is all.'

In fact, Stravinsky had already sent a telegram to the SABC requesting that his concerts be open to everyone. While this was refused, he was allowed to organise what was then referred to as a 'Bantu concert' for a Black audience, in order that he could, as he put it, 'arrange things decently'. That historic free concert by the SABC Symphony Orchestra took place on 27 May 1962, in the township of Kwa Thema, east of Johannesburg. One concertgoer recalls how even as Stravinsky raised his hands to begin conducting, the 1,000-strong audience went berserk. But then, when the music began, 'you could hear a pin drop'. For most members of the audience, it was the first time they had seen an orchestra. In its way, it was as bold and revolutionary a moment as the opening bassoon solo at the first performance of *The Rite of Spring* fifty years before.

Stravinsky's was both an epic physical and political journey; from tsarist Russia to Hollywood, via apartheid-era South Africa. And it was also an epic creative one, coursing through the musical movements of almost an entire century. Yet it is for *The Rite of Spring*, composed when he was still in his early thirties, that Stravinsky remains best known. 'There is still no more influential piece of music in the 20th century,' writes music journalist Tom Service in his *Guardian* piece published to mark the centenary of the ballet's first performance.[29] And Stravinsky himself remained devoted to the memory of his earliest and still most celebrated compositions: *The Firebird*, *Petrushka* and *The Rite of Spring*. When he died at the age of eighty-eight in New York City in 1971, he crossed the Atlantic one last time. His body was flown to Europe to be buried, at his own request, in the Russian section of the cemetery on the island of San Michele in the Venice lagoon, close to his friend and flamboyant collaborator Diaghilev, who had died in Venice more than forty years earlier. Online you can find film footage of his funeral ceremony, which shows his flower-decked coffin being transported to the Isola di San Michele in a beautifully decorated gondola.

Though I've now travelled through an entire winter and into the following spring with Stravinsky's music, I'm conscious that, except for my brief encounter with his *Symphonies of Wind Instruments*, I haven't yet listened to anything he composed during the last six decades of his life. There is so much more to Stravinsky than his early pieces, including an opera – *The Rake's Progress* – composed in tribute to Mozart. But then, as I'm driving home one evening, the fourth and final movement – the Capriccio ('a caprice, free in form and light in style') – of his Violin Concerto in D of 1931 comes on the radio. I sit spellbound in the car in my driveway in the dark. And, as I listen, there are no pictures in my head: no volcanoes, no dinosaurs, no dancing princesses, no fiery feathers, no puppets, no sacrificial ceremonies. There is nothing in my mind but a sublime whirlwind of musical notes, coming from a piece which wrestles more types of sound from a violin than I ever realised were possible.

Five years after composing this glorious Capriccio, Stravinsky wrote in his autobiography, 'I consider that music is, by its very nature, essentially powerless to express anything at all, whether a feeling, an attitude of mind, a psychological mood, a phenomenon of nature, etc. . . . Expression has never been an inherent property of music . . . It is simply an additional attribute which, by tacit and inveterate agreement, we have lent it, thrust upon it, as a label, a convention – in short, an aspect unconsciously or by force of habit, we have come to confuse with its essential being.'[30]

It's a strange statement from someone who so beautifully told through his music the magical stories I heard as a child. But then I am floored by what Stravinsky writes next. 'Most people like music because it gives them certain emotions such as joy, grief, sadness, and image of nature, a subject for daydreams or – still better – oblivion from "everyday life". They want a drug – dope . . . Music would not be worth much if it were reduced to such an end. When people have learned to love music for itself, when they listen with other ears, their enjoyment will be of a far higher and more potent order, and they will be able to judge it on a higher plane and realise its intrinsic value.'[31]

Reading Stravinsky's words makes me realise with a sinking heart that choosing music in response to my mood is all I ever do. A few days earlier I had left the funeral of a friend's mother, craving music to blast through the stilted sadness of the crematorium ceremony. So I drove across the Wiltshire downs with Led Zeppelin's 'What Is and What Should Never Be' turned up high. Jimmy Page's jolting guitar riffs and Robert Plant's uncompromising vocals shook me back into the land of the living in a way that the music of Stravinsky, even at its most arresting, would have struggled to do.

In the pub that evening, I muse with a guitar-playing friend about why it is that, sometimes, there is no simple substitute for the bracing effect of high-voltage, electric guitar playing. 'It's the amygdala,' interjects another friend, back from the bar with a round of drinks. I nod ruefully as I sip my wine. Stravinsky so wouldn't approve of me doping myself with music that I know will go straight to the emotional processing centre of my brain. But while *The Rite of Spring* has opened up a big rift in my sense of classical music as essentially quite tame, listening to it has not, I now realise, been a particularly soulful experience. Armando Iannucci describes Stravinsky as a composer that people 'admire greatly rather than love'. I know what he means. In contrast with my time with Mozart, listening to this small selection of Stravinsky's music, although shot through with chromatic colour and rhythmic surprises, has ultimately been a cerebral business rather than a transformative one. I have found no new state of grace.

Stravinsky's crucial importance to my act of remembrance, however, is that his music has cast my dad in a fresh light. For my father was in many ways the most conservative of men; so conventional that he refused to wear jeans, and only agreed to wear cords after years of chivvying from Mum. But because of Igor Stravinsky, I am having to completely revise my perception of his staidness. Dad loved the work of two composers as contrasting as Mozart and Stravinsky. His music collection is turning out to be far more eclectic than mine. And so I, as Stravinsky demanded, must also learn to listen to it with other ears.

Chapter 3

The Feelings of Ferrier

'Blow the Wind Southerly' (traditional)

Blow the wind southerly, southerly, southerly,
Blow the wind south o'er the bonny blue sea;
Blow the wind southerly, southerly, southerly,
Blow bonnie breeze, my lover to me.
They told me last night there were ships in the offing,
And I hurried down to the deep rolling sea;
But my eye could not see it wherever might be it,
The barque that is bearing my lover to me.[1]

Sometimes, after Sunday lunch, Kathleen Ferrier would make Dad cry.

During Sunday lunch – the one meal of the week we ate together at the dining-room table – I was more often the one in tears. I couldn't stand Sunday lunch, usually tough, greasy meat followed perhaps by apple strudel, sickly heavy on the cinnamon.

My parents would have opened a bottle of Charbonnier red wine, or sometimes a sweet Nierstein or Liebfraumilch white, Dad tying a paper tissue around the neck to catch the drips as he always did.

Once lunch was over, however, the mood would lighten when Dad put a reel-to-reel tape on, most often a vintage *Goon Show* he had recorded from the radio. My younger brother and I were introduced to Eccles and Bluebottle and Major Bloodnok twenty years after their 1950s heyday. Or we'd have Flanders and Swann singing 'The Gnu Song', 'Mud, Mud, Glorious Mud', and 'Have Some Madeira, M'Dear'. Up in my bedroom, I was listening to bands like The Real Thing. Downstairs in the dining room, I was treated to the vintage cream of the BBC Home Service.

At other times Dad would play music, and then the mood was entirely different. I remember darkening winter Sunday afternoons when the tolling bell in Berlioz's *Symphony Fantastique* would mournfully remind me of time running out before my return to school on Monday morning, and send me hurrying upstairs to draw my orange flowery curtains and finish my homework by desk lamp.

And when he played his recording of Kathleen Ferrier singing 'Blow the Wind Southerly', my unemotional, logical, reasoning Dad, who never cried, would weep. It upset me so much to see this, but I never dared ask him why. I was too afraid of what the answer might be. But once I asked Mum and she told me that 'Blow the Wind Southerly' was a very sad song, and that Kathleen Ferrier had died young (at only forty-one), which meant that when you heard her sing it made the song even sadder. Next time Dad put on 'Blow the Wind Southerly', I tried to make sense of what was so upsetting about the song lyrics. But I concluded that the story of a women waiting for her – husband? boyfriend? – to sail home wasn't nearly as tragic as that told in 'Billy Don't be a Hero' by Paper Lace. So I gave up trying to understand and I also tried to forget the sight of my father in tears.

This vivid memory of Dad in tears is painful to recall now. But all these years later I start thinking about his reaction to 'Blow the Wind Southerly' in the light of Stravinsky's disparaging remarks about people who dope themselves with music to induce emotions such as joy, grief and sadness. I want to try and understand why, if he knew 'Blow the Wind Southerly' would upset him, Dad kept on listening to it?

Perhaps he listened precisely *because* it made him cry. My dad was, as I mentioned earlier, the child of dour Victorian parents, a member of a generation for whom the phrase 'boys don't cry' was a mantra. I, his daughter, cry easily, sometimes embarrassingly so. In fact, as a child I was a terrible cry-baby – outwardly confident, but brittle with emotions that always whirled just beneath the surface. As an adult, I still inconveniently shed tears, however hard I try to hide how upset I am in order to appear composed in front of a boss or my children, or try to conceal my sentimental reaction at the end of the cheesiest of films. But tears from my dad were unicorn-rare.

Dad's original reel-to-reel recording of 'Blow the Wind Southerly' has long since gone, so I buy a CD called *The World of Kathleen Ferrier*, an album of nineteen songs which opens with 'Blow the Wind Southerly'. With its cargo of memory, Ferrier's voice is hard to listen to dispassionately. The yearning intensity for a lost love that the song conveys chimes more readily with me now, and I can appreciate the intensity Ferrier brings to her concentrated a cappella rendering of the piece. But something about her highly cultivated voice leaves me a little cold. Her rounded and precisely enunciated singing style sounds contrived at first to ears long attuned to the freeform voices of rock and contemporary folk singers, where attention is focused more on delivering a performance of character, rather than a strict attention to whether each lyric is articulated.

The pitch of her voice sounds weirdly deep, too. Ferrier was a contralto – categorised as the lowest type of female singing voice, its 'tessitura' or range a relative rarity – but since her 1940s and 1950s heyday, the contralto voice has fallen out of fashion. Yet once upon a time contralto singers were everywhere, 'mainstays of all the choral societies in the land, rousing us to action or soothing us with maternal balm', to quote Rupert Christiansen writing in the *Daily Telegraph* in 2010.[2] Historically, while contralto voices abounded in Bach's choral music, early Venetian operas featured them only for grotesque roles like old crones and witches, and by the mid-eighteenth century they had effectively disappeared from the repertoire (there are no contralto parts in Mozart's operas, for example). As a consequence, more recent singers blessed with contralto voices have mostly chosen to major on classical song rather than opera, or train their voices upwards, with singing teachers routinely coaxing 'deeper, darker voices to look up into the sun of mezzosopranodom rather than down into the earth of contraltohood', as Christiansen puts it. Perhaps this is why I find the pitch of Ferrier's voice disconcerting and a little alien.

'Blow the Wind Southerly', a traditional Northumberland folk song which she sang unaccompanied, became a popular fixture in Kathleen Ferrier's repertoire towards the end of the Second World War, just as she was starting to cut her first recordings. Born near Preston in Lancashire in 1912, Ferrier grew up in Blackburn, where her father was a primary-school headteacher. She showed an early talent as a pianist but, as the third of three children and with her father about to retire, her parents did not have the money to send her to music college. So Ferrier left school at fourteen and went to work at the local Post Office, where she was later promoted to the position of telephonist. All the while, she continued with her piano lessons, winning several competitions.

In 1935 she married Bert Wilson, and as, with many other organisations at that time, married women were not allowed to work at the Post Office, Ferrier gave up her job for the role of a small-town bank manager's wife. It was not one she was destined to hold for long. In 1937 she entered a singing competition at the annual Carlisle music festival after her husband bet her a shilling that she wouldn't dare compete. She won first prize, with one of the adjudicators noting that she had a 'very, very beautiful voice indeed'.[3] Over the next two years, Ferrier's singing career began to take off, with bookings for concerts and radio broadcasts.

And then came the war. Her husband was called up, and their enforced separation effectively marked an amicable end to the marriage, which both parties had regarded as a mistake from the beginning. Ferrier apparently confessed to her sister that she knew she'd done the wrong thing in going through with the wedding, but had felt trapped by circumstances and could see no way of calling it off. Free and single and once more known as Miss Kathleen Ferrier, she passed an audition in 1941 for CEMA, the Council for the Encouragement of Music and the Arts, a wartime organisation which arranged for troupes of artists to tour troop camps, works canteens, offices and factories to boost morale and bring entertainment to those who otherwise would have little access to it. Such concerts were enormously popular and Ferrier soon found herself travelling the length and breadth of the country. Once, when she arrived to give a CEMA performance on the Isle of Dogs with her pianist, she found that the canteen in which they were due to appear had been bombed. But someone pushed an upright piano out from a pub and the concert went ahead as planned.

It was through such performances that Ferrier cemented her popular reputation. Reading about her punishingly scheduled tours – for example, taking her from Dover to Bristol to Bournemouth to Bromley to Stourbridge to Stockport to Burnley within the space of mere days – recalls a bygone era when there was a concert hall in every small town and every performance received a review in the local newspaper. Commenting on Ferrier's particular appeal, a fellow CEMA performer, Helen Anderson, said: 'It was partly voice, and partly the warmth of her personality which communicated so strongly to her audiences. She so loved singing to people that they instinctively loved her back.'[4]

In an illuminating piece entitled 'Klever Kaff', an ironic nickname that Ferrier often gave herself, the late writer and editor Ian Jack recalls listening to her at his childhood home in Lancashire in the mid-1950s on 78 rpm records brought home by his elder brother, and feeling a sense of pride, or perhaps amazement, that 'such a voice could have come from such a place: 57 Lynwood Road, Blackburn, Lancashire' (Ferrier's childhood home).[5] She was, Jack writes, '. . . a girl who . . . was as ordinary (and by extension as interesting) as ourselves'. Trying to explain her appeal more than four decades later, he concludes:

> First, I think we felt that Ferrier's was the opposite of a disembodied 'voice'; a personality housed in flesh and blood was singing, and directly, it seemed, to us. Second, the voice made

us respectful and contemplative – even to a ten-year-old it could do this. I suppose we were in the presence of beauty – often a grave beauty; even the jauntiest folk song, 'The Keel Row' had something sad inside it.

In person, Ferrier inspired great affection in her friends for her self-deprecating and salt-of-the-earth sense of humour, as well as for her singing. During the war, she trained her voice to do a very convincing imitation of an air-raid siren. There are film clips of her gurning and sticking her tongue out, and recordings of drunken singing and piano playing. The ribald performance of bawdy rhymes and limericks was also something of a speciality: 'There was a young lady of Nantes/Très chic, jolie et élegante/Her hole was so small, she was no good at all/Except for la plume de ma tante.' Ferrier also loved telling the story of how, when she returned to her old school, someone was heard to whisper, 'You can tell she's a singer, look at the size of her mouth.'[6] Ferrier did indeed have an enormous throat cavity, which gave her voice its deep and rich timbre. 'One could have shot a fair-sized apple right to the back without obstruction,' as her voice coach once said.[7] I begin to warm to Ferrier's spiritedness before I warm to her voice. Classical music is routinely talked about with such seriousness, but Ferrier said boo to all that. This is a woman who enjoyed drinking and smoking, and who referred to Brahms's *Alto Rhapsody* as the 'Alto Raspberry', or renamed the aria 'Softly Awakes My Heart' from the Saint-Saëns opera *Samson and Delilah* 'Softly Awakes My Tart'.

In a typical performance, Ferrier would sing pieces by Handel, Purcell, Schubert, a few operatic arias, lieder by Brahms and Schumann, songs by the likes of Vaughan Williams and Frank

Bridge, and some folk songs. She increasingly sang in big choral works like Bach's *St Matthew Passion* and Handel's *Messiah*, too. And in 1944 she was given a hitherto little-known folk song to perform, 'Blow the Wind Southerly'. It remained her signature piece. While she would eventually sing many classic choral works and operas on some of the world's great stages, popular songs with their vernacular North Country titles and lyrics and their simple themes of everyday joy and sorrow always remained a fixture in Ferrier's repertoire. These songs have wonderfully quaint titles: 'The Fidgety Bairn', 'Curly Headed Babby', 'I Have a Bonnet Trimmed With Blue', 'Drink to Me Only With Thine Eyes', Ben Jonson's 'Song to Celia'. It's a revelation to me how charming and affecting they are. I love 'Come You Not from Newcastle' with its gorgeous simplicity of sentiment: 'Come you not from Newcastle?/Come you not there away?/O met you not my true love/Riding on a bonny bay?/Why should not I love my love?/Why should not my love love me?/Why should not I speed after him/ Since love to all is free?' And I am particularly taken with Ferrier's recording of 'Down by the Salley Gardens', a lamenting folk song by W. B. Yeats, set to music by Benjamin Britten. 'It was down by the Salley Gardens/My love and I did meet/She crossed the Salley Gardens/With little snow-white feet/She bid me to take life easy/As the leaves grow on the tree/But I was young and foolish/And with her I did not agree.'

By the end of the Second World War, Ferrier had divorced Bert and gone up to London on Christmas Eve 1942, moving into a rented flat in Hampstead with her now widowed father and her sister Winifred, to whom she remained close all her life. Before long, work was 'rolling in'. She made her first recordings with Columbia Gramophone Company in 1944 but had reservations about their quality, and worried about the fact that rival company Decca seemed more technically advanced. When the attentions of Columbia's artistic director became less than professional (there were rumours of him making a pass at her in a taxi), Ferrier severed her contract and signed with Decca. She soon became a hugely popular recording artist at a time when gramophone ownership was rocketing. Her first big hit was an aria, originally written for castrato voice, from German composer Christoph Willibald Gluck's 1762 opera in Italian, *Orfeo ed Euridice*. 'Che faro?' is sung by a despairing Orfeo after he has turned to look behind him and with that look returned Euridice to the underworld for ever. In English the opening words are: 'What is life to me without thee?/What is left if thou art dead?/What is life; life without thee?/What is life without my love?/What is life if thou art dead?' Ferrier's recording of 'Che faro?' topped the bestseller charts for months, outselling records in every other musical category, and became an enduring favourite even of those who had hitherto little interest in classical music.

Such was the broadness of Ferrier's appeal at this time that you would have been as likely to hear her singing on the BBC's Light Programme as on the Home Service or the Third Programme (today's equivalent of Radios 2, 4 and 3). Paul Strang, chair of the Kathleen Ferrier Awards – founded after her death to support the careers of talented young singers – writes strikingly of Ferrier's popular appeal at this time, reminding us that she was at the height of her powers just as Britain was emerging from a decade of 'deprivation, misery and danger'. 'The period of the war and its aftermath,' he writes, 'had created a public hunger for music.'[8]

This hunger meant that Ferrier was now also in demand to

sing on the country's biggest stages, including Westminster Abbey, the Albert Hall, where she made her Proms debut on the Last Night in 1945, and the Free Trade Hall in Manchester, where she once travelled to perform a concert by bus. When she got off, the conductor, seeing the huge crowds gathering outside the hall, remarked, 'If you're thinking of going to the concert, love, you'd better forget it. You'll never get in, the place is packed'.[9] Also part of Ferrier's popular repertoire at this time was 'Dove sei, amato bene?' ('Art Thou Troubled?'), an aria from Handel's 1725 opera *Rodelinda*. Again originally written for castrato voice, the aria is addressed by Bertarido, the deposed King of Lombardy, to Rodelinda, his wife, imprisoned by Grimoaldo, Duke of Benevento, who has usurped him from the throne. It opens:

> Art thou troubled?
> Music will calm thee,
> Art thou weary?
> Rest shall be thine.
> Music, source of all gladness,
> Heals thy sadness at her shrine,
> Music ever divine,
> Music calleth with voice divine.

It's a beautiful anthem to music as balm for whatever life throws at us: war, strife, poverty, bereavement, separation. I listen to my recording of Ferrier singing 'Art Thou Troubled?' in English over and over, and slowly begin to appreciate the stilling quality to her voice. Something about the careful and stately way she forms the words and notes takes hold of me in a deeply soothing way. Listening to her feels like having a warm blanket wrapped around one's shoulders, and I can easily imagine the comforting effect hearing it must have had on people who were both weary of war and deeply troubled about what the future might hold.

Does music heal our sadness by giving us a conduit for it? I think of Dad's tears as he listened to Kathleen Ferrier and wonder whether they were in some way healing or cathartic. In 2017, a Japanese study measured the reactions of 154 participants to different pieces of music, and how often they experienced such emotions as goose bumps, shivers, crying or a lump in their throat. Making a distinction between the effect of 'chills' (i.e., goose bumps and shivers) and actual 'tears', the study's authors concluded that 'tears involve pleasure from sadness and . . . are psychophysiologically calming; thus, psychophysiological responses permit the distinction between chills and tears. Because tears may have a cathartic effect, the functional significance of chills and tears seems to be different.'[10]

Although Stravinsky's words have made me wary of giving in to sentimental reactions to music, I start thinking about my own Cathartic Chart Toppers. For a while, the third movement of Mozart's Piano Concerto No. 22 qualified, but I've now moved past a place of grief to somewhere more serene when I listen to that piece. I think of others – Joni Mitchell singing 'Little Green' about the daughter she gave away for adoption. Neil Young singing 'Harvest Moon'. Jeff Buckley singing more or less anything. Nina Simone singing 'The Twelfth of Never'. Anything by Amy Winehouse. Christmas carols, especially 'Silent Night'. And 'Abide With Me'. Tears always begin prickling in my eyes as soon as I sing the words: 'Fast falls the eventide.' I know that this hymn had a similar effect on Dad. He went to almost every FA Cup final during the 1950s and so had a special affection for this traditional anthem sung before those matches.

While pondering all of this, I attend a Cheltenham Science Festival event entitled 'Writing Emotion Into Music' with the TV and film composer Will Gregory, one half of electronic duo Goldfrapp, and neuropsychologist Dr Catherine Loveday. They discuss the role of harmonics and the reinforcement provided by the tonic in setting the tone for our emotions when we listen to a given piece of music. The kind of folk songs in which Kathleen Ferrier specialised, including 'Blow the Wind Southerly', always bring with them a sense of an ending, and of resolution. However keening the lyrics, they do not leave us hanging, and therefore the act of listening, and also singing them leaves us with a sense of closure, albeit alongside lingering sadness.

Then, accompanied by a soundtrack of examples as diverse as Pachelbel's Canon, the Jacksons, Ennio Morricone and John Coltrane, our speakers illuminate the technical devices that composers use to evoke different emotions in the listener. Coltrane's 'Giant Steps', for instance, whirls us around with its minor-third intervals in a disorientating and even exhausting way. Choosing J. S. Bach's Toccata and Fugue in D minor to accompany the title sequence of the 1975 film *Rollerball* is a deliberately dissonant statement. Sequences of notes that lie close together in the scale like this create a disturbance in the cochlea, confuse our brains and make us uncomfortable. And Berlioz's *Symphony Fantastique* makes use of an idée fixe, I learn, in this case the very tolling bell I remember from Sunday afternoons, to give us the sense of being haunted by the music.

At another event, entitled 'Can Science Explain Music?',

neuroscientist, doctor and philosopher Raymond Tallis takes the view that, no, it can't, while musician and physicist Mark Lewney maintains that it can. Tallis quotes Claude Lévi-Strauss, who called music 'the supreme mystery of human knowledge', and asserts his opinion that it would always remain so. Lewney counters by referencing a 2001 study which showed that koi carp could distinguish between an oboe concerto by J. S. Bach and guitar and vocals by John Lee Hooker. So surely, he says, music's emotional qualities ought, neurologically, to be definable, plottable via neural networks. 'We're not just neural networks,' responds Tallis. 'We're the only creatures that enjoy emotion for its own sake.'

I'm with Tallis. Surely our individual emotional reactions to music, or indeed any other art form, can't be explained by neurological triggers alone? After all, the neurological properties of the human brain can be generalised. The effect a particular piece of music has on us cannot. Music acquires such a complex individual cargo of personal memories and associations, and perhaps even Dad himself didn't quite know why listening to Kathleen Ferrier singing 'Blow the Wind Southerly' made him so emotional. It's possible that it just made him rather maudlin – after half a bottle of Charbonnier – to listen to the beautiful lost voice of a woman who died tragically young. But even as a child, I think I sensed something else at work.

I've been reading *This Is Your Brain on Music: Understanding a Human Obsession*, in which Daniel Levitin, a musician and record producer turned neuroscientist, discusses the relatively recent discovery that musical activity involves nearly every region of the brain, and every neural system, in an extraordinarily complex network of firings. The emotions that we experience when we listen to music, for example, 'involve structures deep in the primitive, reptilian regions of the cerebellar vermis, and the amygdala – the heart of emotional processing in the cortex'. And yet, he says, exactly how the brain leads us to experience emotional reactions 'is part of the mystery of music'. Later he admits that 'scientists can't even agree about what emotions are'. Appropriate, given that Dad – a Cambridge-educated scientist – was always interested in what science can't tell us, as well as what it can.

In 1947, Kathleen Ferrier performed at the first Edinburgh Festival in *Das Lied von der Erde*, a cycle of six songs for two voices by Gustav Mahler, which he completed in 1909 but which he was never to hear performed before his death only two years later. This 'song-symphony' was written following a painful period in Mahler's life: in 1907 he had lost his eldest daughter Maria to scarlet fever and diphtheria, been forced to resign as the director of the Vienna Court Opera, and been diagnosed with the congenital heart defect that would soon kill him. He had been reading ancient Chinese poetry, which had made a great impression on him, and used the lyrics– with the addition of a few of his own – translated into German for the songs in *Das Lied von der Erde*. The songs meditate variously on youth, on the beauty of the earth and its transience, and on human mortality. The final song, 'Der Abschied' ('The Farewell') is a long goodbye in which the singer describes the beauty of the nature around her as night falls, as she prepares to bid a final farewell to her friend, and to the world.

The 1947 Edinburgh performance of *Das Lied von der Erde* was conducted by Bruno Walter, a pupil of Mahler's who had conducted the first performance in Munich in 1911. Even though its Edinburgh premiere took place more than thirty-five years later, the programming of *Das Lied von der Erde* still caused controversy, some considering the performance of a major German language work at the inaugural festival in poor taste so soon after the end of the war. The Jewish Mahler's works had, in fact, been banned as 'degenerate' by the Nazis in 1941, although performances by Jewish orchestras and for Jewish audiences in both Germany and Austria took place up until that time. Many of them were conducted by Bruno Walter, who was also Jewish, until he was forced to flee Germany and make his home in the United States for the rest of his life.

The German Dr Walter was immediately taken with the English Miss Ferrier, and their Edinburgh collaboration marked the beginning not only of a considerable revival of Maher's reputation in Britain but of a fruitful musical association between the seventy-something conductor and the thirty-something contralto. In an interview recorded at the Edinburgh Festival a few years later, Ferrier described the experience of working with Walter as 'my greatest good fortune'.[11] Summing up Ferrier's talent, Walter later wrote, 'Whoever listened to her or met her personally felt enriched and uplifted. By her sublime art and by her loving nature she gave happiness and received happiness'.[12]

In rehearsal for the Edinburgh Mahler, Ferrier had to keep breaking off from singing the final song 'Der Abschied' because she was so overcome with emotion. In English, the song concludes: 'Oh my friend, fortune was not kind to me in this world! Where am I going? I shall wander in the mountains, I am seeking rest for my lonely heart.' Walter wrote of Ferrier's tearful rendition that 'with all her willpower and vigour she could not help it, and only by and by did she learn to control her feelings. But nothing could be further from her than sentimentality – in those tears spoke strength of feeling, not weakness, and a deep comprehension for another great heart'.[13] In performance as she sang the final line – 'Ewig ... ewig ... ewig ...' ('For ever and ever') – Ferrier cried unbidden tears once more.

It's fascinating to read about Ferrier's raw emotion while performing the Mahler song cycle, because earlier in her career, after being told by people whose opinions she deeply respected that her singing lacked emotional conviction, Ferrier had sought professional help to inject more feeling into her voice, and to overcome the alleged psychological hurdle of being brought up in a working-class culture which shunned outward display. As the Manchester-born journalist and critic Neville Cardus – whose writing on both music and cricket Dad much admired – once remarked, 'It is a Lancashire custom to lock endearment up in the heart except at weddings, Christmas, and at funerals.'[14] And yet Ferrier often felt her emotions very deeply indeed. In a BBC interview years after her death, her friend Peter Pears, who often sang with her, said: 'If anything, Kath felt things almost too strongly. She often had to fight to control her tears.'[15]

A rave review of Ferrier's Edinburgh performance in *Punch* magazine describes *Das Lied von der Erde* as the 'golden sunset of the Romantic period and the most complete expression in the whole of music of a human's grief at his own evanescence. In it, Mahler unfolds his vision of the universe and of all beauty and colours luminous with agony.' I, however, am having problems digesting *Das Lied von der Erde*, and feeling that tension so often experienced by tentative listeners to classical music of thinking you ought to like something rather than actually liking it. In contrast to the contained sublimeness of Mozart, and the arresting inventiveness of Stravinsky, it all feels rather overwrought, and I find that even Kathleen Ferrier can't make me feel anything very much. I'm reminded of the character played by Maureen Lipman in the film of Willy Russell's *Educating Rita* who says: 'Wouldn't you simply die without Mahler?'

While I doubt he would have considered it a matter of life and death, I know that Dad was very fond of Mahler's orchestral music: there are several recordings of Mahler's symphonies in his CD collection. And we once watched the film of *Death in Venice* together, adopted from Thomas Mann's novella. The final sequence when von Aschenbach (played by Dirk Bogarde) breathes his last on the beach of the Venice Lido to a soundtrack of the sublime fourth movement Adagietto of Mahler's Fifth Symphony had me riveted. At the time, I was studying the book for A-level German, and afterwards found I couldn't read it without hearing Mahler in my head.

I'm still struggling with Mahler's *Das Lied von der Erde*, however. Then I happen to hear the late Jane Birkin on *Desert Island Discs*. She chooses Mahler's unfinished Tenth Symphony for one of her eight records, telling the presenter that once, when she was listening to it in the car while driving in central Paris, she was so overcome by the emotion in the music that – blinded by tears, she said – she scraped her car right along the length of a stationary police car by Les Invalides. Asked to explain herself, she blamed it on the Mahler and, after she had played it to him in evidence, the police officer let her off. Possibly his vision of the luminous – and then mega-famous – Birkin in distress also had something to do with it.

In the wake of her emotional success in *Das Lied von der Erde* at the inaugural Edinburgh Festival, Kathleen Ferrier received invitations to perform all over the world. She sailed for her first tour of the United States on New Year's Day 1948, opening with a series of concerts with Bruno Walter at Carnegie Hall in New York. Overall the tour brought mixed reviews, and Ferrier, who had to pay her own travel and hotel expenses out of her concert fees, revealed her constant worries about money in letters home, even while delighting in shopping trips which yielded a pair of pony-skin boots, a banana and some Lux soap, all triumphantly purchased without coupons. She made no personal profit from the tour at all. But one review from this time tells us something else about why Ferrier was such a treasured performer. Written by the celebrated music critic of the *Chicago Tribune*, Claudia Cassidy, known as 'acidy Cassidy' for frequently taking no prisoners in her reviews, it reads: 'Miss Ferrier is a notable newcomer with a germ of greatness ... Her essential quality is a kind of bedrock simplicity, a native serenity stemming from strength.'[16]

While the realities of touring may have been less than glamorous, Ferrier was steadily cementing her international reputation. She became the first British singer to perform at the Salzburg Festival (in *Das Lied von der Erde*), and in 1950 made her debut at La Scala in Milan in Bach's B minor Mass. Taking a break from Mahler, I listen to a recording of the Bach, in which Ferrier sings alongside famous soprano Elisabeth Schwarzkopf. Her slow solo singing of the 'Agnus Dei' bewitches me. It is utterly spine-tingling, beautiful in its purity and sincerity, and you feel almost compelled to place your hands together in prayer as you listen. According to Schwarzkopf, Ferrier's rendition of the 'Agnus Dei' in rehearsal made conductor Herbert von Karajan – renowned for his toughness – burst into tears. There are some photographs of Ferrier taken at this time by Norman Parkinson in which she looks radiant.

But then, in spring 1951 when in her late thirties, Ferrier found a lump in her breast and cancer was diagnosed. She had always particularly feared such a diagnosis having in childhood witnessed one of her neighbours, an old lady, enduring a slow and painful death from the disease. Consequently, from the early 1940s onwards she nursed a fear that the occasional pains she suffered in her breast were a sign that she herself had been afflicted. In 1949, when she finally plucked up the courage to get herself checked out, she was pronounced fit and well. Just two years later, however, she was being admitted to hospital for a mastectomy, an operation which was followed by long bouts of radiation treatment. In *An Ordinary Diva*, a 2004 BBC documentary, Professor Robert Souhami, the first Kathleen Ferrier chair of oncology at University College Hospital, remarks that Ferrier had obviously had her cancer for a long time but had concealed it 'as indeed a lot of women used to do in those days'.

Neither in those days was cancer something those in the public eye went on TV and talked about. Ferrier's fans were devoted but knew next to nothing about any aspect of her personal life – she gave few newspaper interviews and there are no TV or cinema newsreels of her speaking. She bore her illness entirely in private and, by all accounts, with great fortitude and typical humour: in one letter, revealing her diagnosis, she refers jauntily to 'a bump on mi busto'.[17] Only a few people ever knew what was really wrong with Ferrier: arthritis was the explanation given for her absences from the concert platform.

A few short weeks after her mastectomy, Ferrier was back performing.

In November 1951 she sang in the presence of the then Princess Elizabeth to mark the reopening of the bomb-damaged Free Trade Hall in Manchester. Her performance concluded with a rendition of Elgar's 'Land of Hope and Glory', marking the climax of the evening. I locate a scratchy recording on YouTube, and am moved to tears despite myself by the perfectly pitched majesty Ferrier restores to a song which we now associate with comic bobbing and enthusiastic Union Jack-waving at the Last Night of the Proms. 'Lovers of this tune will fear that, never again, can they hope to hear it in such glory,' wrote Sir John Barbirolli, the conductor that night.[18] His words now seem fateful. For Ferrier struggled to regain her former vigour and, before long, it was clear that her cancer was not beaten. She underwent further radiation treatment throughout 1952, but continued to perform, singing at her seventh consecutive Edinburgh Festival that summer.

In May she had travelled to Vienna to make a recording of *Das Lied von der Erde* with Bruno Walter, and it is this late recording that I have been listening to. I'm finally starting to make some headway with it, but it is the 2004 BBC documentary which finally cracks me open to the music. 'She was in considerable pain much of the time, and it's impossible to listen to the recording they made during those extraordinary, heart-breaking days without taking the personal circumstances of the artists into account,' relates Robert Lindsay in his voiceover commentary. 'Bruno Walter, the composer's friend, and Kathleen, who perhaps knew that it was her own farewell, that she might only see the lovely earth grow green again once more, like Mahler, rose to the challenge of a death sentence by reaching for perfection in her art.' Hearing this, and then listening to her sing the 'Abschied' again, I suddenly feel I've never heard anything so bitterly yet exquisitely beautiful as the parting two minutes of Ferrier singing 'ewig ... ewig ... ewig.'

In February 1953, shortly after being made a CBE in the new Queen's first New Year Honours list, Ferrier was billed to sing in a scheduled four performances of *Orpheus and Euridice*, a new English-language version of Gluck's opera at the Royal Opera House in London's Covent Garden. In the end, she managed just two. Towards the end of the second performance, her femur snapped and partly crumbled, a weight-bearing bone weakened by secondary cancer. The crack was reportedly audible to some in the audience. 'It must have been excruciatingly painful,' says Professor Souhami in the BBC documentary. In a revealing 2012 interview, Irish opera singer Veronica Dunne, who was a soloist alongside Ferrier that night, says that in rehearsal she had no idea how ill Ferrier was. 'Cancer was never mentioned,' she says. But by the final chorus she was no longer in any doubt. 'Suddenly I realised how ill this woman was, and what courage she had.' Ferrier vomited with pain in the wings, but insisted on carrying on and, after a morphine injection, took several curtain calls. 'She knew she was dying and thought, I'm going to give the performance of my life,' says Dunne.[19] Ferrier never performed in public again.

In the knowledge of this extraordinary courage, I now find listening to Ferrier's rendition of the aria 'What is Life?' agonising. I cannot imagine how it must have been for Ferrier to sing those words while in such pain and in the knowledge that she was dying. The undertone of melancholy in all her singing, as if there is a premonition in all of it, is now all too painfully obvious. And it moves me so much to think that Dad must have heard this melancholy, too, and that it made him cry. The foreshadowing of his own death from cancer is also hard to avoid, particularly as Dad also refused to acknowledge he wasn't well for far too long. It took my mother breaking down in tears and begging him to go to the doctor before his diagnosis of prostate cancer was confirmed, too late for any treatment to be effective. What is life, indeed.

After bingeing on Ferrier's voice for weeks, I begin to find it hard to listen to, such are the associations I now feel. If I do listen to her, I am no good to anyone. Only recently, I would have overcome this musical slough of despond by putting on some jaunty pop. But I scroll down my iPod and scan my CD collection in vain. There's nothing else I want to listen to. It's like opening my musical wardrobe and finding I have nothing to wear on my soul.

Kathleen Ferrier died on 8 October 1953 at the age of forty-one. At her memorial service in Southwark Cathedral the following month, a thousand people crammed into the building, far more than the 300 who had been officially invited. Among the congregation that day were Laurence Olivier, Vivien Leigh and Benjamin Britten. And the streets outside were crowded with ordinary people wanting to pay their last respects. 'Shopgirls, clerks, nurses and housewives mingled with celebrities,' writes Ferrier's biographer, Maurice Leonard. 'Her exuberant love of life had communicated itself through everything she sang. She seemed to bring into this world a radiance from another world. Born among the warm hearts of the North Country . . . she knew she was a steward of a great and glorious possession, and was determined to use it to bring happiness into the lives of millions,' said the Bishop of Croydon, a friend of Ferrier's who presided over the ceremony, in his address. Bruno Walter said that the two greatest musical experiences of his career had been working with Kathleen Ferrier, and with Gustav Mahler, 'in that order'.[20]

A wave of grief and affection for a woman who had progressed from a small singing competition in Carlisle to owning the Covent Garden stage in little more than a decade. A woman who had sung her heart out for the people all through the war years and the days of deprivation that followed. 'Housewives who had never been near a concert hall or opera house paused in their chores when her recordings were broadcast on the Light Programme,' writes Rupert Christiansen. 'As she sang, she became every woman who had waited for a loved one to come home or who knew one who wouldn't. Her voice spelt loss and comfort, grief and hope to a generation which had seesawed between those states.'[21]

Now it occurs to me that perhaps Dad was only feeling what so many others felt when they heard Ferrier's voice. Perhaps the essential point about her extraordinary appeal is that, however she did it, she managed to make everyone who heard her feel what she felt. As I've been looking to the brain for an explanation, I'm struck by a slightly bizarre analogy Veronica Dunne makes. 'The brain is a computer, and so everybody in the audience has a computer. And in my lifetime [Ferrier] was the only singer that had a computer that got into the audience and into everybody's brain.'[22]

She has certainly got into mine. Firstly, because I truly love listening to her now. But also because I've realised that, along with Ferrier's ability to make me cry, she's actually very good at giving me a lift when I need one too. Listen to her gorgeously perky rendition of folk song and marital audition, 'Kitty, My Love', or the sublimely triumphant 'Hark! The Echoing Air' from Henry Purcell's *The Fairy Queen*, or her duet on 'Come Ye Sons of Art' also by Purcell, or her memorable version of 'O Thou That Tellest Good Tidings to Zion' from Handel's *Messiah* and your day will go all the better.

Alan Bennett has recalled his parents going to hear Ferrier sing in around 1947.

> Before she was really famous . . . she came to Leeds to sing at Brunswick Chapel. Uncle George made Mam and Dad go with him to hear her, and though they weren't big ones for singing, they came back full of this young woman . . . What makes music inviolable still for me, and preserves it from the poisonous flippancies of Classic FM, are scenes like that, a Methodist chapel in the slums of Leeds lit up and packed with people on a winter night in 1947 and the voice of Kathleen Ferrier drifting out over the grimy snow.[23]

Ferrier's death, Maurice Leonard wrote, 'cast a pall over much of Britain'. The public were stunned at the news, a conspiracy of silence having kept them in ignorance of her illness. Among those who mourned was actress Patricia Routledge, who early on had ambitions to train as a classical singer and who idolised Ferrier. 'She walked onto the platform with this quality that only a few of the greatest artists have – she made you feel that she would be singing just for you . . . I loved her. I cried in the street when I saw the headline announcing her death.'[24] I think again about Ian Jack listening to Ferrier a few years after her death and feeling like crying, even as a ten-year-old lad. Now when I listen to recordings of some of Ferrier's most notable performances, I hear a voice which reminds me that we aren't here for as long as we think. And that's how I come to understand why Ferrier's voice made Dad cry.

I enjoy a melancholy evening alone at home listening to her singing Purcell's 'When I am Laid in Earth', Mendelssohn's 'O Rest in the Lord', and *Das Lied von der Erde*. I put all worries about Stravinsky's doping out of my head and I wallow in the Ferrier blues. I think of my dad, whose prostate cancer spread to his bones too and left any treatment hopeless. I think of Ferrier, in similarly desperate pain, but still singing her heart out. I cry. But while listening to Ferrier reboots my grief, it also brings consolation. For Ferrier's voice still lives and sounds, and my memories of Dad still live, and the music he loved still sounds.

I feel I've gained an understanding, too, of how the act of singing – not merely listening to it, but actually doing it – brings a chemistry of consolation too. I hear a pure demonstration of this while on holiday in Portugal. In a church in Tavira, the Igreja da Misericórdia, I listen to a performance of fado – a melancholic and highly expressive Portuguese song style – by a young female singer called Sarah, accompanied by a guitarist and a lute player. Dressed in a short gold strappy dress and heels, tattoos across her tanned skin, Sarah walks down the aisle, stretching her arms plaintively out to us, and at one point exhorting us to la-la-la along. Even the small children in the audience are enraptured. She doesn't have the sweetest voice, it's true, but something about its lowish register makes it feel as if she is leaning in to tell us her life story. While most of us in the French, Dutch and English audience have little idea of what any of the words she sings mean, their tone is clear. They aren't sad exactly, in fact at times the songs she sings sound positively jaunty, but it is all unfailingly soul-baring, and there are tears in my eyes once more.

Afterwards, as we all stand around in church, knocking back little complimentary glasses of port, I ask Sarah about the content of the songs, hoping she will tell me some of their stories. But perhaps her English isn't up to the task, and my Portuguese certainly isn't. So I have to be content with her brief reply which is, 'Love. They are all about love.' Later I read about fado, which means 'fate'. This traditional song style draws upon the very Portuguese concept of saudade – a kind of unfulfilled yearning – as it laments the harsh realities of life. While its documented origins only go back to the early nineteenth century, and my thinking may be wishful, I feel I hear some kinship between the fado songs and 'Blow the Wind Southerly'. For Portugal, at the very westernmost edge of Europe, is also a seafaring nation, which for centuries has been sending its ships and its sailors across oceans to stake claims and bring home booty and, with it, tales of strange foreign lands. And for every barque that did return to port, how many did not? And how many of the loved ones left behind could be found standing on shore, looking out to sea, and waiting and hoping? Amid the melancholy always lies the hope that a change will come, or at least that the wind will switch direction. And there is certainly consolation in singing or even just listening to such music, whether that consolation is merely blindly hopeful, or has the certainty of religious faith behind it.

Kathleen Ferrier, definitely not one for holy cant, nevertheless sang religious music with a deep sense of spirituality. She once said that Brahms's *Four Serious Songs* were the best sermon that she knew, and the fact that she herself lived by their creed was the reason she found singing them so deeply moving. The songs were Brahms's last works for voice, and set texts from the Old Testament to music. I listen to Ferrier sing them on a 1949 recording she made with the BBC Symphony Orchestra, conducted by Sir Malcolm Sargent, who had transcribed the songs – originally written for piano accompaniment – for orchestra while at the bedside of his daughter Pamela, who was dying of cancer. At the time, I'm on a train to Brighton, packed with families on a sunny bank holiday weekend, which doesn't feel like the right setting at all. Especially when I listen to the third song, 'Oh Death, How Bitter Art Thou', and almost wince at the raw emotion in her voice as she sings the word 'bitter'. When Brahms himself sung this third song to friends in 1896, a few days after the death of his beloved friend Clara Schumann, 'great tears rolled down his cheeks, and he virtually breathed these last words of the text, with a voice nearly choked with tears'.[25] Ferrier put her own faith in the words of the fourth song, taken from 1 Corinthians. 'Though I speak with the tongues of men and of the angels, and have not charity, then am I become as a sounding brass, or a tinkling cymbal.'

Ian Jack quotes an anonymous listener, recorded in a 1955 biography of Ferrier, as saying that her singing 'made you wish you had led a better life'. How did she do that? Deeply buried personal grief, may, some feel, have had something to do with it: Neville Cardus speculated that '. . . disappointment in marriage probably canalised her emotional impulses'.[26] And Ronald Duncan, who wrote the libretto for Benjamin Britten's *The Rape of Lucretia*, once said that he thought that the source of her emotional impact was 'not only her unfortunate marriage but a need for love which life itself could not fulfil'.[27] After her marriage ended, Ferrier had one long-term relationship, but her career put paid to any kind of commitment, and she once wrote of herself that she was meant to be 'a lone she-wolf'.[28] And yet Ferrier, whatever her disappointments in love, and who by the painful end of her short life had more reason for bitter regret than most, still unfailingly thought of herself not only as Klever Kaff but also Lucky Kaff.

In the 2004 BBC documentary about Ferrier, mezzo soprano Dame Janet Baker, whose career was beginning just as Ferrier's came to an end, speaks of what it takes to be a great artist. Once you've established yourself, after all the years of practice and training, she says, you then have to have the courage to walk through the final door and reveal yourself as an individual human being who says, 'I'm giving you this music, but I'm saying it in the only way I can.' Kathleen Ferrier, she says, 'had that courage to a tremendous degree'.

After bathing in Ferrier's voice for weeks, a channel between her cultivated voice and the gulf of my listening inexperience has been opened. I hear now how she manages to make even the most mannered music sound unpretentious. True, I haven't yet cultivated much of a taste for Schubert's lieder, and I fear I might always find Mahler's *Das Lied von der Erde* impossible to love, apart from the very end. But Ferrier's lightness of singing style when she renders folk tunes like 'Ma Bonny Lad' makes my heart glad. And whenever I listen to Gluck's 'What is Life?', I am moved beyond words. Listen to Kathleen Ferrier sing, and think of the state of our world, and your heart will ache for the ephemeral lives we routinely make such a mess of.

And so I return to this question: was it possible that Dad wanted to weep, and that is why he would play that ordinary Lancashire lass Kathleen Ferrier singing 'Blow the Wind Southerly'? He, like Ferrier, came from a culture where feelings were held in: his father, Lancashire-born; his mother from a working-class Leicestershire family; her brothers coal miners. None of them were talkers. I'm more and more convinced that this is one of the things classical music did for Dad. It allowed him to let his repressed emotions course freely as he listened, even to the extent of crying. What I witnessed in my Dad's tears was not distress, but the side effect of music as consolation.

Popular music is explicitly emotional, both in content and intent. But it's hard to entertain the idea that either Bach or Mozart composed specifically with the emotional impact that their music would have on the listener at the forefront of their minds. And in this way, I can see what Stravinsky means. Music is just music: sublime and eternal. The effect it might have on us as individuals, despite some correlation of brain responses, is individual, and therefore trivial by comparison with its essential sublimeness. 'Blow the Wind Southerly' is a deceptively sentimental ditty, sung by a lovelorn landlubber. But I've grown to love the billowing melancholy of Kathleen Ferrier's unadorned rendition and the deep feeling she brings to it. You can listen to it and think of the personal fate that awaited Ferrier, but really it speaks to us of all those we have loved and lost: parents, siblings, friends, as well as lovers. And in that sense, listening unites us. Because we all wish sometimes that those lost to us would sail back over the horizon and into our waiting arms, even though we know they never will. Love is life's price, and its most precious gift.

In the 2004 BBC documentary, Dame Janet Baker says of Ferrier's 'Blow the Wind Southerly': 'To me it encapsulates her entirely. That roundness of vowel, that directness, the glory of this human sound.' In all my decades of listening to popular music, and more often than not to female singers, I've never thought so much about singing, nor understood the emotional places that the combination of music, words and the visceral power of one human voice can take me. In this way, Kathleen Ferrier and her glorious voice that 'reaches right in there', plus my emotional memories of childhood Sunday lunches have brought me a little closer to the emotional heart of my outwardly unemotional father.

Chapter 4

The Love of Brahms

Symphony No. 4 in E minor

I could never spot a piece by Brahms. I always guessed Beethoven, which Dad said was close. But it was still wrong.

The experience of listening to Kathleen Ferrier performing *Four Serious Songs* has reminded me that whenever we did one of Dad's 'name-the-composer quizzes', Brahms always tripped me up. So I'm reluctant to choose his music for my next listening project. But I feel the need to move away from pieces I remember from childhood and take a flying leap out of my musical comfort zone. For as Daniel Levitin writes in *This is Your Brain on Music*, basic structural elements are incorporated into the very wiring of our brains when we listen to music early in our lives. This early exposure, he writes, 'becomes the basis for our understanding of music, and ultimately the basis for what we like in music, what music moves us and how it moves us'.

So it's time Dad gave me a sterner test. I'm almost determined to find some of his music I hate, just as he hated all of mine. Brahms feels like the ideal candidate: the fact that his music failed to make an impression on me as a child, coupled with my more recent tussle with Ferrier's sombre recording of his *Four Serious Songs*, promises a decent struggle ahead. And it's clear from the thick wedge of the composer's recordings in his CD collection that Dad was very partial to Brahms.

I'm not completely ignorant of his music either, because I know the one tune that everyone knows: his 'Lullaby', or 'Cradle Song' of 1868, which I used to play on my recorder at primary school. Then, when I became a parent, I learned some words to this celebrated tune and, every night for months, I sang them to my infant son as he lay in his cot. 'Lullaby and goodnight/With rosy bed light/With down overspread/Is baby's sweet bed/Lay you down now and rest/May your slumbers be blest/Lay you down now and rest/May your slumbers be blest.' My memories of those postpartum nights will be for ever bleary, but Brahms's lulling tune, which I sang on repeat until Alexander slumbered, is still engrained more than two decades later. Online, I discover a Baby Relax Channel, which plays a dreadful clongy electronic version of Brahms's 'Lullaby' on a loop for eight hours.

Aside from his sanity-saving 'Lullaby', however, Brahms to me feels like an in-between composer, somewhere twixt the grace and clarity of Mozart, and the lush pyrotechnics of Stravinsky. I have no idea where to start with his music. Dad's CD collection contains half a dozen recordings covering numerous types of music: serenades, symphonies, variations, overtures (including one called the *Tragic Overture*), fantasias and piano concertos. Do the choosing for me, Dad, I think, riffling the plastic cases. Then I spot the familiar name of Bruno Walter, conducting the New York Philharmonic in Symphonies 1–4 at Carnegie Hall in New York in a recording from the early 1950s. Okay, Dad. I may as well bite off an entire Brahms symphony at once.

In fact, I overdose and listen to all four symphonies – two and a half hours of music – in one hit. It's an unhelpful thing to do. Bar the odd passage that arrests my ear, I find I can't get hold of the music at all. It sprawls in my hearing, sometimes melodramatic and turgid, sometimes nondescript, even tedious. I'm so used to listening to music that is acoustic and stripped-back that I'm wrestling with such dense orchestration. And unlike with Mozart, Stravinsky and Ferrier, there are no memories here to reel me into the music. It's entirely uncharted territory, and I don't know how to orientate myself. Now I've cut loose from pieces I already know, I realise that the whole structure of music is an enigma to me. I know these symphonies have places to take me: my *Oxford Dictionary of Music* tells me that Brahms's symphonies 'are superb examples of his devotion to classical musical architecture within which he introduced many novel thematic developments'. But there's some kind of code I need to crack before I can get anywhere.

I mention to a music-teacher friend that I'm trying to get to grips with Brahms. 'Oh God,' she says. 'He was a seriously screwed-up guy.' Another musical friend tells me he quite likes Brahms's symphonies, but there is no real affection in his voice. I wonder if I should break myself in gently with something more manageable. So, in tribute to Kathleen Ferrier and her 'Alto Raspberry' I listen to Brahms's *Alto Rhapsody* – Dad's CD collection yields up a version by Janet Baker with the London Philharmonic Orchestra, conducted by Sir Adrian Boult and recorded at Abbey Road Studios in 1971. But it strikes me as heavy and indigestible – anything but light and fruity. I try and break the Brahms symphony experience down by listening to all four individually but still fail to focus my mind on the music in any meaningful way. Once again I long to ask Dad what it was he heard when he listened to Brahms, why he liked this turgid stuff.

Then, ahead of a trip to Paris, arranged so my daughter can practise her A-level French, I decide to treat myself to a ticket for a performance at the Théâtre des Champs-Elysées, so I can experience the setting for the turbulent first performance of Stravinsky's *Rite of Spring*. I don't much mind what I go to, but when I look up the programme for the dates of our Paris stay, I discover that Paavo Järvi, whose recording of *The Firebird* with the Cincinnati Symphony Orchestra set off such sparks in my head, is going to be conducting Brahms's symphonies with Die Deutsche Kammerphilharmonie of Bremen. It's a ridiculous coincidence. I gape at the concert details on my laptop, wondering whether Dad is somehow still orchestrating my listening.

I book a mid-priced ticket for the performance of Brahms's symphonies No. 2 and No. 4, without paying much attention to my seat location. When I arrive at the Théâtre, an imposing Art Nouveau concoction in marble and gilt, I discover that my seat lies behind one of a semicircle of numbered wooden doors which lead to the loges or theatre boxes. I rattle and try to turn the handle of the one that corresponds to the number on my ticket, only to find it locked. An usher steps forward, and I show her my ticket. She produces a key, unlocks the door and points me to one of the eight plush red fauteuils inside. Although I've been speaking French to her, my ignorance must be obvious as, when I sit down, she patiently explains that a tip is expected for being shown to my seat. Once I've fumbled some euros into her palm, she departs, locking the door behind me. I've never been imprisoned in a concert performance before and the prospect is a little disconcerting, especially as I'm not at all confident of enjoying the music I'm about to hear. But perhaps a lock-in is exactly what I need to make me engage with it.

I look down at the assembling audience in the corbeille – the dress circle. It's the Parisian bourgeoisie in all its soigné glory: impeccable tailoring, chignons and kitten heels. As a few other concert-goers are ushered into the loge and locked in with me, I look up at the lavish golden frieze which runs round the ornate ceiling and try to imagine the scene 105 years previously, with the rioting audience catcalling from their fauteuils, and the house lights being flicked on and off by Diaghilev. Tonight, however, everyone is beautifully behaved; everyone knows the ropes of dressing well, and the etiquette of tipping and of listening. In fact, the entire audience looks as if it poshes up and comes here every night of the week to listen to Brahms. Except me.

Die Deutsche Kammerphilharmonie begins with Symphony No. 4 in E minor. During the first movement, I scribble something down in my notebook about ebb and flow, and about it being mood music. What on earth do I mean? In the mellow second movement I take note of the beautiful woodwind intro and 'sweet, pillowy, swells of sound', and then in the third, the starring role the triangle plays (probably because it reminds me of how much I liked playing the triangle in primary-school music lessons). I write that I find the fourth movement 'totally exhilarating and colourful'. My reactions are vague and suggest I'm only half concentrating on the music because mostly I note down things about the human spectacle before me. Once again, I'm struck by the sheer physicality of the musicians. Paavo Jäarvi stands, mostly rooted to the spot as he conducts, occasionally taking a step towards whichever part of the orchestra particularly demands his attention. 'Much frantic bowing!' I note. 'I'm surprised the double-bass players don't fall off their perches.'

Even if I'm not bumming the Brahms, I am marvelling at the sounds that simple physics – the properties and shape of wood and metal – combined with human ingenuity and feeling can produce.

After the interval, it's time for Symphony No. 2 in D major. I note that the music is 'flowery, smooth and sweet'. If nothing else, Brahms is starting to seem less stodgy. I like the visual clues as to what is about to happen in the music: the timpani player picking up his beaters, the tubas and trombones raising their horns. And I warm to the finale, the symphony's lush and careening fourth movement, which interjects sweet and reflective passages of string and woodwind into what overall is a headlong hurtle towards the symphony's conclusion. Here is a composer who loved the full power of an orchestra and knew how to use it, that much is evident. But I'm still not connecting with his music. 'How much emotional effect is this actually having?' I write, underlining the word emotional. It's as if Brahms is throwing everything at me at once and asking me to catch it. Instead I am backing away.

Still, as I walk out of the theatre after the concert, with the crowd dispersing around me, I reflect that, if nothing else, the performance has allowed me to make a start with Brahms; shake hands with him, at least. *Now, Dad, please explain to me why you loved Brahms?* I think, as I head towards the Metro in the nippy air of a spring nightfall. I find myself wishing there was more help available. Why couldn't Paavo Järvi have sneaked past all those habitual Parisian concertgoers and delivered a secret idiot's guide to my plush-lined theatre box? 'Here are some clues to Brahms. Here's what to listen for. Here's what each movement does, here's how they fit together, here's the story they cumulatively tell.' Home from Paris, I look at

Brahms's stern and beardy photograph and know I have to work on squaring his stodgy demeanour with the tirade of feeling I can hear in his music.

By the time he died in 1897 at the age of sixty-three, Brahms was one of the most celebrated and most frequently performed composers in the world. His journey to fame and fortune began in 1853, when he was twenty, after a noted violinist of the time, Joseph Joachim, heard him perform some of his own work in his native Hamburg. Joachim was so impressed that he provided Brahms with letters of introduction to two composers with established reputations: Franz Liszt (thanks to Cockney rhyming slang inextricably linked with Brahms), and to Robert Schumann who, equally impressed, set himself to nurturing the young composer's talent, and invited him to move into his home.

The two remained friends until Schumann's premature death in 1856. But Brahms's friendship with his widow, Clara – now belatedly recognised as an important composer in her own right – endured for four decades until she died forty years later. This explains why Clara's name so frequently appears when you research any of Brahms's compositions. Brahms supported Clara when Schumann, who suffered with depression throughout his life, attempted suicide by throwing himself into the Rhine, after which he was confined to an asylum for the last two years of his life. Although Brahms is rumoured to have fallen in love with Clara during this period, the exact nature of their relationship is a matter for speculation. Still, despite their obvious closeness, Clara once remarked that Brahms was 'as much a riddle – I might also say as much a stranger – as he was twenty-five years ago'.[1]

It is thought that Brahms wrote the *Alto Rhapsody* – actually the *Rhapsody for Alto, Chorus and Orchestra* – in a mood of despair after being spurned by Robert and Clara's daughter, Julie. Julie, for whom Brahms was more of an uncle figure, was oblivious to his feelings for her, and in 1869 married someone else. The twelve-minute *Alto Rhapsody* was Brahms's wedding gift to the happy couple, but from its portentous opening bars onwards it is anything but celebratory. With text from a poem by Goethe, it tells of a young man out of love with life. Although its mood lifts a little towards the end, most of it sounds more like a requiem than a nuptial greeting. Still, the piece moved Clara Schumann to write of Brahms, 'if only he would for once speak so tenderly'. But Brahms was clearly a man of much music and few words. His *Four Serious Songs*, so beloved by Kathleen Ferrier, was written to express his sorrow after Clara's death in 1896. By then, Brahms was nearing the end of his own life too: soon afterwards he was diagnosed with cancer and died the following April.

Brahms laboured for almost twenty years to write his first symphony, after Robert Schumann had rather unhelpfully bigged him up by announcing that his protégé would be the man to take over the mantle of Beethoven (ah, so my quiz answers weren't far out after all). No pressure there, then. By the time Brahms's Symphony in C minor received its première in 1876, Robert Schumann had been dead for almost two decades and Brahms was forty-four, an age by which Beethoven had composed eight of his nine symphonies. Still, having broken his duck, Brahms went on to write three more symphonies in relatively quick succession in 1877, 1883 and 1885.

What exactly is a symphony? And while we're about it, why do some symphonies have three movements, as Mozart's do, and some four, as Brahms's do? All those years ago when we listened to Mozart together, Dad told me that the middle movement of the three is usually a slower one. But what happens when you have four? I feel ignorant of even the basics. *The Penguin Dictionary of Music* tells me that a symphony is 'an extended orchestral composition' which found wide popularity in the eighteenth century. The original Italian form had three movements, and this was the form favoured by Mozart, and initially by Haydn, too, as he embarked on the composition of what was eventually to be a body of over a hundred symphonies. But by the end of the eighteenth century, four movements were standard. Then, when Beethoven took the symphony by the scruff of the neck in the early nineteenth century, he turned it into something much more epic, as can be heard in his famous Fifth Symphony, the portentous opening bars of which are one of the most celebrated beginnings to any classical piece. But what, I wonder, am I supposed to be listening for when I listen to a symphony? Progression? Development? Some kind of story? Some kind of resolution?

And even if I learn to listen properly, am I ever going to love Brahms? After the Paris concert, I persevere, listening diligently to both the Second and Fourth Symphonies. And slowly I am warming to the music. It was stupid of me to think that it would all unlock itself after I'd listened only once or twice. I realise that I habitually judge music very quickly – if it doesn't catch my ear after a couple of hearings, I lose patience. If nothing else, Brahms is giving me a lesson in what it is to keep listening.

Around this time, I interview Ali Smith at Stratford Literary Festival about her novel *Spring*. Chatting before our event, I tell her how much I want to read it a second time because I know there is yet more to extract from it. Smith is pleased. 'That's exactly what I want my readers to feel when they read one of my novels,' she tells me. 'It's like with a song. If you only listen to it once, you only hear the outer layer.' Still, I'm finding the inner layers of Brahms's music difficult to peel back. So I decide to focus on just one of the symphonies. I've no idea which one, if any, that Dad liked best, but I go for the Fourth because it has an emotional current running through it that I am starting to respond to. When all else goes quiet, it is now this piece that I hear in my head.

Sometimes called the 'Symphony of Autumn' because it heralded a more mellow and reflective period of composition towards the end of Brahms's life, Symphony No. 4 was first performed in October 1885, with Brahms himself conducting. *The Rough Guide to Classical Music* argues that it was with this composition that Brahms 'reached the culmination of his symphonic style', with the first and fourth movements, which are 'virtually symphonies in themselves'. Harold C. Schonberg's *The Lives of the Great Composers* says that the Fourth Symphony received a lukewarm reception in its early years because it was thought to be too secretive. This puzzles me greatly because when I listen it seems nakedly expressive. The fourth movement in particular was considered 'dry'.[2] I wonder whether this is something to do with its structure, which I discover is a Baroque form called a passacaglia. Sometimes called a chaconne, it's a courtly dance form from seventeenth-century Spain which has been employed by other composers, including Bach and Rameau. At a basic level, it features variations over a repeating bass tune at a moderately slow tempo.

I'm beginning to respond to the drama of the piece. But I still find it overbearing and can't listen to it for long. One day I return to Annie Fischer playing Mozart's Piano Concerto No. 22 for the first time in weeks. Listening to it feels like downing a long cool glass of water with a wedge of lime.

Whereas listening to the Brahms is like drinking a glass of full-bodied red wine that I know is of an expensive and sought-after vintage but that my unsophisticated palette is unable to appreciate. Maybe I can settle for just *quite* liking Brahms in the manner my children would describe as 'meh'. And then I read *Aimez-vous Brahms?* by Françoise Sagan.

In this novella, published in 1959 when Sagan was still only in her mid-twenties, we meet thirty-nine-year-old Paule, who is torn between two lovers. On the one hand, there's Roger, her long-time paramour, who provides her with a certain security despite the hurt he causes her by seeing other women. On the other is Simon, a much younger man who has fallen helplessly in love with her. Paule, however, has yet to acknowledge his overtures. One Sunday morning, with Roger away for the weekend, she finds a note that Simon has slipped under her door. 'Aimez-vous Brahms?' he writes, inviting her to a concert that evening. It's a simple question but musically highly meaningful. Roger, we learn, loves Wagner, Simon loves Brahms.

In *Hear Me Out*, Armando Iannucci writes of the 'vitriolic split' between Brahms and Wagner supporters in the mid-nineteenth century, likening it to 'gang warfare as hostile as any mods-and-rockers beach fight in the 1960s'. So Roger and Simon's diametrically opposed musical tastes are symbolic of the choice that faces Paule between two very different men. Which German composer will she choose? And therefore, which man? However, Sagan's story is not just a tale of a woman caught between two lovers with differing tastes in music. The question, 'Aimez-vous Brahms?' is the catalyst for a long-overdue moment of self-scrutiny in Paule's life. It seems 'suddenly to reveal . . . all the questions that she had deliberately refrained from asking herself'.

Sagan's novella makes me think that Brahms is a composer whose music I need to have a definitive opinion about. The fact that I've been struggling to have one is an indication of my own uncertainty about whether I should like the music or not. I'm torn between trying my utmost to love it because Dad did and trusting my own ambivalence about Brahms. Like Paule, I am no longer sure of what my true feelings are. And I'm learning that immersion in classical music, or in Brahms's music, at any rate, takes time and a level of concentration that I often can't attain. I find myself longing for stripped-back and familiar songs that give me an instant hit, filling my veins with soul. So much so that, after days of entanglement with Symphony No. 4, I slope off and start snacking off bluesy folk as I potter about the kitchen, sorting laundry and preparing supper. By the end of the evening, I've listened to all my albums by Aussie folk rock band The Waifs, one after the other.

But then, suddenly, I remember Dad laughing out loud while watching 'A Touch of Class', the first ever episode of *Fawlty Towers*. It contains a running gag in which Sybil keeps accusing Basil of shirking a couple of jobs she has asked him to do. Catching Basil hiding in the hotel back office with music on, she snaps: 'You could have got them both done if you hadn't spent all morning skulking in there listening to that racket'. 'Racket?!' Basil explodes. 'That's Brahms! Brahms's Third Racket!'[3]

In honour of this memory, I listen to Brahms's Third Racket again – aka his Third Symphony in F major. And I immediately love it. I discover that the third movement – the Poco allegretto – has inspired many writers and musicians, most of whom Dad would have regarded as composers of actual rackets. Frank Sinatra recorded a dreadfully saccharine song entitled 'Take My Love' based on this movement. And Serge Gainsbourg, who was often inspired by classical pieces when composing songs, riffed on it for 'Baby Alone in Babylone', the title track of Jane Birkin's 1983 album.

And, weirdly, I discover that Françoise Sagan also wrote a song to this tune. Entitled 'Quand tu dors près de moi' ('When You're Sleeping Next to Me') it was recorded by Yves Montand in 1961. It's a rather seductive, regret-filled love song, addressed to a woman who still murmurs the name of her former lover in her sleep. Clearly this Brahms composition of 1883 has continued to strike a chord with musicians and composers across the genres and decades. Dad wouldn't have been impressed, though. I remember making the mistake of thinking he'd like ELO's version of 'Roll Over Beethoven' because it begins with the opening of Beethoven's Fifth Symphony. We didn't even get past the disrespectful title of Chuck Berry's original song. If you were here now, Dad, I'd have another go at playing you all this stuff. And you'd just take it down in evidence that pop music would be nothing without classical. Which, unfortunately, is clearly partly true.

Time to return to Brahms's Racket No. 4. I drive north to visit Mum, and on the way immerse myself in Bruno Walter's recording, playing it from beginning to end three times during the three-hour journey. As I clock up the miles, I can feel myself increasingly responding to the drama in the music. My fingers lift and twist in turn from the steering wheel as if I am conducting. But by the third repeat, Brahms's keening strings, particularly in the first and third movements, are making my head throb. This music and I are locked in a kind of stalemate. Sometimes I feel I'm on the cusp of finding it magnificent. But I'm also teetering on the brink of never wanting to hear it again. Staying at Mum's that night, I dream I am stuck in a small lift with awful piped music I cannot escape.

The following day is a Sunday and I walk down to the village churchyard where Dad is buried. The morning radiates spring fever: the village throngs with dog walkers and runners, and gardens bristle with horticultural activity. In the rear corner of the churchyard where Dad lies, it is cool and shady and the long grass winks with forget-me-nots. Buried in the same grave is my brother Richard, who died suddenly following an epileptic seizure in his sleep when he was twenty-three. I cannot ever forget the phone call I received at work from Dad to tell me Richard had died: as soon as I heard his voice, I knew something terrible had happened. I suppose most of us will at some point in our lives be called upon to be the bearer of such news, the one to inflict the shock. I remember trying to stand up from my desk chair in the wake of this call and my legs giving way. Somehow, I managed to return home to my flat and pack a bag, get on the Tube to the station where I could catch a train back north to be with my parents. I have no idea how I did so, but I know I sat on that train too poleaxed even to cry.

In her celebrated book *H is for Hawk*, Helen Macdonald writes of grief that it 'happens to everyone. But you feel it alone. Shocking loss isn't to be shared, no matter how hard you try.' In the wake of the loss of her own father, she tries to explain to some friends what it's like to suffer alongside those you love and yet feel utterly cut off from them at the same time. Imagine, she says, being in a room with your whole family, when someone comes in and punches you all in the stomach, hard. 'The thing is, you all share the same kind of pain, exactly the same, but you're too busy experiencing total agony to feel anything other than completely alone.' I think of my dad – and my mum – experiencing the loss of a child, that most unnatural predeceasing feared by anyone who is a parent. But even with all the empathy I can muster, it is still astonishingly hard to imagine how it must have been – must still be, in my mother's case. I can only know what it is like for me, and even now I am still trying to make sense of it.

I sit on a bench beside these two men who were once ever-present in my life and listen to the soundtrack of this present without them: planes taking off from Manchester airport, the hum of insects, the chorus of birdsong, the drone of traffic on the main road. A robin flutters assertively down, lands briefly, and heads off again. Before me stretches a sea of other graves marked mostly by headstones and, sometimes, crosses. Many are black and shiny with gold lettering, but I prefer Dad's style of headstone – plain stone, which allows the passage of time to be marked by the greenness of the algae that clings to it.

After a while, I get to my feet and look for a stone to leave as a calling card on top of the headstone in the Jewish tradition I have always loved since I first encountered it on a visit to the Jewish cemetery in Prague. I walk into the heart of the churchyard among much older graves that no one is alive to visit any more. Peeping from a curtain of ivy, one bears an epitaph from an age when fewer rewards were expected here on earth: 'They asked for so little but gave so much.'

I don't know why I'm wandering among the dead like this. Perhaps it's my way, on this most alive of mornings, of trying to understand – yet again – that another of my loved ones is dead. When I drive home later that day, I play Brahms Fourth Symphony again, and now it sounds like solace. I listen with new-minted pleasure to the second movement, the Andante, and the way in which its lilts and sweeps appear to mirror the curves of the Cheshire lanes as I turn the wheel to them. England is around me in all its spring glory: the candle flowers of the horse-chestnut trees, the spring green of budding beech woods, the cow parsley which froths in the roadside verges. And yet my sadness is wintry.

My resurgent grief has allowed this music to penetrate somewhere new, and suddenly it sounds different. Now when I wake in the night I hear different passages from the symphony earworming through my mind as I lie still and thinking. And by day, when I listen to the end of one movement, I hear the next one starting in my head before it actually does, something that previously only happened with pop albums that I have obsessively played at one time or other in my life, like *Revolver* by the Beatles, or *Eden* by Everything But the Girl.

A few weeks later, a publisher invites me to meet Daniel Levitin, who is on a visit to the UK. We spend most of our allotted hour talking about his forthcoming book on the secrets of successful ageing (key message: don't retire, or at least, retain a firm purpose in life). Towards the end of our time, I tell him about my listening project. 'Why do I now wake up hearing Brahms's Fourth Symphony on repeat in my head?' I ask. 'Does it mean that it has finally penetrated my brain in some way?' 'It means exactly that', Levitin confirms. 'It's a more elaborative level of processing.' We talk about these levels of processing and how they depend on how well you know something. Levitin demonstrates. 'So if I were to say two, four, six . . .' (he leaves a gap for my response). 'Eight,' I pronounce. 'Exactly. Well-practised, well-rehearsed. The same with music.' 'But does that mean that Brahms will stay there now?' I ask, a little desperately. 'Yes,' says Levitin. He claims not to be as conversant with classical music as he is with rock, which, in a former career, he both played and produced. But as soon as I mention Brahms's Fourth Symphony, he immediately hums me a section of it.

Even without Levitin's scientific confirmation, I know that Brahms's music is changing my brain in some way. But is that the same as loving it? Unlike in the days of 'gang warfare' between Brahms and Wagner aficionados, Armando Iannucci suggests that we, as contemporary listeners, have now gone too far the other way, opting out of any real debate. Instead we put classical music on a pedestal because we consider it 'too perfect, too unchallengeable, too much beyond the whims of those who listen to it'. I think that's precisely my trouble: I feel obliged to revere this music. But what I want is to have an opinion on this music. Aime-je Brahms? I have to keep asking that question because I really want to know the answer.

And several years after his death, I find myself thinking about Dad more than ever. I could blame Brahms, but I also know that it has something to do with the fact that my mother now has a new man in her life. L is a decent, genial, uncomplaining chap who looks out for Mum and makes her laugh. I have met him a few times and I like him. The previous year I had invited them both to stay for Christmas. It was the right and hospitable thing to do, but I also knew that once again I'd find the holiday difficult and emotionally exhausting. A few days before Mum and L were due to arrive, I had a festive drink with a friend and he talked, a tear in his eye, of how each Christmas he feels an obligation to recreate the way his own late father would wholeheartedly embrace the festival. My dad wasn't one for enforced jollity, but he too was always lovely and spirited at Christmas, taking an interest in everyone who came through the door during the festivities, and patiently teaching all of us, young and old, to play poker, a game at which he excelled.

Mum and L arrived with a carload of presents and wine. Once again their festive cheerfulness made me miss Dad terribly. I hid in the kitchen where I necked glasses of fizz while cooking. But when I took them on a hilly Boxing Day walk, which provided a sterner test for Mum's stamina than I should have given her, I observed L's solicitousness to her as she tried to catch her breath, and realised that this very different man looks after her just as well as Dad did, perhaps even better.

I am happy for her, and for me, the only child charged with her wellbeing. But while the pain of loss seems to be easing for her, it is sharpening again for me. I had always considered my mother's bereavement as more profound than mine. When you lose the husband you have lived with for over fifty years, and who was your boyfriend for nearly a decade before that, it leaves a crater in your life. Some left-behind spouses never climb out of it. By contrast, when you lose the father you have already grown up and away from, and see only a few times a year, it initially leaves a shallower hole. But now Mum has found someone new, the pain of loss feels freshly mine to bear. When she and L got together, Mum had asked me if I 'minded', and was horrified when I immediately started crying. I had to explain that it wasn't because I minded. I told her truthfully that I was thrilled for her. But the news breached the carefully constructed dam holding back my own grief.

Over Christmas, Mum tells me that she and L have booked the holiday of a lifetime – a safari to Kenya the following spring. It's a trip she has always longed to go on, but Dad, she says, was 'never keen'. I'm excited for her, sensing what an incredible experience it will be. And she's well into her eighties now – I admire her adventurous spirit. But that night I have another dream. This time I am strolling in my back garden with Dad.

Mum walks several paces ahead of us, chattering animatedly about her forthcoming holiday. As we listen to her talk, I put my arm through Dad's and gently kiss his cheek. It's a gesture of commiseration, and of remembrance.

I brood on this dream for days. I know it signals my determination to hold onto Dad in any way I can. But Mum – in good health, physically active and sharp of mind – still has every use for the years that are left to her. Sensing my discomfort, she sends me an email. 'After nearly sixty years of marriage, your Dad and L's wife are always with us – they are in nearby rooms with the doors closed. We miss them terribly but now our time is running out and we have to do our best to enjoy what and where we can. I do not feel any disloyalty because of it.' I cry again and wonder why again. Am I moved by her new-found happiness? By the thought that it is destined only to be fleeting? Or because Dad is in a nearby room with the door closed?

When I listen to Brahms's Fourth Symphony now, the music seems coupled to the tempest of my emotions: sometimes impeccably controlled, sometimes all over the shop. In this state, I read 'Visions Fugitives', a short story by William Boyd which, like Sagan's *Aimez-vous Brahms?*, which it clearly references, has the music of Brahms as a central theme. Irène Golan, the woman in the story, sits and reads a passage of the narrator's work-in-progress on Brahms, in which he discusses *Variations on a Theme of Haydn*. 'Brahms chose something deeply obscure and through the special alchemy of genius transformed it into one of the best-known tunes in the orchestral repertoire', he writes. 'It's wonderful that, no?' Irène remarks. 'To take something so obscure and make it memorable . . . We should try, when we have that chance . . . to do what Brahms did.'

Make the obscure memorable. Perhaps that's what I'm

trying to do. Save my memories of Dad from fading, at least while there are still people who remember him, people who might visit his grave. Or at the very least, I'm trying to keep the door to that nearby room open. I listen to *Variations on a Theme of Haydn*, which Brahms composed in 1873. Now thought not to be by Haydn at all, the theme's actual composer is a mystery, hence the context of William Boyd's story. In nine parts – the theme, eight variations and a finale, it's an ebullient and cheerful piece, and I love its dominant woodwind chords. Then I find myself thinking: am I listening to a passacaglia? Turns out I am. Perhaps I'm getting better at this.

The music of Brahms finally unlocks for me at an event at Chipping Campden Literature Festival, where I listen to journalist, author and music enthusiast Ed Vulliamy talk about his book *When Words Fail: A Life With Music, War and Peace*. It's a memoir of sorts, in which Vulliamy looks back on a reporting career that has taken him into the heart of some of the world's most terrible conflicts, including the Yugoslav war, and to Iraq following the US-led coalition invasion in 2003. In less harrowing moments, it has also allowed him to interview a wide range of musicians: jazz, rock and classical, and indulge his equally varied musical passions from Verdi to the Grateful Dead.

During his talk, Vulliamy muses on why we turn to music when nothing else will do. He plays us clips of the pieces of music that have spoken most profoundly to him throughout his life: Franz Schubert's *Winterreise*, 'Machine Gun' by Jimi Hendrix, Symphony No. 5 by Dmitri Shostakovich, 'Waiting Underground' by Patti Smith, 'Deportee' by Joan Baez, and 'There Must Be a Better World Somewhere' by BB King. At the end, he leads us in a rousing rendition of Bob Dylan's 'Mr Tambourine Man'.

After the event, I flick through *When Words Fail* at the bookstall and turn to the index, not really expecting Vulliamy to reference Brahms. But sure enough, he does and, what's more, it's the Fourth Symphony, mentioned in an interview he did with celebrated pianist and conductor Daniel Barenboim at La Scala in Milan in 2008 about his West-Eastern Divan Orchestra.

The first Israeli citizen to take dual citizenship and hold a Palestinian passport alongside his Israeli one, Barenboim founded the West-Eastern Divan Orchestra with the late Palestinian writer Edward Said in 1999 to bring together young Israeli-Jewish and Palestinian musicians. The ensemble takes its name from a collection of poems by Goethe – inspired in their turn by the Persian poet Hafez – which bring together and blend themes from the Orient and Occident.

In his interview with Vulliamy, Barenboim says: 'Good music has its technical side, but that is only part of it. I am not interested in getting the orchestra to play the way I want it to play. What I am interested in is getting a hundred people to think and feel alike, to feel like one huge common lung; to breathe the music the same way. That's what is interesting.' At the time of Vulliamy's interview, the Divan Orchestra was about to perform Brahms's Fourth Symphony at the London Proms, and this is the piece Barenboim cites to emphasise his point about the unique effect of this music on the emotions. 'Brahms had something to say that he considered very important, and he didn't write it in words but in sound. Therefore we cannot express in words the content of the music of Brahms: were I able to articulate the content of a symphony or piano concerto of Brahms, I wouldn't have to play it any more.'

That's it. That's why I find Brahms so difficult to translate into words – because it's music for when words fail. I feel a weight lifting. I've been so worried about my lack of knowledge about the technical aspects of music, of what to listen for, of my utter ignorance about the way pieces are structured that, like Paule in *Aimez-vous Brahms?*, I have failed to give enough credence to the way it makes me – uniquely me – feel. Through its performances of pieces, including Brahms's Fourth Symphony, the Divan Orchestra achieves miracles in bringing together people from opposing sides of a conflict. But it is also a miracle, I realise, that I can listen to a Brahms symphony and simply let the music be the bearer of my feelings about Dad.

When I get home, I listen to the Fourth Symphony again. And now I've jettisoned the idea that I have to listen to it in a certain way, it's as if this piece – quite familiar to me now – swells in my hearing. In the first movement – Allegro non troppo – I can hear how the music shifts like a great lake of sound. There's nothing half-hearted about it: this is the music of total commitment, full of weather and expression, from its intense descending string passages and the answering woodwind. It's heroic music which charts the perilous journey that is life, and this movement feels almost complete in itself, so grand and emphatic is the finale.

At twelve minutes, the second movement – the Andante moderato – is almost exactly the same length as the first. While it's calmer and more stately on the surface, I still sense the great channel of emotion that surges beneath. It begins with a plaintive horn tune, followed by lush, quietly building string passages and conversations between woodwind and brass, punctuated by rich, plucking string sounds. A few weeks before, I would have said that this movement was both calming and soothing but now it creates the same emotional intensity as what has gone before. The string passages in particular are extraordinarily full of feeling – of all the instruments of the orchestra, it seems to me most remarkable the effect on the human psyche that the sound of bowing across taut gut strings can produce. This second movement feels utterly transporting, concluding with a long, sustained woodwind chord, poised for what comes next.

The third movement – the Allegro giocoso, 'fast, playful and fun' – is much shorter. It's a joyful and jubilant piece with an all's-right-with-the-world swagger that hurtles along like an express train riding through a bucolic landscape. Here too there is frantic bowing, and great blasts of woodwind and brass that must leave the musicians out of breath.

The three-chord finale that closes the third movement is so emphatic that it almost comes as a surprise when a fourth movement follows, the Allegro energico e passionato, più allegro. But Brahms has something left to say. While equally urgent in tempo as what has gone before, the whole mood has changed. It's as if the sun has gone in, and Brahms is telling us that the joyful moments are just that, moments that cannot last for ever. There is pain here, and doubt, and great trembling uncertainties. And yet this movement, as its designation suggests, is the most passionate yet, and seems to convey raw human emotion at its highest pitch, with its pleading string and plaintive woodwind sections. It seems strange that Brahms chose to make this a passacaglia – any idea that there might be a stately dance in here seems impossible. And yet the theme is there, played over great rumbling bass notes.

This is indeed music about which it is impossible to be neutral. How could I ever have felt it was just washing over me? It has taken weeks of immersion. But I think I might finally have fallen for Brahms. Or at least I now understand why Dad loved his music.

Unlike the physical purging of emotion that takes place when you hear Kathleen Ferrier sing, listening to Brahms has a different effect. It's not so much that it's cathartic – I've never been close to tears while listening to it. Rather, it is music of transference, that soaks up everything you are feeling so you don't have to. When you listen to Brahms, the music is so full of the tempests of life that your own emotions lie down like lambs in the face of it. Clemency Burton-Hill puts it more musically when she writes of Brahms's 'astonishing ability to process raging torments of messy human emotion into disciplined musical forms'.[4] I imagine Dad listening to Brahms on occasions when everything got a bit much, anchoring himself to the mast of the music. It isn't until a few days later that I realise with astonishment the significance of the date on which I finally 'get' Brahms: 7 May. Brahms's birthday. Goose bumps rise up at the coincidence.

As her recommended listening for 7 May in her *Year of Wonder: Classical Music for Every Day*, Clemency Burton-Hill prescribes Brahms's Violin Sonata No. 1 in G major. It feels, she writes, 'like the sun coming out in musical form'. I listen to a recording of this piece by Itzhak Perlman with Vladimir Ashkenazy, one of Dad's favourite pianists, and find it divine. The piece sounds to me more like the sun coming in and out on one of those blustery spring days when clouds scud across the sky. It throws you into chilly shadow at times, but if you wait long enough, it will bring you back into the warmth of the day. That is the light and shade of Brahms, and the light and shade of all our lives. 'Aime-je Brahms?' Dear Dad. I find that I do.

Chapter 5

The Serendipities of Schumann

Kinderszenen, Robert Schumann and
Piano Concerto in A minor, Clara Schumann

My off-piste black run with Brahms has been a blast. But it leaves me craving something calmer, less tempestuous. So once again I consult Dad's CD collection, and find just the right piece in a recording of piano music by Robert Schumann.

Schumann's *Kinderszenen* – *Scenes from Childhood* – is a suite of thirteen short and impressionistic pieces for solo piano which Dad played often. So often, in fact, that I remember being curious enough to ask him what it was. Perhaps we were at home at the time, on one of those closeted winter Sundays that I indelibly associate with the classical music of my childhood, but it could just as well have been in Dad's car on the way to the pub, listening to a tape. I was doubtless entrenched in my conviction that classical music was boring and backward. But I remember being interested in the idea that someone had tried to capture in music what it was to be a child.

I already know a little about the life of Robert Schumann from my time with Brahms, his younger contemporary. Born in Zwickau, in Saxony in central Germany, in 1810, his father

August was a bookseller, and as a young man and voracious reader he considered becoming a writer or a poet. This was, after all, the Romantic era. But then the family history of mental illness cast what was destined to be a long shadow over Schumann's young life. August, who suffered from a 'nervous disorder', died in 1826 when Robert was only sixteen, and a mere few weeks later, his sister Emilia died by suicide.[1]

In 1830, perhaps to make a break with this troubled early life, Schumann left Zwickau to study law in Leipzig, but this venture was short-lived. 'Leipzig was the wrong place for so impressionable a young man as Robert. There was too much music in the city', writes Harold C. Schonberg in his *Lives of the Great Composers*. For Leipzig was at that time the music and publishing heartland of the German-speaking world, and Robert soon abandoned any thought of the law. According to Schonberg, he soaked himself in the musical culture of the city, often rising early 'in a spasm of activity' to practise the piano for eight or nine hours a day, 'smoking innumerable cigars in the process'.[2] Schonberg casts Schumann as the consummate Romantic rake about town, 'affecting a Byronic pose, falling in and out of love, dabbling in the arts, arguing about music, life and aesthetics through the night and well into the morning'. He is thought to have caught syphilis at this time, a disease whose grim later stages may have led to his subsequent mental delusions and his attempted suicide twenty years later. But Robert's first psychotic episodes date from these early music-immersed years in Leipzig. 'If ever a composer was doomed to music it was Robert Schumann,' writes Schonberg. 'There was something of a Greek tragedy in the way music reached into his cradle, seized him, nourished him, and finally destroyed him.'

Prior to his arrival in Leipzig, Schumann had been self-taught in music. But once in the city he became a student of Friedrich Wieck, a music teacher and piano seller whose own daughter, Clara, at ten years old was already a renowned performer. Robert also showed great talent as a pianist. But then he managed to do permanent damage to his hand by overzealous use of a mechanical contraption he had devised to strengthen his weaker fourth finger, although some think the damage was done by poisoning from the mercury he started taking when he realised he had syphilis. Whatever the cause of his disability, from then on he concentrated on composing. His first known piece was published in 1831, and in 1834 he started his own music magazine, the *Neue Zeitschrift für Musik*. As Clara's renown as a pianist grew, Friedrich Wieck seems to have regarded his journalistic pupil as a useful asset when publicising his daughter's burgeoning programme of recitals.

In his *Kinderszenen* of 1838, Schumann attempted to capture elements of childhood, from juvenile games such as 'The Knight of the Hobby Horse' and 'Blind Man's Buff' to locations both real and imagined, including 'By the Fireside' and 'Of Foreign Lands and Peoples', to the capricious moods and actions characteristic of young children like 'The Entreating Child' and 'Child Falling Asleep'. The thirteen short, impressionistic vignettes – each lasting between thirty seconds and three minutes – that make up the whole were selected from an original group of thirty 'curious little things', composed in what the Decca sleeve notes refer to as a 'fever of inspiration'. His *Kinderszenen* are gorgeous and transporting and Dad, I know, loved them.

Dad's CD, which features British pianist Clifford Curzon, opens with Robert Schumann's *Fantasie* in C major, written in

1836. I decide to give this piece, which is entirely unknown to me, a whirl first. As with Brahms, I find its Romantic extremes impressive but also daunting on first hearing. One moment I'm being lulled by its quiet but shimmering tenderness, the next its notes are pounding my ear. While roiling music like this cannot fail to be charged with emotion, whoever plays it, I'm struck as I listen to Curzon's rendition how much a solo piece like this depends on the individual emotional interpretation it is given by the instrumentalist. With Mozart's Piano Concerto No. 22, I had to listen carefully to discern the subtle differences between how Alfred Brendel and Annie Fischer chose to interpret it. But here the notes, stripped of any orchestral support, provide a direct line to the thoughts, feelings and state of mind of whoever is pressing the keys, as well as of the person who wrote the original piece. In Dad's heavily annotated *Penguin Guide to Compact Discs & DVDs* (2003/4), I gulp with emotion a little when I see his big tick against the Curzon CD, Dad convinced to buy it by the authors' description of Curzon's performance of the Fantasie – 'extraordinarily chimerical and romantic . . . depth of poetic feeling' – and his 'equally magical' interpretation of *Kinderszenen*.

I too find poetic feeling in Curzon's playing of *Kinderszenen*. He doesn't overdo the sentiment but still gives the piece a nostalgic wistfulness that is very affecting, particularly in the dreamier vignettes like the fourth, 'Bittendes Kind' ('The Entreating Child'), the seventh and perhaps best-known piece, 'Träumerei' ('Reverie'), and the twelfth, 'Kind im Einschlummern' ('Child Falling Asleep'). I'm struck by how much drama Curzon manages to inject even into the very shortest of these pieces, like 'Hasche-Mann' ('Blind Man's Buff') and 'Ritter vom Steckenpferd' ('The Knight of the Hobby Horse').

Clifford Curzon was apparently a highly self-critical performer who disliked the recording studio because he didn't approve of relying on phonographic trickery to deceive the listener into thinking he could play something in a way that he might not be able to reproduce in live performance. For Curzon, the essence of performance lay in 'catching the butterfly on the wing'; a butterfly he would rather attempt to snare numerous times rather than have his performance engineered to sound as if he had nailed it down first time.[3] Dad's CD is a case in point: Curzon's recording of the Schumann *Fantasie* is described in the *Penguin Guide* as a performance 'so "live" and spontaneous in feeling, that it is difficult to believe it was made in the studio'. And yet Curzon wasn't comfortable with live performance either. Despite practising for up to eight hours a day, he suffered from stage fright throughout his career. According to the *Naxos A-Z of Pianists*, his live performances depended to an unusual degree on how he felt at that particular moment, and as a result were often unpredictable and could be 'disastrous'.[4]

I think about my own piano playing: my woeful lack of practice and application; my inattention to anything but playing the right notes in the right order; the fact that I somehow progressed to Grade 6 without ever really thinking about conveying anything through my playing, or even much enjoying it. I invested so little in it. And yet now I find myself longing to sit down and play again. I rifle through the pile of music I inherited from my piano teacher after she died. I've scarcely looked through it until now, knowing that much of it is way beyond my ability. But, sure enough, among a sheaf of Beethoven sonatas, and preludes and fugues by J. S. Bach, I find a tatty book of Schumann piano works, held together by ageing sticky tape, with cartoons of elephants and kangaroos on it. As I open the book, the tape falls off, having dried out long ago. But inside is the music for 'Träumerei', Dad's favourite of all the *Kinderszenen*. It's a sign, of course. I sit down at the piano and flex my fingers. Dad would be happy just to know that I was playing the piano again, but he'd be thrilled to think of me tackling 'Träumerei'.

Though I'm rusty, I concentrate hard and recognisable bits of the piece start to emerge. But the fingering is tricky, with my hands frequently pulled to full stretch across the keyboard, and there are also chords where I have no idea which hand is supposed to play which notes. Looking for clues, I listen repeatedly to Clifford Curzon's 'Träumerei'. His playing sounds so effortless, and yet every note feels imbued with a finely wrought emotion that is light years away from my hesitant plonking. How will my fingers ever be able to express even a fraction of the essence of this exquisite piece? When played by a virtuoso pianist like Curzon, it conveys so much of the piquancy of our memories of times past, and how these memories, completely unbidden, can suddenly flit from our unconscious to our conscious minds, commanding our attention for the first time in years.

And in my own head as I listen, moving pictures begin to spool in my head: scenes from Dad's own 1930s and 1940s childhood, retrieved from somewhere in my own memory, thanks to my never-met grandfather Fred's work with his cine camera. Sometimes when I was a child, Dad would set up the cine projector in the front room and I'd watch transfixed as a world from before I was born came to life. And thus were those pictures from Dad's childhood transferred to my own memory. Dad later put the footage onto VHS, but in those years when the choice of what we could watch at any given moment was beginning to expand, that footage was packed away and seldom seen again. But I never entirely lost sight of it in my mind's eye.

At my parents' house, I sort through a huge pile of video tapes that Mum wants rid of. Among them I find half a dozen tapes of home movies, most of which contain film of my own children's early years, captured more recently by Dad on his own video camera. But one contains the precious cine footage I am looking for, dating from the early 1930s onwards through to my own screen debut as a baby. We no longer have a VHS player, so back home I go and see Chris at Chris's Shed, one of those indispensable local shops which sells all things audio-visual. Chris tells me he does indeed transfer video footage from VHS to DVD, but points to a shelf stacked with a big queue of waiting video tapes. I must look completely crestfallen because he offers to jump my tape to the front of the line. I accept gratefully.

A few days later, Chris calls to tell me the disc is ready. Once on the sofa at home, I immerse myself in three hours of home movies spanning three decades. About half the footage, from the 1960s onwards, was filmed by Dad himself with his own cine camera, acquired as an adult. I particularly love the film of my parents on holiday in France and Switzerland in the early 1960s, my mother looking glamorous in cat's-eye sunglasses and gaily patterned flared cotton skirts she had sewn herself. And a few years later, I arrive on the scene. I watch myself particularly carefully on the early holiday to Sandbanks in Dorset when I was about twenty months. I think that is my earliest memory. I have a fleeting though clear recollection of being on a kind of dock with water in front of me, and of a garden where there was a large white bird with a long neck. Watching Dad's film of the holiday again makes me realise that it is my recollection of this cine footage that has been masquerading as true memory all these years.

For here I am on Mum's lap, sitting in the front seat of Dad's Sunbeam Alpine in a queue for the Sandbanks ferry, and then toddling about on the quay in a bright red dress with a diamond-patterned collar and matching diamond-patterned tights. In the next scene, we are walking round some gardens, which Mum later identifies as Compton Acres in Poole. The movement of the trees at the edge of the frame tell me it was a breezy day. There are ornamental fountains, pink rhododendrons just coming into bloom, and views along the coast. And there, in front of a cascade in what looks like a Japanese-style garden, stands a large white decoy crane, its head and beak angled upwards as if looking for the source of the water. Then Mum has a go with the camera, and here I am, very briefly in Dad's arms, the bulky leather cine-camera case slung over his shoulder as he jigs me up and down.

What were Dad's own earliest memories? I have no idea. To my infinite regret, I never asked. Instead I avidly watch his own silent film cameos as a small child in the 1930s, which have been spliced together rather carelessly and out of chronological order by my grandfather. One moment we are in colour, the next black and white. But here, unmistakably, is Dad, aged three or four, in a natty, close-cropped felt hat with a little feather in it, and a gaberdine overcoat, riding the amusements at the seafront funfair in Southport, where his father's family lived. Here he is in the garden of his aunt's house, in romper suit and beret, digging a big hole. Here he is on the Lakeside miniature railway along the prom, its carriages packed with holidaymakers in 1930s dress, every single person wearing a hat; and then afterwards, as Dad peers at the locomotive – the *King George* – through the steam, his mother lurking in the background in a coat with a big fur collar. Here he is, trotting about a garden, thumb in mouth, pursued by a gaggle of women, his Lancashire grandmother at the head of them. Here he is a bit later, sailing the model yacht which today sits beached on the windowsill of my landing. I watch him building sandcastles and sloshing water in Blackpool, in Rhyl, in Cleethorpes and Colwyn Bay, and smile at how much this small child already looks like my dad. Same dark wavy hair, same dark eyes, same slightly arch expression.

There is one brief sequence I particularly loved seeing as a child. It shows one of Dad's early birthday parties: his sixth, according to the notes he has handwritten and slipped inside the video box. It was July 1940, wartime, and it's a fancy-dress party, though few of the children seem to have managed to dress accordingly. Instead, the girls wear their best frocks and white bows at a jaunty angle in their hair. The boys are in smart shirts and shorts. Among about twenty children, only my dad and three others are in costume. There are two 'Red Indians' with feathered headbands, and a boy in a blue RAF-type uniform. And then there's Dad, dressed as a cowboy in a red-and-white checked shirt, black neckerchief and a cowboy hat. He carries something in his hand that I can't quite see but may be a toy pistol. As the flickering footage captures the children processing in pairs round the garden, my dad strides along; a twentieth-century version of Schumann's swaggering young 'Knight of the Hobby Horse' a hundred years later.

I'm still listening to *Kinderszenen* and stumbling over my own playing of 'Träumerei' when Mum and I go on holiday to

Italy a few weeks later. And there something uncanny happens, which leaves me wanting to believe like never before that Dad is still somewhere close to us. There's a scene in the film adaptation of Colm Tóibín's novel *Brooklyn* where the priest who looks out for Eilis after her arrival in New York from rural Ireland comforts her following the death of her sister: 'Rose will be looking down on you all the days of your life,' he says.[5] However much I want to, I can't believe that Dad is looking down on me from above: the perspective feels all wrong. But the little I've read and understood about the physics of time persuades me that it isn't completely deluded to believe that a sort of peeping across from a parallel time frame might be possible.

In *Time Lived, Without Its Flow*, her book about the passage of grief, Denise Riley writes of 'the sensation of being lifted clean out of habitual time' after the death of her son Jake. I understand only too well how this skewed sense of the then and now, and the constant ebb and flow of memories, might mess with anyone's perception of presence and absence: and to soothe the agony of this, we tell ourselves many stories. So I try to be sceptical of my own grief fancies, despite the persuasiveness of physics. And yet I can't tear myself from the feeling that Dad is pottering about somewhere nearby, observing what I'm up to, and gently nudging me along, as he always did when I was a child.

During the working week he was usually too tired to talk to me much. But at weekends, he'd often make time to be with me, especially if it could involve going to the pub. A regular Saturday evening scene from my early teenage years: we'd have a quick drink (a pint for him, lemonade for me) in one of the pubs on the outskirts of Leicester (*no* piped music) before heading for the chip shop to pick up fish and chips. In the pub we would talk about all sorts of things. Dad was interested in my youthful perspective on life, and liked to get me to think rationally, probing me about religion, politics, education; never dictating, never pontificating. This careful, measured approach left its legacy: even today I find it hard to form an immediate opinion about anything because I'm still thinking about other sides of the argument.

At my comprehensive school, where going to the toilet at breaktime meant running the gauntlet of a posse of mocking smokers, I was routinely ridiculed for being bright and what would now be called nerdy: 'Brain of Britain' was one of the jibes most often thrown my way. I think one of the reasons I became a writer is that for a long time it was the only way I could enjoy showing off. Afraid of the reactions of others, and lacking in confidence, I often struggled to express myself in class. Now I wonder whether Dad was trying to restore that confidence during our times together. I know he worried about not being able to afford to send me to private school. Though I was mostly miserable at state school, it did in a way prepare me for life in the real world, and in retrospect I'm grateful for that. But it wasn't what Dad wanted for me.

It wasn't just my intellect that was stretched during these outings. Often I'd make Dad do the brainwork instead through the quizzes I liked to devise for him. I'd bring the AA road atlas from the car and turn to the back page, where there was a mileage chart: an isosceles triangle of driving distances between locations that I could test him on. 'Aberystwyth to Tilbury?' I'd throw out, and Dad would screw up his face for a moment and then reply with a number that was unfailingly in the right ballpark. Or I'd pick out obscure place names from the gazetteer and ask him to tell me which county they were in. Again, he nearly always got the answer right.

Maps were always a mainstay of our relationship: from the time I was five, Dad taught me to recite the names of the towns we had to drive through to reach Sheringham on our annual summer holiday: Leicester, Uppingham, Stamford, Wisbech, King's Lynn, Fakenham, Holt, and trace the route with my finger, including the detour off the A47 he liked to take to avoid getting jammed up around Peterborough. I was also devoted to my collection of wooden map jigsaws, including one of the old English and Welsh counties, which had belonged to Dad when he was little. Eventually, I knew the shapes of the counties so well – the banana that was Cardigan, the pointy sock of Cornwall, the heart shape of my own home county, Leicestershire – that I used to flip the pieces over and do the puzzle upside down, just by recognising the bare wood shapes. Dad thought this was a great trick.

So here's the uncanny thing. More than forty years later, at the top of the boot shape that is Italy, Mum and I spend a week at the hotel she and Dad stayed in many times together, in a small town on the shores of Lake Garda, a place they both loved. We've been here together three times now since Dad died, Mum generously paying for me because each year she longs to go back but doesn't want to go alone. I have come to cherish this majestic place too: the misty green of the mountains, the tumbling and exuberant flowers, and all the moods of the great lake. I watch it sparkling and shifting gently in the early morning sunshine when I go down in my chunky hotel bathrobe to swim in the pool before any other guests emerge, or do half an hour of yoga, placing my mat on the pontoon sunbathing area, its wooden slats already warm from the morning rays. At night, as we sit and enjoy dinner on the restaurant terrace, the lake waters smooth themselves out into a barely rippling sheet of mercury.

We while away our days loafing by the lake, people watching as the ferries come and go from the nearby dock; or taking trips to the towns around the lake that Mum and Dad most liked to frequent. We revisit their favourite cafés, and I introduce Mum to Aperol spritz. We drink one and sometimes two with lunch as we watch the stylish Italian world go by. And, as always, Dad is there, hovering in the parallel time frame of my eye. I see him sporting the roll-up Panama hat I bought him for his birthday one year in Jermyn Street, his shirt collar turned up against the sun. That's my dad who wore a collared, long-sleeved shirt every day of his adult life, whatever the weather.

One day, Mum and I take a boat trip up the lake to the town of Gargnano. It's one of the few ferry stops around the lake where Mum has never alighted before. I'm keen to have a mooch there because it has literary history. D. H. Lawrence lived in Gargnano with his partner Frieda von Richthofen between September 1912 and April 1913, when he completed *Sons and Lovers*. It was one of the books I most enjoyed studying for A level, reading Mum's old orange-and-cream Penguin copy, and it sparked an obsession with Lawrence for a while.

Mum and I mooch around Gargnano for a bit, but she grows tired of walking and the trail in Lawrence's footsteps is an uphill one. I don't mind, as it is glorious to sit in a café by the little harbour in the sunshine, watching fisherman fiddling with their boats and trying to understand a few of the words being spoken by the voluble, smoking Italians around us as we sip our lunchtime spritzes. So little will have changed about this scene since Lawrence sat here a century ago. The only modern-life turmoil is the cars zipping along the quayside. I know Dad would have been content here too.

As we wait for the boat to take us back down the lake, I spy a poster on a lamppost advertising a piano recital at the very hotel we are staying in. Back at the hotel, we make enquiries and discover that it is a local music-society event rather than one for hotel guests, which explains why we hadn't heard about it earlier. But the helpful woman at reception is more than happy for us to buy tickets and gatecrash the proceedings.

On the evening of the concert, after an early dinner, we make our way up to the grand first-floor salon of the hotel, which leads onto a big lakeside terrace. I have never been inside it before, but occasionally when a wedding or banquet is due to take place, I've peeped in and seen waiters scurrying about, moving furniture and pushing huge trolleys stacked with tinkling glassware. Mum and I take our seats, conscious that we're the only tourists in the room. I look down at the programme someone has handed me and gasp. A Mozart sonata, two Chopin nocturnes and a Scriabin sonata. And at the top of the bill, *Kinderszenen* by Robert Schumann. 'Do you think Dad's here somewhere?' Mum asks, even though she has no idea that my head is spinning with the coincidence. *Oh yes, he's here*, I think. His atoms, his ions, his particles. All those forensic TV shows have taught us that we leave our DNA everywhere, sometimes with sinister consequences. But at this moment I'm captivated by the idea that some essence of Dad remains in this place that he loved.

Tonight's pianist is a young British performer: Martin James Bartlett, a former winner of BBC Young Musician of the Year, who performed at the Queen's ninetieth birthday celebrations in St Paul's Cathedral. The acoustics in the cavernous room are not wonderful, and to begin with I feel a little distanced from his playing. But Schumann quickly reels me in, and by the time Bartlett plays 'Träumerei', I am in a reverie of my own, back in the 1970s. There is Dad, and there am I, watching the reels go round.

I only beam down into the room again when Bartlett starts playing the Mozart. I look around, struck by how still everyone around me is. Solo piano demands a kind of mindful listening and scarcely anyone moves, not a beating foot, not a bobbing head. And Bartlett too seems entirely to inhabit his performance, oblivious to his audience. After playing the last bars of the show-offy sonata by Scriabin which closes the programme, he jumps straight up from the piano stool as if embarrassed to be caught there. Mum and I mingle on the terrace outside afterwards, drinking Prosecco and stuttering a few words of Italian as we strike up halting conversations with our fellow audience members. But still the wistful chords of 'Träumerei' sound in my head as I look out on the silver metallic waters of the lake. And I revel in my mental capture of another piece of music that will always take me straight back to Dad and to being his child.

Even allowing for the influence of Romanticism at the time he was composing, a movement which set so much store by the innocence and experience of childhood, Robert Schumann spent a lot of time reflecting on what it is to be a child. Ten years after writing *Kinderszenen*, and then with his own three daughters aged seven, five and three in mind, he composed his *Album für die Jugend – Album for the Young* – a collection of over forty short pieces suitable for playing both by children and adult beginners. Back at home, and looking down the list of these pieces, one looks instantly familiar to me: his 'Sizilianisch' or 'Sicilienne', a short piece in A minor derived from a dance form once popular in Sicily. Sure enough, I locate it in a book of the exam pieces I studied for Grade 4.

We have a piano at home that Mum bought for us when my family moved out of London to a bigger house in Gloucestershire. Until 2003 the Stroud valley, where I now live, was home to one of the country's largest piano manufacturers, the Bentley Piano Company, which at its peak exported instruments to thirty countries. A couple of years before we moved to the area in 2005, the factory had closed due to falling demand and competition from overseas. But we benefitted from the expertise of a former factory employee when we bought a second-hand instrument from his local business, which specialises in reconditioning them. I chose a Wilhelm Spaethe piano, manufactured in the second half of the nineteenth century in the German city of Gera, about forty miles south of Leipzig, almost in Schumann country. I liked the tone of it when I first played it in the showroom, and the look of it, too: its chestnut wood and the carved decorative lozenges along the front. When you lift the top lid, its glowing, gold-coloured interior behind the strings is revealed, including the insignia of a double-headed eagle, indicating that Spaethe held a royal warrant of appointment to the court of Austria-Hungary.

On moving day, however, due to a narrow turning circle in our hall, this right royal piano almost failed to go into the room where we wanted to position it. At first, 'he', as it was being referred to – in the Gloucestershire parlance which gives personal pronouns to inanimate objects – by the three local chaps who were shifting it from van to house, moved smoothly enough up over the front doorstep and down the hall. 'Easy,

easy, lift 'im, lift 'im, 'ee's in, 'ee's in . . .' ran the commentary as I watched from a safe distance. But as soon as the men tried to turn the piano to manoeuvre it through the door of the room, it became clear we had a problem. And the moment this realisation dawned, the troublesome instrument changed gender. 'She won't go in there. She won't. You'll have to take the front off her,' said one of the men, mopping his brow. Far from being offended, I was laughing so much that I had to hide in the kitchen while they did indeed take the front off, thus reducing her girth by a few crucial centimetres.

For a time after its eventful arrival, our gender fluid piano was played mainly by my daughter, who took piano lessons for a few years. But once a teenager, she grew too busy with schoolwork and socialising to practise, and these days the piano stands mostly silent. Despite its appropriate provenance, Schumann household we are not. But although I gave up my own lessons when I too grew bored of practising, very occasionally I sit down and play. It astonishes me that, though I'm horrendously out of practice, my fingers can still mostly find the notes of pieces I played over thirty years ago. Simple pieces, it's true, but the neural pathways I laid down when learning them, albeit now grassed over and bumpy, still exist in my mind. Especially for my exam pieces – the ones I practised over and over: a Mozart minuet in B flat; a prelude in F by Bach. For the first time in decades, I have a go at Robert Schumann's 'Sizilianisch', and that, too, I can still sort of play, despite being continually tripped up by its landscape of sharps.

His 'Träumerei', however, presents a tougher challenge both technically and emotionally. I'm on a sentimental mission to master it all by myself. But my fingering issues mean I have a choice. I can struggle through and only tilt at playing it properly, or I can get help. I turn to Catherine, a local music teacher and pianist I know, and while she has a full timetable of students during term-time, she is happy to book me in for a couple of lessons over the summer when she is back from holiday and has time to help put me on the right track.

In the meantime, I continue to fiddle around with 'Träumerei', trying to marshal my sausage fingers. In dire need of instruction, I read *Robert Schumann's Advice to Young Musicians*, originally published alongside his *Album für die Jugend* in 1848. My copy is a recent edition in which the renowned cellist and teacher Steven Isserlis revisits Schumann's original nuggets of advice and adds his own, often witty, take to the mix for modern-day readers. It's ideal reading for an adult piano player like me, trying to pick up where she left off as a child. As early as page eight, Isserlis writes: 'As for those who feel that they really have no talent for playing or singing – don't give up!' There is plenty that Dad would appreciate here too. I smile when I read Isserlis's response to Schumann's advice never to 'play bad compositions, nor, unless compelled, listen to them'. 'What would he have made of the Muzak that assaults our ears almost every time we leave our homes?' Isserlis wonders. As far as Dad was concerned, the introduction by HSBC of piped pop music in its branches marked a new nadir for Western civilisation.

With Schumann's – and Isserlis's – pithy advice in mind, I go for my first piano lesson in thirty years. Catherine helps me decipher the fingering for 'Träumerei' and advises separate-hand practice of short chunks of the piece. It's what my original piano teacher, Mrs Adams, would have told me to do, too, but Catherine's more unconventional advice is to master the beginning and the end first, rather than doggedly working through the piece as written. I explain why I'm so keen to master 'Träumerei', and she advises me to think about the story I want to tell through my playing of it. 'Maybe something about your dad?' she says. I tell her I've been seeking help from *Robert's Schumann's Advice to Young Musicians* and pull the book out of my bag. Catherine smiles and says: 'Have I ever told you my Steven Isserlis story?'

When she was a small child in London, Catherine was taken to the retirement home where her maternal grandmother worked. It was a nursing home for Jewish refugees from the Second World War; Catherine's grandmother had herself fled Germany and come to Britain in 1933. The day of Catherine's visit, Steven Isserlis, then a boy of twelve or thirteen and already an accomplished cellist, was giving a recital for the residents, who included his own grandmother. Catherine recalls how she sat on the bottom step of a wide, red-carpeted staircase and listened entranced. Years later, she queued up to get her programme autographed by Isserlis after he played a concert at Birmingham Symphony Hall. When she got to the front of the very long queue, she told him the story. He was astonished.

For the next few weeks, in the wake of this new coincidence, I practise 'Träumerei' for at least half an hour a day in a show of discipline unknown when I played the piano as a child. I go over and over each bit, playing each hand's part separately ten times or more in a row. I realise how shamefully impatient I used to be, wanting to be able to play without putting in this sort of practice. But I know there are no shortcuts for me now: I have neither the proficiency, nor the chutzpah of youth to carry me through. Instead I call on the more dogged patience of the mature adult to laboriously carve out new pathways in a brain that feels much more sluggish and crowded than it used to.

Still, I'm surprised how quickly my fingers acquire familiarity with the notes, and the piece begins to take shape. With proper practice, it isn't as tricky as I thought it was going to be. And, as Catherine has suggested, I seek out some other interpretations of the piece besides that by Clifford Curzon to inspire me. My *1001 Classical Recordings You Must Hear Before You Die* recommends a recording by the Ukrainian-born pianist Alex Slobodyanik, calling it 'daringly rhapsodic and increasingly somnolent'. I listen and his wistful rendition gives me permission to play more slowly and dreamily than I have yet dared to do. Then I listen to what superstar Chinese pianist Lang Lang has to say. His interpretation is initially very seductive. It squeezes every last drop of Romantic rubato (get me) from the piece, and he suffuses it with an insistent longing. But is that longing perhaps a little too insistent? I feel there's an anchorless quality to Schumann's piece, just as reveries are anchorless, which makes me want to hear it played by someone who appears hardly to be playing it at all. Easy for me to say, of course, when I'm giving the far-too-deliberate performance of someone working overtime just to play the right notes.

Fittingly, the performance that perfectly encapsulates my feelings about 'Träumerei' turns out to be by one of Dad's favourite pianists, Vladimir Horovitz. I find it in a film of him playing the piece as an encore at a concert in Moscow in 1986. This was the year that Horovitz, born in Kiev in 1903, but a permanent resident of the US since the 1920s, returned to play in the Soviet Union for the first time in more than sixty years. As I watch, I suddenly recall seeing this very performance with Dad in a TV documentary about this historic concert called *Horovitz in Moscow*. I buy the DVD, and watching it again is a magical experience.

Clifford Curzon's rendition of 'Träumerei' is exquisite, but Horovitz's performance is both exquisite and profound. In a little over three minutes, perhaps calling up his own childhood in a land from which he had so long been exiled, he renders the innermost thoughts of those present visible on their faces. You can see it as the camera pans across the audience: everyone – young and old – is utterly still, except for those openly weeping and wiping away tears. It's like one grand, communal reverie. But there's nothing grandiose, no ceremony about the way Horovitz plays the piece. Instead, his virtuoso rendition is also childlike; there's a remarkable ease and innocence in the way in which this eighty-year-old man touches the keys, as if it was just an extension of his breathing. Very occasionally he scrunches up his face, but mostly he is entirely without drama in his demeanour as his liver-spotted hands glide across the keyboard. You would not know from his face whether he was playing to thousands or to no one at all. As I listen, it dawns on me that although with dogged practice my fingers will soon be able to play all the same notes that Horovitz plays, I will never be able to infuse the piece with even a fraction of the feeling he does. The feeling which quietly pervades an entire concert hall packed to the rafters with people. One of the online comments below the film reads: 'Träumerei' is 'an easy piece that is difficult to play'.

Here's the human story behind its simple power. Robert Schumann composed 'Träumerei' along with his other *Kinderszenen* when he was twenty-eight. The music was inspired by Clara Wieck, soon to be his wife, who told him how childlike he often seemed to her. At the time, Robert and Clara were three years into a fraught and difficult romance. Until she fell in love with Robert at the age of sixteen, Clara had been in thrall her whole life to her father Friedrich. And from the moment I start reading about her, I am in thrall to her story.

Mute for the first four years of her life, Clara lived at first with her mother after her parents' early divorce. But then, when she turned five, her father reclaimed her, as the law then allowed him to do, and she was sent to live with him permanently. It is then that she began music lessons with her father, and notes on the page became her language. Playing a huge range of works by Mozart, Beethoven and others, Clara began performing in public from the age of eleven, the start of a concert career that would last for more than sixty years. By the time she entered her teens, she had already undertaken punishing tours across Germany, and to Paris, where she met Fryderyk Chopin, whose music she had helped introduce to a German audience. In an imaginative biographical piece, Janice Galloway pictures this teenage Clara polishing knives at home as she reflects on the woman she is to become. 'The great, the good, and the very rich indeed had looked her in the eye and she had looked straight back knowing she had something to give. More to the point, that she worked and she *earned* and that mattered, dear goodness, that mattered.'[6]

In her *Sounds and Sweet Airs: The Forgotten Women of Classical Music*, Anna Beer reflects on how Friedrich Wieck single-handedly turned his daughter into a 'performing phenomenon'. He was a difficult man, prone to violent outbursts of temper, and so from a young age Clara became accustomed to playing on serenely, regardless of what was going on around her. This ability, Beer says, to 'continue a performance in the midst of chaos, illness, even violence, hard-won though it may have been, would sustain her throughout her life'.

From Beer's biography, I also learn that in the 1830s it was customary for performers to play their own pieces at recitals; and so from the age of ten Clara was also composing. Her early works were designed to show off her skills as a pianist, 'such as her ability to play tenths due to her big reach'. I think of my own fingers, stretching to their widest extent and still struggling to play chords ten notes apart in 'Träumerei'. At the age of thirteen, Clara began composing her only work for orchestra, her Piano Concerto in A minor, and two years later it had its first public performance, conducted by Felix Mendelssohn. Many contemporary listeners were impressed: 'If the name of the female composer were not on the title, one would never think it were written by a woman,' wrote one. However, another critic lamented the unconventional key changes in the piece, which he attributed to the fact that 'women are moody'.[7]

And then Clara Wieck fell for Robert Schumann, her father's student and a man she had known since she was ten. Robert – nine years older – had begun writing to Clara when she was twelve, and, somewhat uncomfortably for our modern sensibilities, seems to have become romantically interested in her soon afterwards. Friedrich vehemently opposed the match. He was adamant that Robert would not be able to keep his daughter in the style he believed fitting for her. But perhaps he also had an intimation of this unsuitable suitor's mental instability. Whatever his objection, he did everything he could to separate the pair, and from early 1836 until the summer of 1837 Robert and Clara were prevented from seeing or writing to one another. It was during this period that Robert's turbulent *Fantasie* in C major was composed. Still he refused to give up, and in September 1837 wrote to Friedrich asking for Clara's hand in marriage. He received no reply. You can see Wieck's point of view, argues Harold C. Schonberg. Whereas Clara's father had made his daughter 'the outstanding pianist of her sex', nobody at the time yet thought much of Robert's music at all. And now, just when Friedrich was beginning to reap the financial rewards of his daughter's talent and all his hard work and expense in nurturing it, she was thinking of 'throwing herself away on a penniless composer, a vague idealist, a radical musician whose theories were being called mad, an impractical and disorganised man'. Eventually Robert and Clara had to go to court to obtain permission to marry without Wieck's consent. Their wedding took place the day before Clara's twenty-first birthday in 1840.

According to Schonberg, it was 'an idyllic marriage, the union of two extraordinary minds. She was the stabilising force in his life; he was the spiritual beacon in hers.' That's one way of looking at it when you read her biography. Or you can notice how Clara's intense creativity was increasingly channelled into helping to enhance her husband's reputation rather than promote her own compositions. This dimming of her own identity as a composer and performer began as early as the winter of 1837–8, two years before their marriage. Clara had just completed her most triumphant concert tour yet, to Vienna, where her popularity was such that the police had to be called to control the crowds, and a cake – torte à la Wieck – was named after her. And yet while she was still flushed with her success, Robert was writing to her of his own composing ambitions. 'There's still a lot in me. If you remain faithful to me, everything will come to light; it will remain buried if you don't.'[8] From this time on until his death, it was Robert's talent that took precedence. And this despite the fact that Clara was held in lofty esteem by such famous contemporaries as Mendelssohn and Chopin, who was introduced to Clara by Mendelssohn when he visited Leipzig in the autumn of 1835. On that occasion she played some of her own music, a piece by Robert and then two of Chopin's études. The performance reportedly moved Chopin to tears. Clara was, he said, 'The only woman in Germany who can play my music.'[9]

But then, in early September 1840 in Weimar, the twenty-year-old Clara played her final concert before her wedding, later recording that it was her 'last concert as Clara Wieck and I had a heavy heart'.[10] It's as if she knew how different things were going to be. After only a few months of marriage, she noted in her diary that because her playing disturbed Robert when he was composing, she could no longer play in the morning, 'the best hours for serious practice'.[11] In June 1841, she writes that she is getting out of practice with her playing, 'which always happens when Robert is composing. There isn't one hour in the whole day for me.'[12] While Clara continued to compose and give concerts, many of them with Robert, she was reduced to extreme melancholy at times by her restricted new existence, worrying that her playing would irrevocably suffer. Her first child, Marie, was born in September 1841, the first of eight she would give birth to in the next fourteen years. Within a few months of Marie's birth, Clara was on tour again to bring in much-needed money. Robert joined her at first but then went home as Clara continued north through Germany, to Copenhagen. Then news reached her that Robert was so unhappy he had started gambling and drinking again, so she cut short her tour and returned home.

In 1844 and by now the mother of two daughters, Clara, with Robert accompanying her, embarked on a long-planned four-month concert tour of Russia, taking in Königsberg, Riga and St Petersburg. Commercially it was a success and Clara made a profit. But Robert was miserable throughout. 'He may have found the role of accompanying husband and the circumstances that went with it, to be below his dignity', remarks Monica Steegmann tartly in her biography of Clara. Three months after their return from Russia, Robert had a breakdown and, although he recovered, it presaged darker days to come.

Soon afterwards, Clara and Robert moved to Dresden, and during the six years they lived there, Clara gave birth to four more children; a third daughter and then three sons, one of whom, Emil, lived for less than two years. Her time, says Steegmann, was 'measured out minute by minute': she taught for two to three hours a day, played herself for an hour, worked on arrangements of pieces, went out walking with Robert, dealt with all the correspondence, gave concerts, and managed all matters domestic. Around it all she was still composing, but it was a slog. She writes that audiences were 'tired of concerts' and that there was a 'great shortage of money'. Prior to a concert in Vienna on 1 January 1847, she has only 'one single hour' to prepare. All this time, she continued to play and promote Robert's music over her own.

In 1850 they moved to Düsseldorf, where Robert had been offered a position as municipal music director, but he was not a success in the post, and turned on his wife in frustration, criticising both her person and her playing. 'It may have been because Robert was over-sensitive to his own declining powers compared with the indomitable robustness of his wife,' writes Steegmann of his behaviour at this time. Clara, she believes, was exhausted, bearing the burden both of Robert's health and professional problems, and of a household full of children (her seventh child, a daughter called Eugenie, was born in 1851). Around this time, the twenty-year-old Johannes Brahms entered their lives, and he provided a much-needed diversion, with both Robert and Clara fascinated both by his musical talent and his 'personal magnetism and charm'. So much for all those stodgy late photographs of Johannes Brahms.

But then, following a suicide attempt in February 1854, Robert was confined, at his own request, in a mental asylum in Endenich, near Bonn. Clara was forbidden to visit him. In anguish she turned increasingly to Brahms for support as she set about providing for her husband and children: her eighth and last child, another son, was born in June 1854. Between October and December of that year, she gave twenty-two formal concerts across Germany, playing music both by her husband and by Brahms.

In September 1855, she received a letter from Robert's doctor which put an end to any hope she might have of his recovery. A month later, she set off on her longest ever concert tour, lasting eight months, and by the end of it she had earned enough to support her family for five or six months. In April 1856 she made the first of what were to be numerous trips to Britain. Three months later, however, after receiving grave reports of Robert's condition, she returned to Germany, where she was able to visit him before he died on 29 July. His death left Clara a widow at thirty-seven, with seven surviving children, the youngest only two years old. That autumn, she parted from Brahms after more than two years of close and almost daily intimacy, although they remained friends for the rest of Clara's life. 'There was no question of Clara marrying again, after all she had been through, subordinating and limiting her life as a musician, however great may have been the admiration and intense feelings she had for the young man of twenty-three,' writes Monica Steegmann. Soon afterwards, Clara composed a piece in memory of Robert, her Romance in B minor.

It was her last major composition. For the next thirty-five years, Clara, who died in 1896, concentrated on her concert career, through financial necessity, lack of time, and lack of Robert to inspire her. This, the woman who had once written of composing 'there is nothing that surpasses the joy of creation, if only because through it one wins hours of self-forgetfulness'. No such luxury now. And in any case, argues Steegman, Clara 'lacked a firm conviction in the ability of women to compose'; her temporary joy in composition ('there is nothing better than producing something oneself') was tempered by her doubts in her own potential ('women cannot become composers'). For the rest of her life, Clara continued to promote Robert's reputation and play his music in performances across Europe: in Germany, Austria, France, in Russia and most often of all in Britain, as well as that of Brahms and other male composers like Schubert and Chopin. Their mighty reputations today owe her a considerable debt of gratitude. At the end of the 1860s in London, Clara played Robert's *Kinderszenen* for the first time in public. The fact that 'any over-sentimentality was always anathema to her' meant that she played 'Träumerei' 'rather faster than it is usually played nowadays', notes Steegmann, and I note this as well.

Clara's own music languished in obscurity for well over a century. The attitude of the influential Harold Schonberg – for years the music critic of the *New York Times*, and the first in his field to receive the Pulitzer Prize for Criticism – is typical. He does acknowledge Clara's supreme talent as a pianist in his chapter on Robert in his *Lives of the Great Composers* (there is no chapter on Clara). But of her music he writes that while it is 'fluent, tasteful and thoroughly attractive', its composer 'never had many original ideas as a composer', and that 'hers was not a strikingly creative mind'.

Clara the composer's long dwelling in obscurity is not only Schonberg's fault. Flick through virtually any book on the lives of 'great composers' and you'll find Robert's music lauded to the exclusion of Clara's. Even in *1001 Classical Recordings You Must Hear Before You Die*, there are more than twenty recommendations of pieces by Robert Schumann; there are none by Clara. Only in Clemency Burton-Hill's *Year of Wonder* do I find two suggested pieces: her Scherzo No. 2 in C minor and her Three Romances.

Getting caught up with Clara and the unjust neglect of her work has diverted me from my path. For Dad probably never heard any of her music and, what's more, there is not a single female composer in his CD collection. *Why not, Dad?* I wonder. While I can't help being disappointed that he wasn't more adventurous, I know it wasn't for any discriminatory reasons. After all, plenty of female soloists feature among his CDs, from Annie 'Ashtray' Fischer and Jacqueline du Pré, to Rosalyn Tureck playing Bach's *Goldberg Variations*. He just hadn't been exposed to any music composed by women for the same reason that so few people had – none on the radio, none on concert billings, little available on CD. So I feel vindicated in shaking up a dead white man's record collection of music by other dead white males just a little. And I think about how Dad would probably have loved it if I'd bought him a CD of music he didn't know for us to listen to and discuss. In fact, it makes me sad that I never did this.

After all, Dad never gave up trying to get me to listen to his music, often bringing me CDs to borrow when he and Mum came to stay. 'I thought you might enjoy this,' he'd say. And I'd place the CDs on top of the stacks of Nanci Griffith and Bruce Springsteen and Lucinda Williams by my CD player in the kitchen and say, 'Ooh yes, I'll have a listen.' But I almost never did. Why didn't I? I was busy of course, running a home, running a freelance career from home, running around after two children. There was no time to listen. Correction: I made no time to listen. I made no time to listen with Father.

So I find a small way of putting this right. I've heard some Robert Schumann performed, so now it's time for some Clara. By another of those serendipitous coincidences I am now coming to expect, Cheltenham Music Festival has not only programmed a concert to mark the 200th anniversary year of Clara's birth, but a concert that takes place two days after what would have been the eighty-fifth anniversary of Dad's birth. So as a birthday present, I treat us to an event called 'Schumann Square', billed as 'an immersive chamber music adventure' in which the audience will be walked between four different Regency town houses in the centre of Cheltenham to hear a series of recitals 'inspired by the consummate artistry of Clara Schumann'.

Eighty of us gather in Imperial Square and are divided into four groups of twenty by different coloured wristband. I am in the teal group. We crocodile off, led by a pink t-shirted festival volunteer to the first venue – a Regency townhouse on the other side of the square. We troop through the solid front door and up the stairs to the first-floor drawing room, where a bank of chairs and sofas facing the floor-to-ceiling windows awaits us. As we sit down, we nose around the room, taking in the family photos on the piano, the tasteful Farrow & Ball shade on the walls.

The first soloist is Xuefei Yang, a revered female guitarist from China, and one of the first Chinese guitarists to achieve international recognition after the Cultural Revolution. Yang plays us three charming short songs by Brazilian guitarist and composer Dilermando Reis, followed by a piece by Argentinian composer and virtuoso guitarist José Luis Merlin, his *Suite del Recuerdo – Suite of Memories*. I particularly enjoy this wistful piece, which feels so appropriate to the occasion I'm here for. It wraps me up in thoughts of Dad, scarcely conscious of anyone around me, despite being tightly packed into this room with my fellow festival-goers. I'm brought back to earth, however, by a man sitting in an armchair by the window. When each piece finishes, he goes 'mmmmmmm' quite loudly, as if a voiced response is immediately required. Someone else asks Yang what kind of guitar she is playing. She tells us it's a Spanish guitar made in Australia, and this unexpected reply is met with silence, even from the man by the window.

As we leave the house and walk to the next venue, another man comes bustling up behind me. 'Is that what you were expecting?' he asks. *Nobody expects an Australian Spanish guitar* . . . I think about saying, but instead ask him what he means. 'I thought this was an event of music by Clara Schumann,' he says as if the issue should be obvious. I indicate the bit in my festival programme that says the music will be partly inspired by Clara and partly by the chamber setting, but he doesn't seem mollified and stalks on ahead of me. I notice he's carrying his own festival programme, which bristles with Post-it-note markers. He's clearly an aficionado, and he makes me feel like an arriviste. But I'm enjoying myself immensely, and apart from hoping for a little Clara Schumann, I don't much mind what music I hear. I'm happy because I know Dad would be enjoying his birthday treat, too.

At the second house, we ascend once again to a first-floor drawing room where a Steinway grand piano awaits. I perch on a chair at the back, behind the 'mmmmm' man, who is squished onto a sofa with three others. And then our soloist arrives: Isata Kanneh-Mason. I glance at the Post-it man, as I know this means we'll be hearing some Clara Schumann. Hopefully that will make him pipe down.

Kanneh-Mason is the eldest of seven remarkable and musically gifted siblings, her brother the superstar cellist Sheku, who played at Prince Harry and Meghan Markle's wedding in May 2018. I'm thrilled at the prospect of hearing her play live because her debut album *Romance*, music by Clara Schumann, is due to be released in a few days' time. Tall, with long, braided hair, Kanneh-Mason cuts the slightest of figures as she greets us and announces the short programme: Clara's Scherzo No. 2 in C minor; the final movement – the Rondo – of her Piano Sonata in G minor; and 'Widmung', the tune she wrote to accompany a song of Robert's. The piano, Kanneh-Mason tells us as she seats herself, is from 1870, and therefore from the period when Clara herself was still performing. I'm very taken with the sweeping Scherzo, by turns towering and fierce, and then clement and shimmery. The pensive and delicate Rondo puts me in mind of wandering fantasies, given brief rein and then pulled back under control. Both pieces date from the early years of Clara's marriage, after the birth of her first child, Marie, and they seem to speak eloquently of her emotional quest to fulfil so many roles in her life: that of loving wife and mother; of a working, earning woman; of an artist with a burning creativity so often thwarted.

The music, the sound, the setting are glorious, and Kanneh-Mason's performance is all too brief. I'm realising what a special experience it is to be so close to a soloist, to witness their emotion at close quarters as they play, with only inches between you and the source of this sublime music.

Similarly, at the third corner of the square, Franco-Belgian cellist Camille Thomas gives us an exquisite recital of pieces by Pablo Casals and by Bach, and her great sighs are clearly audible as she plays. At the fourth recital in another private drawing room lined with books and paintings, we hear more Clara Schumann, this time played on the piano and violin by Tom Poster and Elena Urioste, two members of the Kaleidoscope Chamber Collective. Stupidly, I've never really thought about the term 'chamber music' before and the intimacy it implies. This must have been the chief attraction of chamber concerts in Clara Schumann's time, too: the sense of soundwaves being created for you and just a few privileged others.

Poster and Urioste play Clara's *Three Romances*, Opus 22, and then throw in a piece by Robert, his 'Abendlied' – 'Song of Evening'. And despite my new devotion to Clara, it is the melody of this song that I find most transporting of all. There is something freeing to the mind about the closeted comfort of the chamber setting that allows you to commune with your own thoughts. It might sound fanciful but, as I descend the steps of the final venue, I do feel as if Dad and I really have been on an outing together. I sit on the grass in the middle of the square and sip my complimentary glass of fizz, thinking back with relish on all I have heard. But later, my mood turns melancholy as I wait on Cheltenham station for a train home and remember all the train journeys I took north from here to visit Dad when he was gravely ill. And I remember trying to get on with life and hoping for the best when I knew deep down, almost from the moment he was diagnosed, that it would not end well. I think of the photograph I took of us in my parents' conservatory, the summer before he died, the one where I put my cheek against Dad's and took a selfie on my phone. He was baffled by the selfie business, but I knew the day was fast coming when I would treasure that photo.

I buy *Romance*, Isata Kanneh-Mason's newly released recording of Clara Schumann's music. It opens with Clara's Piano Concerto in A minor, the piece composed between her early and mid-teens and whose unconventional key changes caused its composer to be dismissed as 'moody'. From its strident beginning – the Allegro maestoso – onwards, I'm wowed by this dramatic and ambitious composition, and astonished that it could have been composed by one so young. Mindful of its snide and sexist reviews, I listen on, but find nothing to complain about. It is undoubtedly a piece full of high-rolling emotions of the kind that are worn on the outside rather than held inwards, as perhaps one learns to do when one grows older. But for me this only adds to its rousing drama. I picture the physical effort that must have been made by Kanneh-Mason's slender frame as she recorded this movement.

The second movement – designated as Romance: Andante non troppo con grazia – features a gorgeous solo piano passage, joined halfway through by a cello. This movement takes the piece back to Clara's chamber roots: there's something loving and giving, too, about the way in which the piano lets another instrument shine at this point, its finale making a feature of the rich, sonorous cello chords.

And in the final show-offy movement – the Allegro non troppo – the orchestra returns to provide backing for Clara's virtuoso use of the whole keyboard. In the breathtaking final forty seconds of the piece the music races to the conclusion at such breakneck speed and clamour that you imagine Kanneh-Mason almost taking off as she pounds the piano.

Clara's music grips me. And my sympathies lie firmly with her, because of the injustice of her neglect as a composer, and of her struggle to pursue a creative life despite all the obstacles fate threw in her way. My own experience of attempting to write while dealing with the domestic and raising two children as well as earn a living pales into insignificance by comparison. But despite resenting Robert a little for all he demanded from her, I can't let it affect how I feel about his music.

And I feel his tragedy, too. Especially after reading Mary Oliver's poem 'Robert Schumann', in which she writes of thinking almost every day about the composer and his life in the asylum. When I play 'Träumerei' on the piano, which I can now mostly do without faltering, I think, too, of this sensitive and deeply troubled man. My performance of the piece isn't in the same universe as that of Clifford Curzon or of Vladimir Horovitz for its fluency or tone or depth of feeling. But I've tried to take another piece of Robert's advice to heart. 'Do not aim for mere dexterity, or so-called "bravura". Try to recreate the spirit intended by the composer, nothing more; anything else is a caricature.'[13] While technical brilliance is in any case beyond me, this is not a particularly difficult piece to play. But now I need to feel it as well as play it.

'An honest approach to music will not necessarily whip an audience into a frenzy,' writes Isserlis. 'But people with true sensitivity will feel your sincerity and be moved by it; and moving people is more important than impressing them.'[14] With this advice in mind and pressing the keys as gently and lovingly as my fingers will allow, I try and make my playing say something about Dad. I think about a ten-year-old in a cowboy hat. I think about upside-down jigsaw puzzles. I think about discussing the state of the world with him over beer and lemonade. I think about the number of miles there might be between Carlisle and Chelmsford. And I try and make the music reach him, wherever he now is.

Chapter 6

The Swan Songs of Sibelius

*Symphonies No. 5 in E-flat major,
No. 6 in D minor and No. 7 in C major*

I'm driving home from a frustrating shopping errand, something to do with the hard-drive failure of my daughter's cheap and not very cheerful laptop. Within seconds of turning on the car radio in search of something soothing to listen to, I know the piece playing is a Sibelius symphony.

I'm amazed that I'm so certain about this. Once again it astonishes me how much classical music is stored in the hard drive of my brain. I can't remember which Sibelius symphony it is (it's the Fifth, in fact, played by the Estonian Festival Orchestra and my old friend Paavo Järvi), but there's something so characteristic about that resonant, concentrated string sound.

That I know it's Sibelius is Dad's doing, of course. Once, when I was a student, home for the holidays, we watched a documentary together about the life of Finland's most famous composer. I'm sure I watched it initially to please him; classical music played almost no part in my life at that time. During my first year at university, I heard the opening of what

I later discovered was the Simple Minds track 'Waterfront' thundering up through the floor of my college room. Desperate to find out what I was hearing, I knocked on the door of the room below and met its occupant, Tim. Before long, I was listening to U2, The The, The Chameleons and The Smiths in his company, as well as Simple Minds. We sang our hearts out to both those last two bands at City Hall in Newcastle-upon-Tyne, and later went to a recording of *The Tube* at Tyne Tees studios; where we saw live performances by the Alarm, Shriekback, and Grandmaster Flash and the Furious Five.

But then I watched that film with Dad and, though at the outset I knew nothing about Sibelius, I was bewitched by scenes of his house in the country, viewed through whirling snow, and accompanied by a haunting soundtrack of his music which seemed to perfectly echo what I was seeing. I remember also being struck by the fact that a deep depression had led Sibelius to stop composing music altogether, and even to burning some that he had already written. And I liked the music I heard so much that I went out and bought a cassette of Sibelius music to take back to university with me. I still have the tape, of the Third and Fifth Symphonies, played by the Bournemouth Symphony Orchestra, with Finnish conductor and noted Sibelius interpreter Paavo Berglund presiding. On the front is a chilly photograph of snow-dusted fir trees climbing up a mountainside.

I hear Sibelius's Fifth Symphony again by chance in the car at a time when I'm feeling the need to break out of my own introspection. I've spent much of the summer listening to the music of Robert and Clara Schumann, thinking about mental instability, thinking too much about the past, drinking wine every night, becoming maudlin and playing 'Träumerei' over and over again on the piano, trying to hone my emotional storytelling. I'm stuck in a bit of a brooding reverie I need to snap out of. I need to throw open the shutters to wide-open spaces and listen to something rich and expansive. Some Sibelius might be just what I need.

Among Dad's CDs is a recording of the complete symphonies – all seven of them – along with some other orchestral pieces, played by the Philharmonia Orchestra conducted by Vladimir Ashkenazy. After catching it on the car radio, I reacquaint myself with the Fifth Symphony and it is as magical as I remember it; its rising, quivering string sounds which evoke the wind whipping up at sea, or a wild wood filled with insects, perhaps. So I start listening to the other symphonies in turn, and before long I am gorging myself on all of Sibelius's music, as if it is a TV boxed set. I listen to all seven symphonies, one after the other, and it's such an assault of sound that I struggle to hold onto anything I've heard. The symphonies are so full and so rich that I can't take it all in. No sooner have I listened to one then I drop it while I try and concentrate on the next.

I also listen to *Finlandia*, a rousing, seven-minute anthem which opens with trumpets and a drum roll and sounds like a call to arms until suddenly, close to the end, it unexpectedly morphs into a hymn tune I recognise: 'Be Still My Soul'. There's also *En saga*, an unsettling piece which puts me in mind of Stravinsky's *Rite of Spring* in its balletic weirdness, and *The Swan of Tuonela*, the most popular of a suite of four tone poems called *Lemminkäinen*, which mournfully evokes a mystical swan which swims on the lake surrounding the island of the dead. And Sibelius's *Karelia Suite* is full of gorgeous and arresting melodies that gain such a hold over me that I find myself staring into space for several minutes after the music has finished.

I'm also taken with *Tapiola*, one of the last pieces of music Sibelius wrote. Tapiola is the god of the forest, and Sibelius's music conjuring up the legend is alluring in its bosky strangeness. As I listen, its frenzied strings evoke pictures of the Moomins from the Finnish books I so loved as a child, and the weird creatures which emerge from the Hobgoblin's enchanted hat after Moomintroll has thrown eggshells into it.

And I listen to Sibelius's Violin Concerto in D minor through big headphones in a sun lounger in the garden one hot summer's day. I get goose bumps as I lie there, my eyes deep in the clouds above me. The concerto's emotional intensity is extraordinary, particularly in the second movement, 'a mercilessly beautiful, eight-minute benediction', as Clemency Burton-Hill calls it in her *Year of Wonder*.

My Sibelius binge leaves me longing to see the documentary I watched with Dad again, so I track it down. It's a two-part film from 1984 made by Christopher Nupen, who is noted for his documentaries about music and musicians. I buy the DVD and from the opening scenes of Ainola, Sibelius's country house wadded with snow, I am once again entranced, just as when I first watched it with Dad.

Part One – 'The Early Years' – focuses on the first half of Sibelius's life. Born in the southern provincial town of Hämeenlinna into a Swedish-speaking family in 1865, Janne Sibelius, as he was then called, his mother, brother and sister moved to live with his grandmother in Helsinki after the death of his bankrupt doctor father before Janne was two years old. It was Sibelius's aunt, with whom the family holidayed by the sea in Loviisa, along the coast from Helsinki, who encouraged all three children to study music, and Janne, who also played the piano, nurtured his youthful passion for the violin. His early ambition to be a violinist was, Nupen asserts, 'to remain with him long after his talent as a composer had determined the course of his life'. Janne began composing at the age of ten and his first piece was a delightful pizzicato piece for violin and cello called *Vattendroppar* (*Water Drops*), an early signal of how nature would come to provide inspiration for so much of his later music.

Sibelius's adult composing career began in what Nupen calls 'an almost unprecedented blaze of glory and patriotic fervour'. Finland was at that time a Grand Duchy of the Russian Empire but, as the turn of the twentieth century approached, Tsar Nicholas II began to deprive the country of much of the autonomy it had traditionally enjoyed, sparking a wave of Finnish patriotism. This popular uprising took inspiration from the epics of Finnish mythology, and Sibelius's early compositions borrowed from this mythology as well. He began to build a reputation with his musical settings of folk songs and epic poetry, such as *Kullervo*, an interpretation of another myth from the Kalevala. First performed in 1892, the prodigious success of this piece transformed Sibelius's artistic prospects, propelling him to prominence as a spokesperson for Finnish culture at a time when the country didn't yet exist as an independent nation.

This status as a Finnish cultural icon, cemented by patriotic pieces like *Finlandia* – originally called *Finland Awakes!* – which was to become one of his most celebrated compositions – was one that Sibelius would in time find burdensome. But initially the popularity of *Kullervo* gave him enough confidence in his future career as a composer to enable him to propose to Aino

Järnefelt. She came from a highly creative Helsinki family and Sibelius had come to know her through his friendship with Armas, one of her brothers. Janne Sibelius had now become Jean, adopting the French form of his first name, as was the Finnish custom of the time when travelling abroad. He and Aino married in 1892. A contemporary photo shows a rakish-looking young man with an exuberant head of floppy hair and a full moustache. Nupen quotes a telling letter to Aino from this period, in which Sibelius writes prophetically, 'you must not die as long as I live, and you will not either. I still feel I am going to do something great.'

And great things were indeed beginning to happen for him. At the age of thirty-three in 1899, Sibelius unveiled his First Symphony, and it brought him his first dose of acclaim from outside Finland. It has, says Nupen 'a voice of ringing authority', and 'full of the confidence of youth', it also takes what he calls a 'major step forward in orchestral imagination and symphonic thinking'. I have already listened to enough Sibelius to understand a little of the orchestral imagination Nupen is referring to: the distinctive way that Sibelius combines intense string and woodwind sounds, for example. But what Nupen means by 'symphonic thinking' I have little clue. Finnish conductor Simon Parmet once referred to the First Symphony as 'the music of a young giant, full of a fiery love for his country and flaming defiance against its oppressors'.[1] For indeed Russian oppression continued to grow, and Sibelius's Second Symphony, first performed in 1902, is also imbued with the idea of Finnish national identity. It must have been rousing indeed if you were a poor oppressed Finn at that time. Ironically though, when I listen to the First and Second Symphonies, they remind me of the music of Tchaikovsky, a quintessentially Russian composer. They sound theatrical in the way that Tchaikovsky's ballet scores do, but also classically contained.

But I can also hear qualities I'm learning to recognise as quintessentially Sibelius: lush orchestration, a merry-go-round of moods, a plethora of memorable melodies. There's something elemental about his music, a sense of drama and of the seasons of the soul. It packs exuberance and wonder but also darkness and foreboding, as if the joys and agonies of life are tussling for supremacy. The existential thinking which seems to underpin these conflicting moods is encapsulated by an orchestral setting Sibelius wrote in 1903 for a poem with the same title by Finland's national poet, Johan Runeberg, whose work Sibelius loved. 'Since Then I Have Questioned No Further' is, as Christopher Nupen puts it, 'a highly condensed and intensely personal lament of transience of life and love' which seeks to convey the fleeting duration of all our lives and all that we love. 'Why does spring pass so soon?/ Why can summer not last? . . . Deep in my soul/I have come to know/That beauty is transient/And happiness won't last,' it concludes. Sibelius was not yet forty, but already seemed to be anticipating the end.

It's perhaps no wonder. For at the time he composed this song setting, beautifully rendered in the Nupen film by Swedish soprano Elisabeth Söderström, Sibelius was struggling with growing debts and embarking on bouts of drinking which left him hungover and incapacitated for days. His early fame had left him with a taste for the high life that he never lost, and socially he was in high demand. His brother urged him to stop drinking, while Aino was clearly distressed at his behaviour. The composition of his now famed Violin Concerto between 1903 and 1904 precipitated yet more hard-drinking sessions.

'Janne has been in the throes of it all the time. And so have I,' wrote Aino to one of her husband's closest friends and supporters during this period. 'He has had so many ideas forcing their way into his mind that he becomes quite literally dizzy . . . But if I have been excited by all of this, I have suffered too. A woman cannot cope with all the turbulent ups and downs of a creative artist's temperament which changes so violently that I become alarmed. Of course I am happy to have been able to be near him all this time. Sometimes he speaks of our partnership and then I feel proud.'[2]

The first part of the Nupen film sets the scene for Sibelius's exacting and often deeply introspective creativity. But it is the second part, 'Maturity and Silence', that I most clearly remember watching with Dad, its footage of wintery snowscapes of close-knit birch trees that speak of isolation and hardship, etched onto my mind after only a single viewing. When I watch the film again, thirty years later, I realise that this vividly recalled section is only a few minutes long. But during my initial gorging on Sibelius's music, I immediately recognised the exact passage in the Seventh Symphony which accompanied this section of footage: a menacing combination of howling strings and portentous brass. I saw myself sitting on the sofa next to Dad in my parents' sitting room, transfixed by a film I had feared might be boring. If only Dad knew of the legacy of music he placed in my head that day, without either of us even realising it.

There's no doubt that my long-standing emotional attachment to Sibelius's music has been rekindled. But can I cultivate a more critically astute ear for it, too? After overdosing on his music for weeks, I know I need to narrow my focus if I'm to get under the skin of it. I want to choose a symphony, but which one? On first seeing the Nupen film, the Third and the Fifth were my takeaway favourites, and their lush melodies still have a familiarity which is seductive. But the fact that I've retained such vivid memories of Part Two of Nupen's film means that I'm now more drawn to later Sibelius. So perhaps the searing Seventh, his final symphony? Or maybe the Sixth, which on my brief initial listening feels equally elemental? But then again, I'm reluctant to turn away from the Fifth, given that it was my gateway to re-engaging with Sibelius. Each symphony has its own distinct character, and each one feels as if it has the potential to become my favourite.

I start trawling through the pile of music books I've collected, hoping to find something that will help me decide. Dad's copy of *1001 Classical Recordings You Must Hear Before You Die* has entries for Nos 1, 2, 4, 5 and 7, which naturally makes me wonder what it has against 3 and 6. For the Fourth, it suggests Herbert von Karajan conducting the Berlin Philharmonic – although I'm intrigued to read that this recording has been considered 'too beautiful', with Sibelius's biographer Robert Layton finding it at first like 'the Finnish landscape perceived through the window of a limousine'. I ponder the meaning of this. Eventually I take it as a sign that whichever symphony I choose, I need to immerse myself totally in it, although I wouldn't mind doing so from the window of a limousine while being driven through Finland.

Distinguished music critic Fiona Maddocks selects the Third for her book *Music for Life: 100 Works to Carry You Through* but reveals that she too found it hard to choose a single symphony: 'The choice of the Third, over his Fourth (a particular favourite of composers), Fifth (rightly popular), Sixth (wonderful if neglected) or Seventh (one movement genius) caused much hand-wringing.' In the end she goes for the Third because it is the 'child most overlooked'. I feel quite gratified that the Third is one of the pieces I know best, but I'm no closer to deciding which symphony to choose.

In *Hear Me Out*, Armando Iannucci writes that Sibelius, 'perhaps more than any other composer, has been my gateway to classical music'. When he first listened to the opening of the Third Symphony he says, 'that settled it for me. Classical music wasn't the fey, light-headed, drippy background noise for "cultured" people to play at dinner parties; it was so much more . . . something deeply human.' But then, to demonstrate how far musical opinions can differ, he quotes critic Theodor Adorno, who wrote that 'the work of Sibelius, perhaps more than any other composer, is not only incredibly overrated, but it fundamentally lacks any good qualities'. It's hard to imagine a more damning dismissal.

In *Play It Again: An Amateur Against the Impossible*, his account of learning to play Chopin's fiendishly difficult Ballade No. 1, former *Guardian* editor Alan Rusbridger recalls an interview he once did with Daniel Barenboim. 'If it were a score, it would not resemble a sonata, or indeed anything with a recognisable beginning, middle or an end,' writes Rusbridger of their far-from-linear conversation. 'It is much more like a Sibelius symphony – a multitude of thematic gems, which occasionally fuse into a big theme.' There are moments with both Sibelius and Barenboim, he says, where 'it's not entirely clear where it's all going'.

I frown at this. When I listen to Sibelius, I'm so caught up in all its dramatic lushness and its tapestry of textures that I haven't ever stopped to wonder where it's all going. Should I? The more I read about Sibelius's music, the more I realise how few opinions about music I have that are in any way objective. I want to try and apply some critical listening but don't really know how to go about it. When I review books, my opinions are contextualised against my knowledge of other books I have read, which allows me to make statements like: 'this is the best travel book I have read this year', or 'her writing reminded me of early Anne Tyler' (i.e. it is brilliant). But beyond this modicum of critical thinking, my opinions about books are still mostly driven by intensely personal feelings. My heart will always be welded to Helen Macdonald's *H is for Hawk* because I read it only three months after Dad died. Why should music be any different?

Still, despite the fact that I'm on a musical quest that is emotional by its very nature, I do feel I want to come away from it, as Dad did from those early 1950s lunchtime sessions at his grammar school, with a little more appreciation of classical music, what it has to say and how it seeks to say it. I'm much less familiar with the nuts and bolts of music than I am with the way in which words are put together, but I dare to hope it's a language I can learn to converse in at least a little.

And as I embark on listening to the work of another composer, I know I've already come to appreciate the particular depth and power of classical music, its ability to articulate emotions in a way that words cannot, to convey, as Iannucci puts it, 'something deeply human'. Words and the way I express myself verbally are so much a part of my life that listening to orchestral music, where words are not used, has required a shift in my patience, my tenacity, my ability to hear. I realise now how much I listened to the words of songs rather than the music. It's not that I don't appreciate a beautiful melody, rather that – in my world made of words – melody has always taken second place in my hearing. Now, however, I'm undergoing a transformation, and my musical 'needs' have changed quite markedly. I now rarely put on background music while I'm cooking or cleaning, and I no longer garden along to favourite albums on my iPod. Mozart, Stravinsky, Brahms, Clara and Robert Schumann have all seized my attention, so much so that I would now rather work in silence if I can't give my undivided attention to what I am listening to. Dad would be delighted.

Occasionally, I feel a bit square and wonder if it's less an epiphany and more a sign that I am getting older and more ponderous. So one day I sidle up to my eighteen-year-old, deeply on-trend daughter and ask her what she's listening to at the moment. While we prepare supper together she plays me tracks by Brockhampton, Frank Ocean, Kofi Stone, Rex Orange County and her favourite, Loyle Carner, enjoying my interest and taking pleasure in sharing them with me. I find I love the upstart energy of so much of this music, and rejoice in my own child's omnivorous and entirely independent listening habits. Sibelius might as yet be a step too far for her, but Julia listens to Fleetwood Mac, Frank Sinatra and Aretha Franklin as well as Stormzy and SZA. In fact, her open-mindedness stands in stark contrast to her late grandfather's abhorrence of any music that urged him to get with the beat.

And yet, just as for his daughter and granddaughter, music was one of my dad's abiding pleasures, and the CD collection he left behind is testament to his love and appreciation for the work of many different composers, in wholly different styles and from different periods. 'Overrated' it may be, but if Dad loved Sibelius's music, then that's all I need for my own burgeoning attraction to it.

In the end, my symphonic decision is made for me in the

space of an impulsive couple of hours. In the throes of my Sibelius addiction, I do something as wild as the wood sprites who haunt *Tapiola*, and I act on my longing to visit Finland. Flicking through a music magazine, I notice an advert for a five-day trip centred on the annual Sibelius Festival in Lahti, and run by one of those upmarket companies which specialise in fancy cultural holidays. The cost of the trip isn't given (if you need to ask the price . . .), but looking it up online, I find that it is an outrageous £3,500. I can't possibly afford it. So, 'just for fun', I challenge myself to see if I can put together a similar trip for less. In less than an hour, I have discovered that concert tickets for the Sibelius Festival are available from around £20; that Finnish trains are cheap and efficient, and will transport me easily from Helsinki both to Ainola – Sibelius's country house, and the main location for Nupen's film – and to Lahti; that there are lots of cheap and lovely Airbnbs in Finland; and that a return flight from Helsinki can be had for less than £200. In a matter of hours, I have researched and booked my own five-day trip to Finland for less than a quarter of the price. And included in this is a ticket to a concert by the Royal Stockholm Philharmonic Orchestra at the twentieth annual Sibelius Festival, of Symphonies 5, 6 and 7. I still can't really afford it, and there definitely won't be any limousines, but as the trip is to take place in my birthday month, I make a gift of it to myself, and, of course, to Dad.

And so, in preparation for my first visit to Finland, I concentrate on listening to not one Sibelius symphony but three: the Fifth, the Sixth and the Seventh. *The Rough Guide to Classical Music* tells me that these three later works represent the composer's most original handlings of the symphonic form: 'The mature symphonies of Sibelius progress from scattered and fragmentary ideas into fully formed themes and sections.' Fortuitously it also recommends the recording of the symphonies I have already been listening to for its 'wonderful consistency of vision', and for marking one of Vladimir Ashkenazy's 'finest achievements as a conductor'.

Sibelius's final three symphonies were composed in the ten years between 1914 and 1924 when Sibelius was in his late forties and early fifties. While he was a national and to some extent an international celebrity by this time, he began to find composing more and more exacting, and the Fifth Symphony's huge popularity, and its soaring, upbeat confidence, belies the labours behind its composition. None of his other symphonies went through such a protracted process of revision: it was an artistic battle that Sibelius described as 'wrestling with God'.[3] He began writing the Fifth in 1914, buoyed by the success of a triumphant visit to the United States, where he was acclaimed by public and critics alike. And while it would take five years for him to be satisfied with the piece, Ainola brought him the winged inspiration that set it in motion musically. 'Today I have melodies like God,' he wrote. 'At 10 to 11 this morning, I saw 16 swans, one of the greatest experiences of my life. Oh God, what beauty . . . The mysticism of nature and the agony of life.'[4]

The Fifth had its premiere in late 1915 as one in a series of events to celebrate his fiftieth birthday. But even as Finnish shops were marking the occasion by displaying his portrait in their windows, Sibelius's money worries continued. He narrowly avoided the repossession of a Steinway piano given to him as a birthday present. And his dissatisfaction with the Fifth Symphony, which he had felt rushed into completing, led to a resumption in his drinking after seven years' abstinence.

It was a turbulent time in Finland's history, too. In the wake of the Bolshevik Revolution in 1917, Finland seized its chance to become an independent nation. Preoccupied with the continued turbulence in Russia, Lenin granted Finland's demands and Russian troops were withdrawn. No sooner had independence been achieved, however, than Finland was plunged into its own brief civil war between pro-Soviet Red factions, and the provisional White government formed after the Russian withdrawal. Ainola was among properties searched by Red Guards, and for a time Sibelius and his family moved back to the relative safety of Helsinki until peace was restored in mid-1918. The following year, he declared the Fifth Symphony finished and the final version was performed in November 1919. Two years later it received a triumphant reception in the US, where the first performance was conducted by none other than Leopold Stokowski (who was later to appear in *Fantasia*).

The Fifth sounds like an old friend now. The Sixth is almost entirely new to me. Sibelius took years over the composition of this symphony, too, as his financial situation – and relations with Aino – worsened. He had begun to sketch out ideas for it while still working on the Fifth but set to in earnest during 1922/3. It's a very different piece in mood: Sibelius biographer Guy Rickards writes that it captures in sound 'the rarefied, limpid quality of the Nordic countries . . . seeming to depict the streams and forests of his country in the full flood of spring', while Christopher Nupen comments in his film that this 'more restrained and intimate' piece has a 'quietism and harmony of spirit . . . unmatched in any of Sibelius's other works'. It is pastoral in feel, its tranquil and almost wistful opening giving way to increasing vigour, as if evoking the slow but accelerating awakening of the natural world, of spring on the march after the winter hibernation. It is forceful in places but never tempestuous, and the overriding impression it leaves is a harmonious and optimistic one.

Sibelius's Seventh, which emerged just over a year later, overturns everything I think I've learned about symphonies, with their progression over several movements expressing different aspects of the whole, for it has only a short single movement of a little over twenty minutes. Beginning life as what Sibelius referred to as a 'Symphonic Fantasia', it effectively condenses four movements into one integrated piece. Working through the night, and fuelled by whisky, Sibelius eventually came to refer to the composition as his Symphony No. 7. Aino, whose patience with her husband's drinking and carousing and spendthrift fondness for fine living, was by now near breaking point, refused to accompany him to Stockholm for the premiere in 1924. But the new work brought him fresh acclaim, not least from the English composer Ralph Vaughan Williams, who said that Sibelius had 'lit a candle in the world of music that would never go out'.[5]

The symphony's concentration of moods is astonishing. I watch again the section of the Nupen film which features the Seventh, and am mesmerised by the sight of Vladimir Ashkenazy conducting it. At one point he almost seems to be in elemental combat with the sound that surges towards him. Nupen calls it a symphony of 'towering grandeur', and this exactly conveys how I feel about it. It's awesome, gripping, epic music.

I find such worlds in these symphonies: I feel I could listen to them every day for the rest of my days and not tire of them. They keep me constantly on my toes, each piece so different in mood and character, but all unmistakably Sibelius. But while I hear new things each time I listen, I grow more and more convinced that hearing them in the land where they were composed, in a country I have only ever seen on screen but has for so long been turning in my imagination, will unlock another dimension in this deeply patriotic music that I need a sense of place to understand. I am impatient to leave for Finland.

On the plane to Helsinki, I settle into my aisle seat. Two Finnish women arrive to sit in the same row. When the drinks trolley arrives, I copy the one next to me by ordering a delicious glass of blueberry juice. 'Mustikka. Typical of Finland,' she says. We strike up a conversation. I've noticed she's been reading some exhibition brochures, so we chat for a while about her visits to the Wallace Collection and the Royal Academy during her trip to London. She introduces herself as Leena, and writes her name down for me in my open notebook, correcting my pronunciation to 'Layna' when I read it out. Then she asks me why I'm going to Finland. I explain that I'm on a musical pilgrimage to Sibelius's house and the Sibelius Festival. 'Ah,' she says. 'You do realise you're sitting next to two musicians?' Leena, it turns out, is a retired cellist from the Helsinki Philharmonic who has been accompanying her friend on a work trip to London. And her friend runs the Finnish Radio Orchestra and has been in London to meet the orchestra's new British conductor: the first non-Finnish conductor it has ever appointed. We chat for a bit longer and then Leena goes to spread out and snooze at the back of the plane where there are plenty of empty seats. Meanwhile I sit and marvel at this fresh coincidence, this new sign that I'm on a true quest.

In Helsinki I stay in a studio apartment close to the centre of town. It's very small but provides a pristine and impeccably designed home from home. I go into solo raptures over the Marimekko duvet cover and mugs, and the little tube of Moomin toothpaste in the tiny bathroom. I roam all over town on foot, taking in the white wedding-cake edifice of Helsinki Cathedral, the waterfront and the main shopping avenue. It's the calmest capital city I've ever visited, and at night I sleep like a baby. On Leena's recommendation, I also visit the Ateneum art gallery late one afternoon to see some Finnish artists, including Eero Järnefeldt, brother of Aino Sibelius. Afterwards I sit in the café, which stays open into the evening, drinking red wine, thinking of Dad, and feeling lucky and adventurous.

My auspicious encounter on the plane has set the tone and I'm enchanted to be in Finland. I think of how I thrilled as a child to the spookiness of Tove Jansson's Moomins: the terrifying yet pitiful Groke in my favourite book, *Comet in Moominland*, the Hobgoblin, the creepy Hattifatteners. I think of the four female Finnish students I briefly befriended when I lived in the South of France, all of them stereotypically white-blonde and striking. I think of Lasse Virén, the 'Flying Finn' and celebrated long-distance athlete who won gold in the 5,000 and 10,000 metres at both the 1972 and 1976 Olympics. I remember watching the 1972 Munich 10,000 metres final on TV with Dad, and being astonished at how long the race lasted: twenty-seven minutes, which felt like an eternity for a running race. Being Dad, he asked me if I could work out how many laps of the track 10,000 metres was – and I remember the maths being a bit beyond me. Virén won gold in spectacular world-record-smashing style, with a final lap-and-a-half sprint of astonishing velocity.

The next morning I walk to Helsinki's central station and

take a commuter train to Ainola. About twenty miles outside Helsinki and close to the shores of Lake Tuusula, Ainola was home to Sibelius and Aino for more than fifty years. It is this house which provides the chief backdrop for the Christopher Nupen film, appearing by turns shrouded in thick snow, and then surrounded by summer colour. I'm longing to see it for myself. It's a balmy early autumn day, and on the kilometre hike from the station to the house I throw off my coat to walk in my t-shirt, listening to the Fifth Symphony on my iPod as I stride eagerly along.

From the film, I'd imagined Ainola to be in the middle of deep countryside, but while the setting is semi-rural, to my right the path is flanked by a busy road, to my left new-build timber houses, painted in tasteful Scandi shades of moss-green and brick-red, are under construction. Further on, the path is flanked by birch saplings and rowans bright with berries, but beyond I can see fields and forests stretching into the distance. As my eyes scan the horizon and my ears fill with soaring strings and the rumble of timpani, I get a frisson of how this expansive landscape inspired the epic and elemental qualities in the music I'm listening to, so thrillingly close to its place of composition. I can't quite believe I'm almost at Ainola, and I feel both ecstatic and a little tearful to be walking this path, a path that Dad unknowingly set me on. I almost break into a run, propelled by my emotions and the tremendous forward thrust of the third movement – the Allegro molto of the Fifth Symphony. I'm actually here, Dad. Can you believe it?

Jean Sibelius bought the plot on which Ainola stands in 1903, when he was in his thirties and already famous. After he and Aino married in 1892, when they were both in their twenties, they settled in Helsinki. But before long, Sibelius's drinking and carousing began to drive a wedge between them, particularly after the birth of their first daughter in 1893. Aino was increasingly left holding the babies, as her husband stayed out until all hours, drinking heavily and smoking cigars with his buddies in an intellectual drinking circle known as the 'Symposium'. He also began to travel abroad more frequently, visiting Germany, Austria and Italy on a quest for musical inspiration.

As Sibelius's reputation as a composer grew, so did his debts from living the high life, such that he would not be free of them for decades to come. It was a vicious circle, for his depression about the amount he owed led to more heavy drinking in binges that often lasted for days. 'There is much in my make-up that is weak,' he wrote to his brother Christian around the time he was composing his violin concerto.[6] Friends and family began to urge the couple to leave Helsinki with all its temptations and settle in the countryside, where they could live more simply and cheaply, and eventually Sibelius came to see the sense in such a move. Another of Aino's brothers, Arvid, an author, had co-founded an artists' colony in the small lakeside village of Järvenpää. Sibelius had a house built to his own design on the plot of land he bought a little further down the lake. He called it Ainola: Aino's House. Jean, the long-suffering Aino and their four daughters moved into the house in September 1904. 'This house is vital to my art,' he wrote at the time.[7]

It's still early in the day when I arrive, and there are hardly any other visitors at the ticket desk in the modern building by the entrance. Through the trees, I get my first tantalising glimpse of the house, but I'm feeling too fluttery with excitement to make straight for it. I still can't quite comprehend that I'm here in this place that I first saw on film, sitting next to Dad on a sofa the other side of Europe. Instead I heighten the anticipation by ambling around Aino's gardens while I have them to myself, admiring the roses and colourful dahlias that are still in bloom. A bed of nasturtiums kindles a memory of growing them from seed myself when I was a child. I wander on and pick a path which leads into the wood beyond the house, and imagine Sibelius himself walking this way, weaving the sounds of the Finnish countryside into the music in his head.

Today, Ainola is not entirely tranquil: the sound of traffic carries from the road, and I can hear aircraft making their descent into Helsinki's Vantaa Airport. But the noises off recede as my imagination takes over. Ainola is a place heavy with atmosphere and, as I ramble through the garden and surrounding woodland, I have the spookily delicious sense that whoever lived here has only just left. As I pick my way through the trees, the hissing of the breeze in the birches seems to conjure a past that still loiters in the wings. I stop to admire a tomato-red fungus sprouting from the springy soil, and pick up and pocket a fir cone and a fallen orange birch leaf to take home as souvenirs.

Just as I've resolved to approach the main house, I run into a large party of Finnish schoolchildren about to go inside, already bored and foot-shufflingly unruly. A patient Ainola guide is clearly giving them an introductory talk about one of their most famous compatriots, but it seems to be falling mainly on deaf ears. I don't fancy sharing the house with them, so instead I walk back down to the wooden building which houses the sauna (this is Finland, after all) and laundry room, and I peer inside. Here, too, the past is thickly present, and I feel that if I wait a while, a servant of the family will turn up to deal with the week's washing. Round the back of the laundry I discover a raised porch which looks out onto the surrounding countryside. I sit there for a while and gaze out across fields as I nibble on my packed lunch of rye bread and smoked salmon from the corner shop near my apartment in Helsinki. A sharp shower descends and, as I cower under the wide eaves of the building, I watch mist blow across the pine trees in the distance, and feel it moisten my face. It leaves me feeling intensely alive and entirely content.

When the rain eases off, I walk back up towards the house past Sibelius's grave, which is marked by a large flat edifice of bronze. 'JEAN SIBELIUS' it says across the middle in large upper-case letters. 'Aino Sibelius' it says some distance beneath in much smaller, cursive script. I stand for a moment paying homage while I watch the birch leaves waft to and fro like little silvery discs of paper. Then at last I make my way up the steps of the front porch and into the house.

Viewed from a distance, Ainola, built on top of a small rise, with lofty eaves, red pantile roof and its smartly painted cream and forest-green exterior, looks like quite a grand house as it rises impressively from the woodland floor, surrounded by lofty Scots pines. Inside, however, it is compact and cosy, thanks to its wood-panelled interior and bright and artistic decor. Kept almost exactly as it was when the Sibelius family lived here – the only people ever to do so – it feels less like a museum and more like a house one is visiting while the occupants are temporarily away.

Downstairs is mostly given over to one large open-plan drawing room, the walls full of paintings by artist friends like Akseli Gallen-Kallela; Pekka Halonen, whose tactile, almost furry snowscapes I'm particularly drawn to; and Aino's brother Eero, whose work I was only last night admiring in

Finland's National Gallery. On one wall is a painting of a woman, prostrate and distraught at the bedside of a dead child. In the far corner stands the almost repossessed Steinway piano, Sibelius's fiftieth birthday present from 1915. The English notes I'm handed at the door tell me that he 'rarely used it for composing since he composed everything in his head'. I ask one of the young female guides on duty if Aino – the daughter of a highly cultured and artistic family – played it too. 'She was the best pianist but also conservative,' I'm told. 'She believed her place was to be there for her husband.'

The room is dominated by a green-tiled floor-to-ceiling stove. The guide notes refer to the composer's synaesthesia: in his mind, different chords brought forth different colours. The bright peppermint green of the stove was F major; the sunny yellow of a nearby painting led to it being dubbed 'the D-major painting'. The upstairs of the house is out of bounds, but I peep into the other downstairs rooms which, frustratingly, are roped off at the door: the library, apparently Sibelius's favourite room in the house, with a whole wall of books and its corner for smoking cigars in; and the study, which became a bedroom later in Sibelius's life when the stairs became too much for him.

The novelist Julian Barnes visited Ainola and later wrote an illuminating piece about the house. He relates how he became acquainted with the music of Sibelius as a young man, enjoying its 'cool yet turbulent melancholy' which, he writes, seemed to harmonise with his 'unrestful late-adolescent soul'.[8] Like me, Barnes senses the almost-presence of Sibelius at Ainola, as well as that of Aino, their five daughters and two long-serving housekeepers.

Everywhere in the place that bears her name is the sense that

Aino, the wife who believed utterly in her husband's genius, was the one who sewed the fabric of his life together: home-schooling their five daughters while he travelled; waiting anxiously for news when he went on benders that lasted for days; and economising in the face of the crushing debts he constantly ran up. It was Aino who designed the garden shortly after moving to Ainola, and it was she who cleared the stony ground. 'I hoed and dug continually. Sometimes I cried and then I went back to my hoeing,' she is reported to have said.[9] I'm moved almost to tears to think of this talented, artistic woman working here, year in year out in her kitchen garden and orchard, where she grew berries, fruits and vegetables for the family's own consumption, aiming for self-sufficiency, finding satisfaction in that, and consolation in tending the flowers she grew everywhere else.

As I stand on the station platform waiting for the train back to Helsinki and sheltering from the rain which has now set in, I think of Aino and all she invested. Given the glories of her husband's creations, I can hardly wish it any other way. But I'm mindful of what it cost her, for the beautiful home and garden she created at Ainola is testament to the fact that Aino too was an artistic, creative soul, a woman who spoke several languages. And yet unlike Clara Schumann, that other muse and mother to a large family, she never had the opportunity to nurture her own talents in any professional sense. It is some justice that this place of pilgrimage for those who love her husband's music still bears her name.

That evening, holed up in my Helsinki studio drinking herbal tea from a Marimekko mug, I sit and reread my Sibelius biography by Guy Rickards while listening again to the Third Symphony, the first major work Sibelius composed while living at Ainola. For a while after leaving Helsinki, Sibelius felt rejuvenated in his work. The Third Symphony, premiered in 1907, feels even-keeled and optimistic in character, with a gorgeous repeating tune which seduced me when I first heard it, the blended string and woodwind alternating to lead a wonderfully satisfying circularity of melody. Nupen calls it 'arguably the first of Sibelius's symphonies that is worthy throughout of his genius'. For one night only, it feels like my favourite symphony again. Yet the fonder I grow of all Sibelius's music, the less fond I grow of him, especially after reading about one particular example of his bad behaviour. It occurred on a family trip to Italy in 1901, a year after the death from typhoid fever of his third-born daughter, Kirsti, at the age of fifteen months.[10] During the trip, their second daughter Ruth fell ill with the same disease. While Aino nursed her back to health, her husband couldn't cope and ran away to Rome for two weeks until the danger had passed.

Is this what it takes to be an artist: selfishness, coupled with the unconditional love of a wife who is made miserable by your behaviour but who has resolved never to leave you, come what may, because she believes in your greatness above all things? I'm angry on this wife's behalf, but my anger feels spurious given my now ardent love for Sibelius's music. Had I been married to a man who could create such music so long as all his needs and whims and cravings were indulged, I'm not sure I would have had the selflessness to bow to them. Aino found the strength and resolve to support her husband through it all.

But I am not devoid of sympathy for him. For then, as now, it was hellishly hard to support a family as a creator, even with an international reputation. The Nupen film reveals that while

Sibelius's Second Symphony, in its composer's own words, 'brought fame and credit to Finland on countless occasions', it cost him 18,000 marks to produce it, while he earned from it only 1,500. The story of his *Valse triste*, a short, wistful piece composed in 1903 as part of the incidental music for *Kuolema*, a play by his brother-in-law Arvid Järnefeldt, is even worse. The melancholy charm of this six-minute waltz made it a contemporary hit around the world, versions in all kinds of instrumental combinations proliferating, but under the terms of his original contract Sibelius was paid royalties only on his own original score. 'Time and time again for the rest of his life, he encountered this simple, wistful tune in concerts, restaurants, cafés, almost always in arrangements other than his, earning his publishers the small fortune the near penurious composer had missed out on,' writes Guy Rickards. Despite Sibelius's worldwide fame, much of it — unlike Mozart's — achieved in his lifetime, I have a sense of what this man suffered as he tried to continue composing works that would both make him worthy of that fame, and also pay the bills.

In 1909, and in the long shadow of multiple operations to remove a tumour from his throat which had left him with a terrifying sense of his own mortality as well as more debts, Sibelius went through another time of crisis, writing that his 'domestic harmony and peace are at an end because I cannot earn enough to supply all that is needed, let alone pay off my debts'.[11] He wrestled 'to harmonise what is right for me as an artist with the necessity to produce income', and the burden of this towering challenge led to a more introspective kind of life at Ainola during which he began to 'turn away from the world and search for his inner voice'.[12] Self-doubt had always plagued him but, from now on, composing seems to have become a kind of agony, and he was plagued by what he called 'the terrifying creatures of eternal silence' and beset with fears of not being good enough, soon enough. He wrote that he missed his youth terribly: 'O tempi passati . . . This wonderful life that I love so much, and which is yet so difficult to live . . . May I just live long enough; for now I am sure of my artistic path.'[13] The Fourth Symphony, premiered in 1911 with Sibelius conducting, did little to boost his creative confidence. At the end of the piece, the audience did not know if it had actually finished, and it was received not with applause but with bewildered silence.

Back in Helsinki, before I go to bed I listen again to the Fourth. Armando Iannucci describes it as 'almost wilfully downbeat and morose', Nupen as the 'strangest and most personal of all Sibelius's symphonies . . . in some ways perhaps the greatest, but certainly the most intensely revealing and the most intensely Sibelius'. I find it a strange piece, too: it's by no means all solemnity, and some passages are positively jaunty, but it's a rather manic jauntiness, and I can't help remembering Alan Rusbridger's remark about it not being entirely clear where it's all going. Perhaps it is my upbeat, exultant mood, but I still don't take to it as I do to the Third and the Fifth. Tellingly, Nupen remarks that with his Fourth Symphony, Sibelius 'had to accept that he had misjudged his ability to communicate with his audience'.

The next day I pack up and bid farewell to my little Helsinki pied-a-terre and head to the station for the train to Lahti and my date with the Sibelius Festival. Though I'm sad to leave a city I've already fallen in love with on our short acquaintance, I'm ecstatic at the prospect of hearing Sibelius's music performed live in his native land. Early in the journey, small towns of modern apartment blocks alternate with stretches of arable farmland, topped with immense green combines working the fields. Before long, however, this dormitory town scenery gives way to acres of forest and rocky outcrops of peach-coloured stone. Occasionally, beyond the trackside rowan trees in full berry, older red-roofed buildings flash by, which make me think of the paintings of Carl Larsson or of Villekula Cottage, home to Pippi Longstocking. It's showery and, as the forests grow thicker, a great banner of a rainbow spans the stormy sky. There is nothing particularly dramatic about the scenery, but it affords a great sense of space: a canvas on which nature and the elements can make their mark in the kind of dramas that are integral to Sibelius's music.

Lahti feels very different from Helsinki – a modern working provincial town with little of the capital's grace or atmosphere. The steps down from the platform spit me out in a dark underpass beneath the tracks and, though I have a map to help me find my Airbnb, for a moment I am completely disorientated. But then I manage to strike out in the right direction, and mercifully the rain which greeted my arrival holds off. Twenty minutes later, I've made it to a peaceful Lahti suburb, and to the front door of the characterful timber house painted egg-yolk yellow that belongs to my Airbnb host Risto and his wife Terhi. They live with their three children in an artfully furnished interior filled with Terhi's paintings and papier-mâché sculptures, and my tranquil double room upstairs looks out on the garden. When I ask her the best way to get to the Sibeliustalo – the Sibelius Hall – by public transport for my concert, she offers to lend me her teenage daughter Petra's bike. And so a short while later, off I go, a little wobbly at first – unaccustomed as I am to riding a Dutch-style bike – cycling across a Finnish town on my way to the twentieth anniversary Sibelius Festival.

It feels completely exhilarating to be travelling this way as the autumn sun sinks in the sky. I stop for a while en route, parking Petra's bright yellow bike by a lake fringed with birch trees which couldn't look more quintessentially Finnish. At Ainola, I expected views of Lake Tuusula from the house: the Christopher Nupen film has numerous scenes of birds on the lake. But no water was visible, and it puzzled me so much that when I got back to Helsinki, I immediately emailed the museum about it. A reply came back very quickly from Anne, one of the guides. She told me that in Sibelius's time the trees on the lake shore had not yet grown up, and so the lake could clearly be seen from the windows of the house. Anne also informed me that Sibelius took walks by the lake every day.

Although it isn't Sibelius's lake, my presence here beside Lake Vesijärvi feels like a kind of destiny. Or at least a miracle that somehow I'm sitting here, contemplating the water in Lahti in glowy evening sunshine as a curtain raiser to a concert of Sibelius's music, in the land that so deeply inspired it. Look where destiny, and considerably less than £3,500, has brought me, Dad. And all because of you.

With the shadows lengthening, I cycle the last few hundred yards along the waterfront to my destination and lock my bike to a stand outside the gleaming dockside façade of the Sibeliustalo. Built in 2000 in the shell of an old brick factory beside Lake Vesijärvi, the glass waterside frontage of the Sibelius Hall glows gold in the evening light. It's a stunning building. Inside, its gorgeous pale-wood interior was inspired by Finnish forests and, when completed, it was the biggest public wooden building built in Finland for over a hundred years. I gaze up in awe at the ceiling of the expansive front-of-house area, supported by thick wooden floor-to-ceiling masts and criss-crossing beams which create a stunning 3D tessellation of beautiful star shapes. The lights in the ceiling pick out the exact configuration of the constellations in the night sky on the day that Sibelius was born: 8 December 1865.

I'm early but my fellow concert goers are already starting to arrive. I make my way up the stairs into the auditorium to find my seat. It is in a spur on one of the upper levels, which means I am right over the orchestra and level with the conductor. The music will rise straight up to me. How Dad would have loved this, I think, wishing with all my heart that he were here.

As soon as I hear the horn call and timpani roll that opens Symphony No. 5 in E-flat major, I start crying. It's the effect of the spectacle before me: the physical presence of the orchestra, this sublime music with its exquisite orchestration rising up to meet me, the sensitivity of the bowing that produces the quivering string sounds of the first movement, which evoke so powerfully the beat of birds' wings, of sixteen swans a-rising. As the conductor Thomas Dausgaard gets into his stride, his great mop of grey hair quivering, the whole orchestra begins to sway back and forth with the communal rocking of the bows in the string section. There is both joy and melancholy in this music. Dausgaard, a hugely expressive conductor, exhorts the orchestra to give full attention to the whole gamut of its moods. As I watch from my close vantage point, he stands on tiptoe one moment, the next he bends down with one hand on his haunch and inclining his head as if to hear better. He is open-mouthed, he screws his face up tight. Then he makes great swoops of his arms before raising them in supplication, as if imploring the orchestra to give of its best.

When it comes to the astonishing six sharp blasts of sound with which the third and final movement of the Fifth concludes, my closeness to the orchestra means I can hear the collective intake of breath made by the musicians between each note. *You don't get this punctuation of human emotional response with a studio recording*, I think to myself. Reflecting on the glorious melody of the final movement which feels, he says, 'like the traditional basis for a stirring climax', Armando Iannucci notes that the expected climax never comes and instead the symphony concludes, he says, 'as if the drama immediately preceding it is being swept away like a distraction'. Iannucci thinks this is Sibelius's way of subverting the expectation brought by a good tune. I have had my own theory, however, since I learned from the Christopher Nupen film about that first disastrous performance of Sibelius's Fourth Symphony, when the audience could not tell if it had finished or not. Ending his Fifth Symphony so emphatically was surely Sibelius's way of making sure there was no doubt this time.

An interval follows, but I feel too emotional to move. So I remain in my seat, reflecting on how much I've gained from hearing classical music played live. Although I've been to many rock concerts and music festivals, and have always thought of myself as an aficionado of live gigs, I somehow didn't think I'd gain as much from listening to classical music played in this way. I suppose I thought there'd be less drama, less of a sense of performance from a static orchestra. But from going to concerts featuring Mozart and Stravinsky, Brahms, and Robert and Clara Schumann, and now Sibelius, I realise how much watching the physical act of the music being played has enhanced my appreciation of it.

As the members of the Royal Stockholm Philharmonic file back onto stage. I smile when I notice that the timpani player – Sibelius symphonies make extravagant use of timpani – has the longest hair and the longest beard. He's definitely the drummer in the band, I think. Just in front of him, a harp is carried onto the stage and tuned, ready for the performance of Symphony No. 6 in D minor. I read through the programme notes but their academic tone is at odds with my buoyant mood. The symphony begins and once again I'm riveted by the sheer physicality of the music: I feel as if I could lean from my perch and grab a handful of notes as it ascends. The moments of silence, particularly in the first movement, are strikingly effective here, holding so much at bay in suspended animation. Dausgaard is like a karate-chopping conjuror: bending the orchestra to his will as he wields his baton like a weapon of destiny. The orchestra's rendering of the fourth and final movement is particularly sublime and, when it comes to the final moments of slowly subsiding strings, Dausgaard makes sure that every ounce of quiet feeling is teased out from the long final chord.

A short break between symphonies and then it's on to the Seventh, with its at first more elegiac and introverted feel, which builds ravishingly in this beautiful space to the elemental whirlwind halfway through its single movement. The scrunching concentration of sound, particularly in the final minute, is mesmerising. Never have I been as spellbound in a concert hall, and I don't want it to end. So much so that when the orchestra members file out at the close of the evening, I am still gazing down into the auditorium, dazed, barely able to comprehend that my Sibelius experience is over.

On my cycle ride back to my billet on the other side of Lahti, under a darkening teal-blue sky, I reflect on the epic physical journey I've been on with this music: to a small town on the other side of Europe, to a new country, so often conjured by Sibelius's music, but until now only imagined. And this has been an epic stage in my remembrance journey too, the sheer inventiveness and expansiveness of Sibelius's music a revelation. It's music that envelops your senses, capturing the experience of being outside in nature in all its wild glory. And if Dad were giving me one of his music quizzes now, I know I would not now fail to recognise a piece of Sibelius. This at least, I have achieved, dear Dad.

A few weeks after returning from Finland, I drive back from chairing an event in Cheltenham late one clear and chilly autumnal evening. As I head towards the Cotswold escarpment, the Seventh Symphony is playing in the car and a waning crescent moon hangs in the sky ahead of me. As I ascend into the hills, the moon disappears, visible only intermittently through the branches of the beech trees which line the road. The symphony finishes and I drive on in silence. And silence was all that followed the composition of the Seventh Symphony too. For although he lived another thirty years, dying in September 1957 at the age of ninety-two, Sibelius produced almost no new music during the final third of his life.

It was an astonishing time to bow out, creatively. With the Seventh Symphony, and with *Tapiola*, Sibelius's symphonic poem first performed in 1927, Sibelius was at the height of his powers. With these compositions, says Nupen, he entered into an 'entirely new world of orchestral sound', and the acclaim he received encouraged him to believe that he could go even further with his Eighth Symphony. In early 1928 he wrote: 'It is going to be wonderful; giving it form just seems to be taking so long.' Three years later: 'I am writing my Eighth Symphony and I am all youth.' Then more than a decade later, in 1943: 'My life is nearing its end and I should like to get this one work finished. If I die in the middle, everything will have been in vain.'[14]

Then, sometime in the mid 1940s, Sibelius burned a laundry basket full of music manuscripts in the fireplace at Ainola, including, it is believed, the completed pages of his Eighth Symphony. 'We started a big bonfire here,' recalled Aino.[15] 'I did not have the strength to be present and left the room. I therefore do not know what he threw onto the fire. But after that my husband became calmer and gradually lighter in mood'.[16]

In a scene I remember vividly from watching it with Dad, Christopher Nupen's film recreates the burning of the Eighth Symphony, flames consuming a sheaf of music. I remember even then feeling bereft at the sudden cessation of Sibelius's immense creativity. Now, compounded by the loss of Dad, who first introduced me to his music, this duet of silences – by my father and by the composer – distresses me. I have experienced such highs with this music, particularly in the country where it was composed. And yet now, after all the furious sound and deep visceral pleasure, I feel suddenly alone and bereft, wrapped in my own lonely, moribund silence. Without the remembrance channel of the music, I feel a cold mist of grief enveloping me once more. It's a sign that I need to keep on listening and find my next composer.

Sitting at my desk at home, I look at a photograph of Sibelius taken at Ainola in his twilight years. Dressed in dark clothes, he stands, walking stick in hand, glowering out at me from under his hat. Behind him, against what looks to be a scudding, cloudy sky, rises one of the tall pines that surround

Ainola. Then I turn to the photograph of Dad as a young man that I keep under my computer screen so it is constantly in my eyeline as I write. Dressed in jacket and tie and v-necked sweater, hands in the pockets of his pleated-front trousers, he too stands against a background of pine trees. The youthful man and the elderly man stare out at me from their respective black-and-white photographs, but neither of them says a word. I sit looking at them both for a while, my nose and chin resting broodily on my steepled fingers. Then I stand up and walk off, ready for the next chapter in my musical journey.

Chapter 7

The Consolations of Chopin

Études, Opus 10

Lockdown in the springtime of coronavirus, and we are watching TV at home. These days it's rare for us all to be together, but my son has moved home from university because of the pandemic, and my daughter has a night off from her gap-year supermarket job, which has turned into a frontline occupation. We are watching *Life of Pi*, the 2012 Ang Lee film of Yann Martel's Booker Prize-winning novel. I've already seen it twice before, the second time on DVD at my parents' house when Dad, by then weak and exhausted, was dying.

Watching the film again now, for the third time, seven years later, I start to cry at the memory of that awful time, and it is the sight of the tiger, Richard Parker, which sets me off as he lies sprawled in the stern of the lifeboat, his emaciated condition so strongly recalling Dad's own diminished state. When Pi and the tiger reach Mexico, having drifted across the Pacific Ocean, Pi watches Richard Parker heading across the beach towards the jungle beyond, hoping that the great beast will turn to look at him once more, as if to acknowledge what they have been through together. But the tiger does not, and Pi beautifully articulates the agony of that sudden parting.

Try as we might to stay positive and count our considerable blessings during this bleak time of pandemic, I feel death lurking just beyond the barricades of the normality we are striving to preserve. It is there in emails from friends, and it is there every time I look at Twitter, my go-to place to see how other writers are faring. 'My lovely Dad died early this morning due to Covid 19. The grief is immense,' someone I follow writes one morning. You ain't felt nothing yet, I think, cruelly. Seven years on, it doesn't take much for me to feel the bewilderment of bereavement anew. And yet I also know that I have no right to indulge feeling. I have come off lightly compared to so many others – I laugh, I have a zest for life, I have my mother still, my family and wonderful supportive friends. And my Dad died of a common disease after a full life.

I think of Dad on his birthday – one of the hottest days of the year so far – while reclining on a sun lounger in my garden, a place which has become such a haven during lockdown. I can't go to a concert to celebrate Dad's birthday this year because there aren't any. So instead, I am looking up and listening to the house martins chirruping as they duck and dive in that shimmering way they have, across a hazy blue sky. More than six years after he died, I still can't reconcile the fact that I feel Dad's presence so strongly still with the reality that nowhere on earth can he be found. I think about what people mean when they speak of 'moving on'. If it means being able to laugh once more, to speak of the dead person without breaking down, to look at an object that belonged to them, or at their photograph without weeping, I can do all of those things. But have I faced the fact that I'll never see him again? Not entirely, no. Some days I suddenly miss him so much I feel the very breath has been taken out of me.

A few weeks later, I am travelling south through France on a train bound for Marseilles, listening to Chopin's Études, Opus 10. After the expansive, well-ventilated landscapes of Sibelius's symphonies, the intimacy and containment of these solo piano pieces feel entirely right for the present times. As I watch the grey clouds and lush green pastures of northern France slowly give way to the bosky uplands of its central regions, and then the spikier vegetation and blue skies of the Midi, I think about Chopin travelling this route in reverse.

I've been reading Paul Kildea's *Chopin's Piano: A Journey Through Romanticism* and his account of the harsh winter of 1838/9, which Chopin spent holed up in Mallorca with novelist George Sand and her children. There, over a few short weeks in his tiny room at the Carthusian monastery in Valldemossa, high in the mountains of the Serra de Tramuntana, he composed some of his celebrated Preludes, Opus 28, despite bouts of ill-health due to pulmonary congestion, poor weather and the hostility of the locals. 'We were treated as outcasts in Majorca – because of Chopin's cough and also because we did not go to church,' wrote Sand in a letter from Barcelona after they fled the island in February 1839, having spent only three months of an intended year there.[1] From Barcelona, they travelled on to Marseilles, where they stayed for three months while Chopin recovered his health and strength. By the autumn of 1839 he was back in Paris once more, the city to which he had moved from his native Poland almost ten years previously. In another ten years he would be dead from tuberculosis, a disease he probably contracted in childhood and which at that time affected one in four of the population across much of Europe.

As I look out of the train window, I keep getting distracted by my alien reflection: my face barely visible behind my disguise of mask, sunglasses and earphones. On our long train journey from London, the effect is stifling, and yet I am feeling miraculously fortunate. Our destination is Avignon – lockdown has been eased enough to allow us to go ahead with a long-planned week's stay in a friend's place in Provence. When we reach the pink-hued house, with its dove-grey shutters and sparkly blue swimming pool, each blue Provençal morning feels like a miracle after the restrictions and privations of the previous months.

And yet death is still on my mind, as I knew it would be, as soon as I decided to make Chopin's Études the new focus of my listening. I have chosen them because they are some of the last pieces Dad listened to before he died. When he left home for what turned out to be the final time, first for a stay in hospital, and then for the hospice where he spent his last weeks, he left behind a small pile of the CDs he had most recently played on the table in his living room. On the top was a 2002 recording of the Études, played by Murray Perahia. I want to try and understand why, of all the recordings he could have picked out while weak and in pain, it was this one he chose.

I have no memory of Dad listening to Chopin during my childhood, although in the months when I'd just started primary school and still came home for lunch, I got to know the so-called 'Minute Waltz' – actually Chopin's Waltz in D flat, Opus 64 No. 1 – because it was the theme tune to the long-running BBC Radio 4 programme *Just a Minute*, which I'd hear each week as I ate my midday meal perched on a stool at the breakfast bar, Mum bustling about behind me. Years later, a friend from my first year at university took to playing me Chopin in his room on Sundays, and bought me my own Deutsche Grammophon Double Time cassette. I still have it, and, looking at it now, I think of him for the first time in years, remembering his fondness for the Hungarian pianist Tamás Vásáry, who plays both of the two études (in E, and A minor) which are included on the tape. I remember that even the jauntier Chopin pieces struck me as a little mournful then, as we listened, closeted away from the north-eastern winter chill.

Dad didn't receive a terminal diagnosis when prostate cancer was detected, but his decline was devastatingly swift, and he was dead in a little over six months. Mum, with the sixth sense of a spouse who had lived with him for over fifty years, had suspected he wasn't well for a year or more, but Dad stubbornly refused to go to the GP for a check-up. His stoic view was that the 'old age' aches and pains in his back and legs, only really noticeable when negotiating stiles on his walks in the nearby Peak District hills, were a trifling matter, and not worth fussing about. He relented after Mum broke down in tears one day because she was so worried. The aches and pains proved to be a symptom of the fact that the cancer had already spread to his bones, and it wasn't long before palliative care was all that could be done for him. Shortly after he was first diagnosed and we were still full of a brittle optimism that he could be successfully treated, I had a long and vivid dream that I was giving Dad's funeral tribute. When I woke, I tried to pretend to myself that it wasn't a premonition. But I sensed in my own bones that it was.

Losing an elderly parent is not a tragic event, it is a routine one. That my seventy-nine-year-old father's becoming ill was a crisis waiting to happen made me a little more stoical at first, perhaps. But nothing prepared me for watching my steady, dependable dad, who had barely had a day off sick in the forty years of his working life, being so radically changed by his illness. His alert and agile brain, trained by decades of chess and scientific thinking, became confused. Always interested in optics, and the owner of several pairs of binoculars, he conceived an obsessional desire in his final weeks to buy a huge spotting scope, of the type used by people who venture out onto the African savannah to view lions and elephants from a safe distance. Just when Mum or I thought we had talked him out of it and persuaded him to drop the subject, he brought it up again. Mum, who bore the brunt of this compulsion and often had to listen to him talking about it for hours, was driven to distraction. It was almost funny. Almost. But now I find it awful to contemplate, this strange longing Dad had to see far out of his own self, as if the prospect of things in the distance could at least give his mind flight from the body that was so rapidly turning on him.

It was at this grave time that he chose to listen to Chopin's Études. The Murray Perahia CD is only one of several Chopin recordings in his collection, which also includes the Nocturnes played by Portuguese-born pianist Maria João Pires, and the aforementioned Preludes, played by the French Canadian virtuoso Louis Lortie. Since reading Paul Kildea's engaging account of Chopin's time in Mallorca, I've felt drawn to the Preludes, twenty-four short pieces, which, says Kildea – a distinguished conductor, writer and formerly the artistic director of the Wigmore Hall concert venue in London – marked Chopin out as 'the lodestar of Romanticism'. But it was the

Études which Dad chose; earlier works, composed between 1829, when Chopin was still a teenager in Warsaw, and 1835, by which time he had left his native Poland to make a permanent home in France, his father Nicolas's country of birth.

An étude (study) is a short instrumental musical composition containing some technical difficulty, and designed to provide practice material for perfecting a particular musical skill. The tradition of composing études emerged in the early nineteenth century with the rapidly growing popularity of the piano across Europe. Chopin played a Broadwood piano in the final public concert of his life, at the Guildhall in London in 1848.

This made the étude natural territory for Chopin the composer, too. A musical child prodigy, he left Warsaw at the age of twenty and spent almost nine months in Vienna before travelling to France. Newly arrived in Paris, then considered the musical capital of Europe, he earned a tidy income teaching piano to members of the Parisian haute monde. There he also struck up a friendship with the composer and celebrated pianist Franz Liszt, and it was through him in 1836 that Chopin met the novelist George Sand, real name Aurore Dupin, one of the most famous, and notorious, women of the time. Their relationship, which lasted for eight years, enhanced his celebrity.

Chopin's Études are arranged in two sets of twelve: Opus 10 and Opus 25, together making up what Kildea refers to as a 'startling, complex collection'. In his sleeve notes that accompany Dad's Murray Perahia CD, Tim Page, who won the Pulitzer Prize for Criticism in 1997, asserts that the Études are 'rightly considered Himalayas of the piano literature, magnificent and treacherous'. The first set – Opus 10 – published in Leipzig in 1833 under the title 'Douze Grandes Études', when Chopin was twenty-three, were dedicated to Franz Liszt, then regarded as the greatest pianist of his age. Liszt was in the audience, applauding furiously, when Chopin made his Paris concert debut in early 1832. 'Never before had there been piano music of such expansive sweep and muscular energy; it is as if Chopin had somehow managed to yoke a simple chorale melody to the rushing fury of a waterfall,' writes Page.

Étude No. 1 from Opus 10 is an arresting piece: I marvel at how Chopin was able to cram its short (less than two minutes) duration to bursting with such acres of notes. Lying in the shade of an olive tree, I am listening to the Études, with no distractions for the first time, and marvelling at the effect of hearing them, my mind emptied and my eyes trained on the perfectly clear azure sky above me. I feel so alive to every note of these jewel-like pieces, but they also give me the sense that I am not quite present here on this sunbed: in levitation, somewhere between it and the infinite realm above me. Though I'm trying to train myself not to immediately hear concrete things in the music, I find it hard to resist discerning the humming of an insect in Étude No. 2 while watching the wasps beside the pool. Murray Perahia's interpretation is so liquid and shimmery, too, and I think of all the great lumps in my own piano playing. I listen with awe to the galloping pace and exhilarating acceleration of Étude No. 4 in C-sharp minor, and the tinkling bells of Étude No. 5 in G-sharp major, played entirely by the right hand on black keys.

I decide I particularly love Étude No. 8 in F major, with its beautiful left-hand melody accompanied by further great supple sweeps of rising and falling notes in the right hand. And I close my eyes, better to concentrate on the extraordinary sound of Perahia seeming to massage the notes of Étude No. 11 in E flat, as if he is plucking at a harp, all the way to the gorgeous tiny tinkle of the final note. Then to finish, the arresting contrast of Étude No. 12 – the so-called 'Revolutionary' Étude – with its great swathes of roiling notes, its plaintive rallying cry of a melody, and a final pounding flourish capable of levering an entire concert-hall audience from their seats.

In these short, short pieces, ostensibly written to allow pianists to perfect their technique, reside such worlds of meaning and feeling. They are so delicate and yet so muscular at the same time; and so concentrated that when they end, the silence you hear is thick with absence. I cry a little thinking of Dad listening to this music and taking a heightened pleasure from it at a time when he could barely eat or move, barely concentrate or sleep. I think of him losing himself among these perfect miniatures, letting the stairways of the notes carry him briefly away from the fear and the pain.

I haven't purposely arranged to listen to Chopin's Études in the composer's adopted homeland, but somehow it feels appropriate. And the daily act of speaking French, a language which I studied to degree level, and in which I am fairly fluent still, also reminds me how often Dad's interests and preoccupations became my own. While he didn't study French beyond School Certificate level (as GCSEs were called in those days), I know from his school magazine *The Ashbeian* for 1948/49, that he received a Very Good for French, and a Credit in his optional oral French test. Later, when I was still at primary school, he decided to introduce me to foreign language learning via *Basic Conversational French* by Julian Harris and André Léveque, a *Daily Express* language course published in 1955.

Looking at that book now, I realise just how entirely unsuitable it was as a first French primer for a young child. It launches immediately into long and involved narratives which even an adult beginner would find it hard to follow. But as a young child who had never been 'abroad' but longed to travel there, I remember how much I loved studying the black-and-white photos of France that appear throughout the book. And with Dad's help, I tried to decipher bits of the conversation lessons which charted the various exploits of 'John Hughès, jeune ingénieur-chimiste', recently arrived in Paris from Philadelphia. 'Pardon, où est l'hôtel du Cheval blanc?' asks John, translated for the student as 'Pardon me, where is the White Horse Inn?' Later, in Conversation 6, 'Having Lunch', he orders, 'Du rosbif et des pommes de terre frites.'[2]

No matter that it was hopelessly old-fashioned even then. That book – and my dad – kindled in me a love of languages. Once I got to secondary school and began proper French lessons, I was already in my element, and went on to study the subject at university, and to work as a language assistant in two schools in the South of France during my undergraduate year abroad. Now, because of Dad, I'm trying to learn another language entirely – that of music, and somehow translate that into words too. It's an intractable process. The composer Felix Mendelssohn, who also attended Chopin's Paris debut concert, and who came to know him well, once said that, 'What the music I love expresses to me is not thought too *indefinite* to put into words, but on the contrary, too *definite*.'[3]

Back home after the miracle of my week away, I feel sufficiently fortified to tackle the black binbag of death that my Mum has given me to deal with. With a move to a smaller house in the offing, she has been sorting through more than three decades of accumulated possessions, and the rubbish sack contains items which she knows she must get rid of but cannot face doing so herself because they belonged to loved ones now deceased. Among them is a woollen check sports jacket – chest size 40R. Pure new wool, made by Aspen & Court. I recognise it immediately as one which Dad wore almost daily for years. The lining is torn and worn along the front edges, and Mum, regarding it as tatty, tried and failed to persuade Dad to part with it, even though he was usually completely uninterested in clothes. I put the fabric to my face and breathe deeply. Does it smell of him? I decide that it does not. It smells only of Mum's house and the wardrobe it has been kept in.

All the other items in the binbag felt devoid of any connection to the people they once belonged to and I have little trouble in disposing of them. Dad's sports jacket gives me pause, however, because he would not let Mum throw it out. Then my daughter comes into the room and looks at me questioningly. I explain the problem, and she who loves mannish, vintage clothes, just as I did at her age, carries it gladly off.

Her adoption of Dad's jacket makes me smile. But I remain in a morbid mood. It occurs to me that my dad was a person bereaved too – a man who lost his only son, a man orphaned of both his parents in the space of two years when he was in his early thirties. And listening to Chopin and thinking of my dad in a time of global pandemic also prompts me to think about how all these life burdens: grief, illness, and the awareness of one's own impending mortality might give music some added significance, either in the composing, or simply in the listening. All those whose music I have listened to so far understood only too well what it was to be gravely ill or to mourn. Mozart, who lost four children, and experienced the death of his mother while far from home. Stravinsky, who lost both his wife and eldest daughter to tuberculosis within a few months. Kathleen Ferrier, who continued to perform even while she knew she was dying. Brahms, who lost his father and sister, as well as his close friend and mentor Robert Schumann to mental illness. Sibelius, whose young daughter died of typhoid fever. And now Chopin, whose perpetually delicate health would lead to his early death at thirty-nine. In fact, of all well-known composers, perhaps he most famously suffered ill health, leading to a public image that Adam Zamoyski, author of the biography *Chopin: Prince of the Romantics* refers to as 'a sugary blur of sentimentality and melodrama'.

His lover George Sand was always trying to put into words what Chopin was seeking to do with his music. As I have come to understand, writing about music always involves a grappling for the right vocabulary, even for those who have a facility for language. In the cause of trying to write something – anything! – it forces you to settle on a choice of words which never feels wholly satisfactory. Still, the quest to try and describe what has moved you and why it has feels like a worthwhile one. Writing of the Preludes, Paul Kildea singles out their evanescent quality as the source of what is so 'risky and radical' about them. When I read this, I realise that 'evanescent' is exactly the kind of word I love to use, without really knowing precisely what it means. 'Fleeting', I have always thought, but I look it up and find that is not quite right correct. Evanescent means 'fading', 'dying', 'something that quickly disappears from sight or from memory', 'like a vapour which vanishes'.

Though Kildea applies the word to Chopin's Preludes, I recognise the same evanescence in the Études, too. It derives from their improvisational quality: the sense that the pianist has sat down at the piano – par hasard – and created the piece at that very moment, in its entirety, just for you, the listener. A review of a concert Chopin gave at a private house in London's

St James's Square in 1848 makes much of the way in which Chopin as performer seemed to 'abandon himself to the impulses of his fancy and feeling, to indulge in a reverie and to pour out unconsciously . . . the thoughts and emotions that pass through his mind'.[4]

Robert Schumann's 'Träumerei' has this sense of reverie, too, and in my clumsy way it's something that I've been trying hard to capture when playing it, although trying too hard makes it more difficult to do. It's paradoxical that this idea of a piece of music that fades quickly from memory and is soon forgotten could apply to such famous and oft-played compositions. But it's also a matter of wonder that even a piece with which you are familiar, as I am coming to be familiar with Chopin's Études from Opus 10, can have this quality of evanescence when beautifully played. It's the opposite of the earworm effect, in fact: it is while you are listening to the piece that it wholly occupies your senses. Afterwards, it is as if the music has entirely evaporated, but you nevertheless remain changed by it.

In the context of my quest for remembrance, this feels radical. My approach to all the pieces of music I have so far singled out in memory of Dad has been to listen to them over and over again, striving to describe and capture in some concrete way what they are all about, to understand some of the reasons why they sound as they do to me. I loved discovering that Sibelius had had an encounter with swans while working on his Fifth Symphony. It meant I could listen for the swans! And travelling in Finland made it much easier for me to fancy I could hear the sounds of different weathers passing over lakes and through forests. But, I think ruefully, this means I have progressed very little from the *Peter and the Wolf* level of music appreciation that I had already attained as a small child. Listen for the clarinet . . . it means the cat is coming!

And yet plenty of others have adopted this approach. Many of Chopin's compositions have nicknames which seek to capture the essence of each one. For example, in compiling his edition of Chopin's Preludes, the French pianist and renowned twentieth-century Chopin interpreter Alfred Cortot dreamed up portentous titles for each piece. No. 4 is 'Beside a Grave', No. 15 is 'But death is there, in the shadows', and No. 24 'Blood, Passion and Death'. Not one of the titles under which his works were later popularised was dreamed up by Chopin himself.

Paul Kildea appears to hold George Sand partly responsible for starting this posthumous meddling. Her 'mundane' descriptions of Chopin's works were, he writes, 'always too literal, in a way that would come to dominate their presentation and scholarship in the decades that followed'. In her *Histoire de ma vie*, she writes that in Chopin's Preludes written in the Mallorcan monastery, 'visions of long-departed monks', and 'the sound of long-departed funeral plainsong that so oppressed him' could be heard.[5] And in the so-called 'Raindrop' Prelude – Number 15 – also composed in Mallorca at a time of prolonged and driving winter rain, she imagines she hears the vision which came to Chopin in a dream – of himself floating dead in a lake, with raindrops drumming rhythmically on his chest – or at least on the monastery roof tiles above his head as he sat composing at the piano. Listening to this prelude, it takes little imagination to hear gentle raindrops, gradually increasing in force until they become a downpour. But, writes Kildea, Chopin 'did not believe his job was to capture a physical phenomenon in music'. In George Sand's defence, Kildea records that she later wrote with great insight of music's power to take hold of the heart without ever having to explain itself in words.

Here, with this notion of Chopin's music owing nobody an explanation, I feel I'm tilting more closely at what made the Études such consolatory listening for Dad as he neared the end. They are both ravishingly easy listening, which allows you to enjoy the music without having to strive to understand it. But it is also music which makes the ultimate demand: that you put aside every other sensation, great physical pain included, so that, for a short while, this one piece of music is all that exists for you.

And it is a marvel to me that so many worlds of feeling can come from the simple range of sounds that one instrument affords, an instrument that is, after all, 'just' a wooden soundbox fitted with hammers and strings of varying lengths. As its title suggests, *Chopin's Piano* tracks the life story of one such box: the small and rudimentary piano – the pianino – on which Chopin composed some of his preludes in Mallorca. It's a gripping account of that one piano's fate through the late nineteenth and early twentieth centuries and beyond. Paul Kildea also introduces me to a renowned female pianist of whom I have never previously heard: the Polish-born Wanda Landowska, who owned Chopin's Mallorcan piano during the early part of the twentieth century. Prior to the Second World War, Landowska taught a host of future concert pianists, including Clifford Curzon, with whose recording of Robert Schumann's *Kinderszenen* I have become so familiar.

Kildea writes of the piano's development as an instrument, speculating on how Chopin would have responded to the prestige instruments of today – the Steinways and the

Bechsteins whose manufacture only began in the 1850s, after Chopin's death. With their revolutionary methods of stringing, they transformed the sound of the piano, empowering it to fill the concert halls that were springing up all over Europe in the second half of the nineteenth century, thronged with audiences composed of the new kind of affluent middle-class listener who still mainly fill them today. While Chopin played only thirty public concerts in the course of his career – the vast majority of his performances taking place in private salons – it was the boom in popularity of such larger-scale concerts which allowed Clara Schumann to have such a lucrative and wide-ranging performing career after the death of her husband in 1856.

It is on a Bechstein, loaned to the Kanneh-Mason siblings while in lockdown at the family home in Nottingham during the coronavirus pandemic, that I hear seventeen-year-old Jeneba Kanneh-Mason, younger sister of Sheku and Isata, and a former BBC Young Musician of the Year keyboard finalist, play Chopin's Étude No. 3 in E major from his Opus 10 Études. In *This House is Full of Music*, a BBC1 programme in the series *Imagine*, Jeneba explains that as a lockdown project, she and her sister Isata have decided to learn all of Chopin's Études, and she particularly loves No. 3, partly for being in the key of E major, which she likes because it's 'bright and it sings'. Interrupted during her first take on camera by the postman ringing the doorbell, her second playing nevertheless sounds wholly spontaneous, like a thought process in train, with fleeting moments of rubato where the tune almost but not quite comes to an end. But she never overdoes the ponderousness, even as the piece gathers pace and the mood darkens. Her unmannered performance couldn't be less flashy, and yet somehow we hear the piece afresh through her controlled and youthful rendition of it: she captures its delicacy and its evanescence but also the depth of concentrated feeling it contains while it lasts. Her performance perfectly captures the sad stoicism that lockdown has required of us.

At this stage of my musical remembrance journey, it strikes me as interesting that my dad – an outwardly pragmatic man, devoted to facts, and to constructing reasoned arguments – was so partial to music composed during the Romantic era. Aside from Mozart, his favoured pieces so often seemed to hail from the heart of the nineteenth century and the Romantic era of Beethoven, Brahms, Robert Schumann and Chopin. I take a short and 'super-scientific' online Classic FM quiz which claims to be able to tell me whether I'm logical or emotional based on my taste in music. I fully expect to come out as the latter. However, despite expressing a preference both for Chopin's Nocturne in C-sharp minor, and for the key of A-flat minor ('I'm a little complicated') over C major ('No sharps, no drama') in answer to two of the multiple-choice questions, I come out LOGICAL. 'When solving a problem, your head usually leads the way – and your taste in music is no different. Just like a Baroque masterpiece, logic always wins,' the quiz analysis tells me.[6]

The quiz is clearly quite tongue-in-cheek, but listening to Chopin's music shows me that neither music nor people are always as simple to categorise. Compared with his Romantic contemporaries, Schumann – who was born in the same year – and Brahms, there's a delicacy about Chopin which speaks of the inner self laid bare but without any storms or sobbing. If Romanticism is essentially about the legitimacy of feelings and giving vent to their full and honest expression, then the music of Brahms and Schumann seems to fit the bill precisely.

While belonging broadly to the same tradition, Chopin was something of a Romantic lone wolf. And his music feels less publicly heart-on-sleeve to me, and more confiding, as if I, the individual listener, am the only person he is interested in talking to. It is intimate but controlled; it is music that never bursts its banks emotionally. 'They (the virtuosi) try above all to stress Chopin's romanticism,' wrote André Gide in his 1948 work *Notes sur Chopin*. 'Whereas what seems to me most admirable in his work is the reduction to classicism of the undeniably romantic material.'

This sense of intimacy and controlled emotion fits the profile of my unflashy dad, who felt the need for the unflashy profundity of Chopin at a time when his need of consolation was greatest. And somehow it fits my profile, too. I like to think of myself as someone who wears her heart on her sleeve: even now, in my more stoical midlife, when it should be easier to hold my feelings in check when I need to, I still feel as if I live with emotions that simmer just under the surface just as I did when a child, ready to burst forth whenever someone pushes the wrong button. But my emotional self constantly battles with the tendency to containment that I grew up with, for saying less than one might. Some might call it emotional constipation, the kind often unflatteringly associated with the English middle classes. But for me it's the essence of my relationship with my dad. We didn't talk about feelings much. But those feelings were there and we both knew it. And knowing it, I found, was enough.

I think about all this when I listen to Chopin's Études, music that is both capable of articulating our inner pain, sadness and fear but also somehow to reassure by its very honesty. Being gravely ill, as Dad was, must put you into continued dialogue with your inner self, and listening to Chopin feels like the ultimate expression of that. It's an analgesic which still allows you to feel. His compositions have the power both to turn you in on yourself, to bring you close to that which ails you, to feel your pain, to hold your hand and console you, but also not to spare you from things you must face. They are gentle truth for the soul. And so perhaps they have a particular power to speak to someone for whom everything else has fallen away as they try to deal with the reality that life is coming to an end.

After his early death in 1849 at the age of thirty-nine, some were critical of Chopin's music, dismissing him as a sick man who enjoyed his suffering. But perhaps this says more about how his compositions were routinely performed in the nineteenth century than how they were written. Paul Kildea explains how the power of the new Bechstein and Steinway pianos encouraged performances that were 'too flashy and full-blooded'. Liszt, a famously explosive, show-offy performer as well as composer, was often quoted as saying 'dans les arts, il faut faire grand'– in the arts, one should go big! But if you do so with Chopin, something is lost. Kildea argues that the 'astounding young Polish pianist and scholar' Wanda Landowksa was one of the first of a new generation of pianists who sought to strip back their interpretation of Chopin to its essence, without letting off fireworks or excessively showing off their virtuosity. Intimacy over power was the order of the day with Landowska.

While Chopin's pieces have now been performed in public hundreds of thousands of times in the almost 200 years since their composition, André Gide – himself a keen amateur pianist – expressed his feeling in *Notes sur Chopin* that this music was 'too full of private grief and torment to be performed to others', asserting that it should be 'played in a whisper for oneself alone' and that 'its indefinable emotion can not [sic] be exhausted, nor that kind of almost physical terror, as if one were before a world glimpsed in passing, of a world hostile to tenderness from which human affection is excluded'.

Though originally announced in 1892 as *Notes on Schumann and Chopin*, Gide's eventual text barely mentions Schumann, because in the intervening years, he writes, Schumann's compositions have become 'less and less important' to him. There is something about Chopin's music, however, that concentrates the attention on life, he argues. 'His sole concern, it seems, is to narrow limits, to reduce the means of expression to what is indispensable.'

Paul Kildea quotes pianist Stephen Hough as saying that Chopin himself would not have been able to play more than a few bars on a modern Steinway. He presumably means its power would have knocked his socks off, and not in a good way. And I get this. Somehow in Chopin, whatever emotions the music expresses, a calm centre still holds. And there are always parameters to the emotion, as if something is always held back. Reflecting on Chopin's own playing, André Gide writes that 'he always seemed to fall short of the fullest sonority; I mean almost never made the piano yield its full sound, and thereby very often disappointed his audience, which thought that it hadn't gotten its money's worth'. The authorities in the Soviet Union entirely missed this subtlety when they banned Chopin's music for its 'extreme sentimentality'.

I find an NPR interview with Murray Perahia, recorded on

the release of the recordings of Chopin Études on Dad's CD.[7] Introduced by presenter Fred Child as the 'boy from the Bronx who grew up to become an honorary Knight Commander of the Order of the British Empire', Perahia, who has lived in the UK for forty years, talks in the interview about Chopin having 'something of the common touch'. He was a composer who 'felt suffering, he felt pride, he felt joy. All of the human emotions he encompassed in a way that everybody understands. It's absolutely extraordinary,' Perahia asserts. Following in the tradition of Wanda Landowska, and similarly valuing intimacy over power, somehow it is the very purity and precision of Perahia's playing which floors me when I now listen, thinking once again of my dad in his Richard Parker state; the tiger who never would get up and stroll nonchalantly off into the jungle.

And yet throughout the unprecedented twenty-four-hour news story that is the global Covid-19 pandemic, Chopin's Études, Opus 10 becomes the music which transports me to a calmer, stiller place. But it isn't merely a place of safety from the enormity of what is going on. Rather, this is music that seems able both to tune into the pain of trauma while also making it somehow more bearable. For weeks on end I listen to very little else.

Much of Chopin, Paul Kildea argues, is essentially the music of youth, with its sense of 'unrest and romantic passions'. And yet this is the music that Dad chose to listen to at the very end of his life, with all vitality and fight gone from him. Am I being fanciful to imagine that listening to Chopin was not only consolatory, but also a way of calling up a little of the youthful energy and intellectual spark he had once possessed to mitigate against the knowledge of what cancer had reduced him to? I think of the young school footballer described in a report for *The Ashbeian*. 'At full-back Sanderson played well; in technical skill he has still something to learn, but his positional play was first class and he is one of those players whom forwards find it most difficult to get by.' All that youthful energy, and effort, and intellect.

One of the most moving moments in the final days of Dad's life in the hospice where he died came when the visiting relative of another patient brought in a tiny Border collie puppy. I spotted it while crossing the lobby, heart-stopping in its cuteness, and I asked the owner if she would mind bringing it over to show Dad. My parents never owned a dog during their married life but, as a boy, Dad had several, including Nipper, a cairn terrier, and Toby, a Jack Russell with a screw loose, captured in one of my grandfather's early cine films chasing his own tail. Now, near the end, that puppy gave Dad a perceptible lift, his face lighting up at the sight of it for a few moments I now treasure the memory of. But the contrast between that small, rumbustious puppy, bristling with life and possibilities, and my Dad, so ill, so weak, so reduced, also hurts my heart when I think of it.

Dad died a few days later. It was a mid-December night and Mum was resting in the adjoining bedroom as I kept vigil by his bedside. He had been unconscious and unresponsive for many hours, and while he looked peaceful most of the time, occasionally he would screw up his face and we'd worry he felt pain and ask the nurse to up his dose of morphine. I had my laptop with me and passed some of the time trying to hit an impending work deadline (no compassionate leave when you're freelance). But mostly I'd just sit there, keeping watch and holding his pale, veined hand, listening to his quiet, slow breathing, my heart clenching as the long gaps which occasionally punctuated his quiet, slow breathing became more frequent.

I now know from reading Kathryn Mannix's illuminating and empathetic book *With the End in Mind* that this is the so-called Cheyne–Stokes pattern of breathing, and it signifies a state of deep unconsciousness. Nevertheless, his irregular breathing convinced Mum that Dad was ready to leave us, but was hanging on, worried about whether he could. So while she rested, I bent my head down and talked softly into his ear. 'It's all right, Dad,' I told him. 'You can go now. I'll look after Mum. We'll be okay.' And then I told him I loved him very much. Until the last few months of Dad's life, I had so rarely said these words to him, and very seldom had he said them to me. It was not how we were. But impending death changes even the habits of a lifetime. One day, at the end of a visit when he was still at home but declining fast, I put my arms round him as he sat in his armchair and gently hugged his skeletal body. 'I love you,' he responded.

Being with someone when they die is, I now know, one of the greatest privileges that life can bestow. I will be eternally grateful that I had the chance to hold Dad's hand in mine at the end, to tell him at least a little of what he meant to me. Consequently, throughout the pandemic, I keep thinking of the many who have lost a loved one but who were unable to be present when it happened, leaving strangers to provide comfort and love at the end. Though the nurses in the hospice were wonderful, had I not been with Dad at the end I do not know how I could have borne it. And then, at Dad's funeral at his local parish church, I gave the eulogy I had dreamed of and I did not falter. Not once. I felt a raw, adrenalised determination that nothing and no one was going to stop me telling everyone who my dad was, and what he meant to me.

And perhaps it was also because I was trying to compensate for that fact that I felt I had failed him towards the end. I did not try hard enough to find a way for him to listen to music either in hospital or in the hospice, where the staff would, I know, have bent over backwards to help me arrange it. I thought about it but dithered because the complexities of an MP3 player would, I knew, be beyond him. Eventually I bought him an old-fashioned Walkman with which he could play his favourite CDs through headphones, but he was already too weak and ill to manage it.

And I still berate myself that we didn't play him music in his final days either, when he lay seemingly unconscious. Our hearing is said to be the last of our senses to shut down when we die, and during this pandemic year I hear a wonderful testimony that this is so. During the summer a friend of mine, Jo, lost her husband to an aggressive brain tumour after a happy ten years together. It's an awful story: one of those times when you cannot compute how life could be so unfair. And yet I envy her one small thing: that on his final day of life, she played him Schubert's Impromptu No. 3 in G-flat major, a piece that he loved and used to play her on their baby grand piano; a piece which they chose to have played on their wedding day.

Jo agrees to talk to me about Simon's final hours, so we Zoom and talk for more than two hours. Four months on, she is brave and beautiful and funny, and though we both keep reaching for tissues, our plain speaking about the death of her husband seems to console her. 'I think about him three times a minute, every minute,' she tells me. On the day Simon died – at home, in a large hospital bed that had been wheeled into the large ground-floor kitchen extension in their cottage – he had been unconscious and unresponsive for almost a week, even though Jo had kept a constant vigil at his bedside, talking to him, and playing him music that they both loved: Tom Lehrer, David Bowie, Lou Reed; comic songs that made them laugh like 'Hole in the Ground' by Bernard Cribbins, or sometimes just whatever was playing on Radio 3 that day. He was, says Jo, completely unresponsive throughout all of it, even when she played him 'Dream a Little Dream of Me' by Louis Armstrong and Ella Fitzgerald, the record which accompanied their first dance at their wedding party. Still then, no sign that he was listening. Then, that evening, she played him the Schubert impromptu as she sat by him, holding his hand, and stroking his arm. And out of the blue, Simon squeezed her hand. She told him she loved him, and he squeezed it once again. That was the last time he communicated with her before he died at three o'clock the following morning.

'How he found the strength to swim up to the surface from wherever he was, I don't know,' says Jo. 'But I know he was saying goodbye and telling me he loved me. I couldn't have asked for more proof.' At Simon's funeral in the same church where they had married only five years before, Jo followed his coffin down the aisle, while the same friend who had played piano at their wedding played the Schubert piece once more. After our conversation, during which we both break off to pour a glass of wine, I drink another one and listen to the Schubert in a sublime and wistful recording I find online, played by Vladimir Horovitz. I think about what Jo said about the way the music switches back and forth from the major to the minor key. 'It makes my heart sing.' With an improvisational quality that is similar to the Chopin Études, the impromptu is so beautiful and mournful and perfect that I cry a little more for Jo. I think about what Mendelssohn said about music being too specific to put into words, and about how this piece by Schubert seems to encapsulate everything Jo has told me about her relationship with Simon, and so much else besides that only she will ever feel and know.

I wish that I could have worked out a way to play music to my dad at the end, too. But what would I have chosen for him? Reading one of the instructive stories in Kathryn Mannix's book makes me realise that this is a decision I would have had to take with the utmost care. Describing the final weeks of a music lover and Mahler connoisseur in a chapter entitled 'Transcendence', Mannix writes: 'Since he had realised that he was dying, he was no longer able to indulge his lifelong love of the music of Mahler. The pathos and beauty of the music now resonated too deeply with his sense of approaching farewell.' Which music would you choose to die to? My dad chose Chopin. And because of this I am astounded when, in his NPR interview, Murray Perahia says of Chopin's music that 'you have to play it last on the programme. Because nothing can follow Chopin.'

Fryderyk Chopin died in Paris on 17 October 1849. His funeral took place at the church of the Madeleine and he was buried at Père-Lachaise cemetery. All of him that is, except his heart, which was returned to his native Poland to be interred there by his sister, Ludwicka, who had travelled to France to be with her brother at the end. At his graveside, the so-called *Marche funèbre* from the third movement of his Piano Sonata No. 2 in B-flat minor was played. While this piece has accompanied many other significant funerals since, including that of J. F. Kennedy, Winston Churchill and Margaret Thatcher, it has also become something of a cliché, and also when needed, a morbid joke. There's a 1956 Looney Tunes cartoon that Dad would have loved in which Granny threatens to sell puddy tat Sylvester to the violin-string factory if he so much as touches one feather on Tweetie Pie's head while she is out. To emphasise the point, she mimes playing a violin while singing the pounding riff from Chopin's funeral march. When an undaunted Sylvester creeps up on him again, Tweetie responds by cheeping out the same riff and, at the end of the cartoon, caught in the act and his fate sealed, Sylvester brings out a violin and plays the tune again before falling backwards into the violin case, which slams shut like a coffin. That's all, folks.

I listen to Murray Perahia playing Chopin's Études once more, while thinking again about this idea of evanescence; the notion that this music comes, fills your life, and then goes. Perhaps, like my dad, I must let it go without seeking to hold on to it in any meaningful, material way. But it is also music that will always hold the power to return and wholly take hold of you again any time you hear it. Music as a metaphor for human existence. People live, and then they die, and with the passing of time start to fade in the memory of those who knew them. But you can be sure that our loved ones will live again, if only for an evanescent moment, when we accidentally come across their photograph, see their features and mannerisms in a descendant, or listen again to a piece of music that they loved.

And so, when I listen now to Chopin's Étude No. 3 in E major, this piece in particular, the so-called 'Tristesse' Étude, seems to speak of everything that I feel when I think about my dad: the grief; the gratitude; the tenderness; the anger and incomprehension that I feel at his loss; the consolation I take from all my memories of him, and from the legacy he left in the person that I am. And I know that I will always now be bound to this piece, just as I will always be bound to Dad.

In his NPR interview with Murray Perahia, Fred Child, referring to the suffering that Chopin experienced in his short life, asks, 'Do you hear that, can you feel that in his music?' 'Not alone,' responds Perahia. 'You hear a great nobility, and you hear a great strength. All the music is brave. It's the contradictions that he had. Small and frail, and yet noble and brave.' Perhaps that is why my dying dad chose it, this music of feeling and steeling; this music of courage.

Chapter 8

The Soul of Strauss

Ein Heldenleben

So, then: what requiem for the man who was my father?

After Dad died, Mum and I received dozens of cards containing heartfelt messages of sympathy. Almost every one of them described Dad as 'a lovely man'. Lovely. Usually the most unimaginative of words, but for those who knew him it must have seemed the apt one. Searching for a poem to read at his funeral, set for two days after Christmas, I found Robert Burns's 'Epitaph on William Muir', ironically one of the mock tributes that the poet was in the habit of writing for friends who were still very much alive. I'm not sure how Dad, a longtime agnostic, would have felt about being described as 'blest' with God's image. But Burns's references to knowledge and to warm virtue instantly spoke to me of him:

An honest man here lies at rest
As e-er God with his image blest;
The friend of man, the friend of truth,
The friend of age, and guide of youth:
Few hearts like his, with virtue warm'd,

> Few heads with knowledge so informed:
> If there's another world, he lives in bliss;
> If there is none, he made the best of this.

Now, seven years later, attempting to settle on a piece of music that will provide a fitting epitaph, I am dithering. I have a piece in mind; a piece that I know Dad loved, but I am queasy about it, not only because I am worried that it might be too grandiose, but also because of its composer.

Richard Strauss's *Ein Heldenleben* (*A Hero's Life*), completed in 1898, is another piece I heard Dad play often: I remember so well how he used to relish saying the title to me in German, and how he always pronounced Richard as 'Rikard' with a flourish in his voice. I don't know why he made such a thing of the composer's first name, but it was his surname which used to confuse me as a child. I'd already heard of Johann Strauss, because each 1 January my parents would listen to the Wiener Philarmoniker's New Year's Day concert from the Musikverein in Vienna, an annual festival of Johann Strauss's waltzes, polkas and marches. So when I heard Dad mention Richard Strauss I confused the two composers, thinking for a long time that they were somehow related, or even the same person. Now, however, I know more about Richard Strauss and his giant reputation, compromised because of his associations with the Nazi Party.

When *Ein Heldenleben* premiered in 1899, it caused a sensation because of the perceived arrogance of its then thirty-five-year-old composer, not only in presuming to write his autobiography in music at such a young age, but also by daring to call it *A Hero's Life*. Responding to his critics, Strauss denied that the piece was all about him, stating that it was only partly so.

Divided into six parts, *Ein Heldenleben* is a tone poem: an instrumental piece intended to convey a particular story, scene or mood. This innovative musical form which dates from the Romantic era was employed by a diverse range of composers in pieces ranging from Modest Mussorgsky's *Night on a Bare Mountain* to *The Swan of Tuonela* by Jean Sibelius. It was a form that Richard Strauss embraced enthusiastically, too. Perhaps his best-known tone poem is *Also Sprach Zarathustra*, inspired by the philosophical work of the same name by Friedrich Nietzsche.

After all the time I've spent training myself not to construct an accompanying narrative in my head for every piece of music I listen to, I feel like I'm playing hookey by tuning into the blatant tone-poem storytelling of *Ein Heldenleben*. Especially after the 'abstract explanation' of my feelings I experienced when listening to Chopin's Étude No. 3 in E major. But perhaps this quest has required of me two different types of listening: the figurative kind I did as a child when Dad played me such storybook pieces as *The Firebird* and *Kinderszenen*, and the other kind, the more rigorous but also more mysterious Mozart, Brahms and Chopin kind, when how the music makes you feel is what you must grasp in order to make sense of it.

The sleeve notes in Dad's CD of *Ein Heldenleben*, a recording made in 1960 by the Philadelphia Orchestra and featuring Hungarian American conductor Eugene Ormandy and American violinist Anshel Brusilow, reflect this notion, too, referring to 'two famous definitions in musical aesthetics': 'musical forms in motion' and 'music as expression'. Richard Strauss apparently regarded these two definitions not as 'antithetical opposites but as mutually complementary'. Whatever I listen to, I still fret that I do not have the technical knowledge to hear classical music properly. All this time I have been striving to listen to it in a less amateurish way, to stop trying to deal with it as if I am reading words and to learn to hear it in a way that is more, well, musical. But what if the kind of listening I have been reaching for doesn't actually exist? After all, books do not demand to be read on a certain 'level': ultimately, whatever the author's intent, books are only what the individual reader finds in them. The glory of much instrumental music, as Armando Iannucci says in *Hear Me Out*, is that it is what you yourself hear in it, whether it be a story, an emotion, or even a colour. So now, as I approach the end of my journey of remembrance, perhaps it's time to liberate myself from the striving, and content myself with being the listener only I can be.

Though it is decades since I last heard *Ein Heldenleben*, the piece kindles in my memory as soon as I hear the scrunch of strings with which the opening part, 'Das Held' ('The Hero'), begins. In the sallying, stirring melodies of this first section Strauss conveys the optimism, energy and egotism of youth. In part two, by contrast – 'Des Helden Widersacher' ('The Hero's Adversaries') – the melodious strings, which signify the hero's confident path, are checked by dissonant and anarchic woodwind sounds, supposedly representing Strauss's critics. The hyena-like hooting of the mocking clarinets and oboes makes me think of the crazier passages in Stravinsky's *The Rite of Spring*. The hero's strings reassert themselves, still strident but this time racked with doubt as the mocking woodwind continues. And then, right at the end, a solo violin said to represent Strauss's wife, Pauline, comes in. Part three of *Ein Heldenleben* – at twelve minutes the longest section – is devoted to 'Des Helden Gefährtin' ('The Hero's Companion'), given voice by this solo violin, alternately cajoling, flirtatious, pleading and persuasive, and answered by orchestral passages representing the hero. This sometimes tempestuous but gorgeous intertwining dialogue builds to a lush and serene climax, but then as the third part concludes, the taunting voices of the hero's adversaries can be heard in the background.

I wonder if Dad first heard *Ein Heldenleben* at school, at his sixth-form lunchtime classical-music club. Because of its heroic theme, it feels like exactly the kind of piece a master at a boys' grammar school in the 1940s and 1950s might choose to play for his pupils. Dad's copies of *The Ashbeian* provide a salutary reminder that such schools had spent the last decade striving to turn out young men fit to become heroes in the battlefields of Europe and beyond. The magazines I have from 1944 and 1945 include long lists of the old boys and staff who were serving in His Majesty's Forces, including those 'Discharged, Unfit', 'Prisoners of War', 'Mentioned in Dispatches', 'Missing'.

I wonder how this might have influenced Dad's character; a boy too young to serve but growing up on the heels of those who did. There is plenty of evidence that he was highly able academically, featuring routinely on the annual prize lists from Christmas 1945 onwards. He was awarded a Higher School Certificate in science in July 1950, and, the following year, an Advanced and Scholarship paper in science, with his results good enough to net him both a state scholarship and a Leicestershire County major scholarship to study mathematics and physics at Cambridge. His name also appears in the annual school sports reports, playing First XI football, and cricket, too, being mentioned in dispatches for his 'occasional useful innings' and registering sixth in the leading batting averages. Even without any mention of his chess triumphs, his profile is that of one of those admirable but annoying boys who is successful both academically and on the sports field.

Mum gives me an envelope she has found of miscellaneous letters and newspaper cuttings relating to Dad, most of them about his chess playing. One mentions him beating the captain of the Oxford chess team – 'a player with a fine international reputation' – while he was at Cambridge. And years before that, a letter dated 7 July 1944, just after Dad's tenth birthday, sent to his father from the headmaster of Bridge Road Junior School in Coalville. 'For your information only. In order of merit of the children in my school, Peter was second . . . His marks for general intelligence were very good indeed . . . I consider this exceptionally good for an underage boy.' Meaning, I suppose, for a summer-born child.

But then also in the envelope, another letter, this one dog-eared, as if it has been folded and unfolded many times. Dated 17 December 1947, it too is addressed to Dad's father.

> Thank you for your letter . . . Peter is a <u>most promising</u> boy and like you, I am anxious that every help should be given to make a fine man of some grand material, for he is that. The point I had in mind when I wrote what I did was an instance of bullying in which he was concerned: two or three lads, including Peter, maltreating a form fellow – not a strong lad, with an impediment. I took the matter up very sharply at the time, and I have reason to believe that there has been no repetition at all, and that Peter, perhaps more so than the others, took the matter to heart. My remark therefore was a reminder that anyone who has the natural gifts that he has, has on that account a greater responsibility for a high code of behaviour: and I believe we have the responsibility of trying

to keep him to that by any means in our power. There is nothing else that I know of — nothing at all. I have never found any attempt at deceit or evasion — on the contrary, an admirable frankness. You will, I am certain, have a son of whom you will have cause to be even more proud than you rightly are at the moment.

While this letter contains the only bad report I have ever read about my dad, I am struck by his form master's reference to him being 'a fine man of some grand material'. This teacher's sense of his duty to mould the moral character of his prototype hero pupils is unmistakable. I can understand my grandfather keeping this letter, more in pride than in concern, perhaps, but why did my dad keep it? As a reminder of past misdemeanours which he still took to heart? As a salutary reminder of his privilege, and consequent responsibilities?

I also have the Bible which was presented to Dad by his godfather, Richard Whitford, on his confirmation in June 1949. On the first page, Mr Whitford has inscribed the date, his name, and then '6 ch Galatians 17v', a verse he has also bracketed in ink in the text. 'From henceforth let no man trouble me: for I bear in my body the marks of the Lord Jesus.' I can imagine Dad, always a reluctant churchgoer, being glad to have the whole business of confirmation done and dusted, marks of the Lord Jesus notwithstanding. That letter from his form master I suspect did more to form his moral character than any Bible quote, though the line 'anyone who has the natural gifts that he has, has on that account a greater responsibility for a high code of behaviour' brings to mind one of the few Bible verses I know by heart: 'For unto whomsoever much is given, of him shall be much required.'

And what of the moral character of Richard Strauss, composer of *Ein Heldenleben*? In a curious continuity, Strauss crops up in *Chopin's Piano*, in the chapters where Paul Kildea traces the journey across Europe of the said piano during the Second World War. Referring to the Wiener Philharmoniker, of New Year's Day concerts fame, Kildea states that 'fully half' its members were card-carrying Nazis, and that the orchestra expelled 'thirty Jewish players, five of whom later died in ghettos or concentration camps, and exiled others because they were married to Jewish women'.

As for Strauss, aged sixty-nine and a world-famous conductor and composer by 1933 when Hitler came to power, he did not hesitate, writes Kildea, 'when asked to replace Bruno Walter on an international tour with the Leipzig Gewandhaus Orchestra after Walter, a Jew, was publicly removed from his position'. To him to whom so much had been given – a glittering career, public recognition, a villa in the German Alps – could an outspoken stand against abhorrent Nazi policies not have been expected? Instead, as composer Howard Goodall puts it in his contextualising book *The Story of Music*, Strauss, then the most famous living composer in Europe 'had a relationship with the Nazi government that oscillated between polite acquiescence and obstinate stand-offishness'. When Hitler came to power, he gave his Propaganda Ministry, headed by Joseph Goebbels, the right to take control of 'all areas that influenced the mind, including complete control of cultural affairs.'[1]

Goebbels established a Chamber of Culture for the Reich – the Reichskulturkammer, divided into seven areas for music, fine arts, theatre, literature, press, radio and film – of which anyone involved in the production of culture would be legally bound to be a member. When it came to music, the Nazis decided it would be a coup to have Strauss signed up, especially when so many other leading musicians were leaving Germany. Strauss was duly nominated as president of the music section, the Reichsmusikkammer. 'I was not consulted,' Strauss later wrote. 'I accepted this honorary office because I hoped that I would now be able to do some good and prevent worse misfortune.'[2]

The following year, 1934, the year Dad was born, Strauss's seventieth birthday was celebrated across Germany, and both Hitler and Goebbels sent him signed photographs. Strauss later composed a hymn for the 1936 Berlin Olympics, and in 1938 conducted a *Festive Prelude*, also of his own composition, at the opening of a music festival for the Reich, convened by Goebbels. Moreover, Strauss was close friends with the culture-loving and culture-appropriating Nazi, Hans Frank, appointed Governor-General of the occupied Polish territories following Germany's invasion of Poland in 1939. During Frank's tenure, he presided over the mass murder of Jews in the lands under his jurisdiction. In *East West Street*, Philippe Sands records that Strauss wrote a piece of music in Frank's honour after the latter intervened to prevent the composer's driver being conscripted to the east in 1943. After the war had ended in 1945, Strauss gave an interview to an American magazine in which he said that Frank had 'really appreciated my music'.[3] Meanwhile, Hans Frank stood in the dock in Nuremberg, on trial for crimes against humanity and for genocide. Crimes of which he was found guilty and subsequently hanged.

From the early 1930s onwards, Strauss must have already known what was happening to Jewish musicians all around him, not least because the librettist for his operas at that time was the Vienna-born writer Stefan Zweig, who was Jewish. From 1934, anti-Jewish laws explicitly forbade their collaboration, although technically this did not apply to Zweig, who was still an Austrian citizen. However, Strauss later insisted that Zweig's name was included on the posters for his opera *Die schweigsame Frau* at its premiere in Dresden in 1935, a defiance which incensed the Nazi regime and led to the opera's closure after only three performances. It also lost Strauss his job as president of the Reichsmusikkammer, from which he was ordered to resign on the grounds of 'ill health'. He wrote a grovelling letter to Hitler, protesting his innocence and requesting a personal audience so he could explain. Hitler did not reply. Strauss took refuge in his Bavarian villa, and from then on his relationship with the Nazi regime turned into a cat-and-mouse game.

Some have attributed Strauss's actions, or rather, inactions in the face of the Nazi regime to a blinkered and self-centred obsession with perpetuating his status and career by any means possible rather than as out-and-out anti-Semitism. And it is also possible to interpret his actions somewhat differently when you consider that Strauss's much-loved daughter-in-law Alice, the wife of his only child, Franz, was Jewish, meaning that his two young grandsons, Richard and Christian (born in 1927 and 1932 respectively), were also Jewish. As a consequence, the whole family was regarded with suspicion by the people of the town where they lived, and the two young boys were bullied at school. On Kristallnacht, 9 November 1938, even though Franz had by now joined the Nazi Party, the Gestapo arrived to arrest Alice, who, luckily, was away at the time. Instead, Strauss's two grandsons were dragged to the town square, where they were forced to publicly spit on other Jews being held there. After Strauss appealed to Hitler, it was agreed that the boys would be treated as Aryans.

The official commissions Strauss accepted after this time were undertaken on condition that his family was left alone. In 1941, they moved to Vienna after agreeing to help Baldur von Schirach, former head of the Hitler Youth and now Nazi Governor of Vienna, in his ambitions to turn the Austrian city into the cultural capital of the Reich. But the protection this was supposed to ensure only extended to Alice and her children. When deportations to the concentration camps began in earnest in the autumn of 1941, the rest of Alice's family, including her grandmother, Paula Neumann, were stripped of their possessions and held in the Prague ghetto. From there, some were sent to the ghetto in Łódź, and others to Theresienstadt, including Frau Neumann.

In his 1999 biography of Richard Strauss, Tim Ashley relates that on learning of Paula Neumann's internment at Theresienstadt, Strauss drove to the gates of the camp, told the guards exactly who he was and demanded to see her. The guards turned him away, telling him he was insane. Paula later died there. In all, twenty-six members of Alice Strauss's family were murdered by the Nazis in the Final Solution. Then, as the Reich later began to fall apart around him, Strauss, who turned eighty in June 1944, witnessed the destruction wrought by Allied bombing raids, which reduced to ruins such iconic buildings as Munich's National Theatre, where his horn-player father had regularly performed, and the theatres of Dresden, where the premieres of so many of his operas had taken place. In 1948 Strauss was cleared of having any ties with the Nazi regime by an official de-Nazification tribunal in Munich. And yet suspicion still surrounded him: Thomas Mann for one, dubbed him a 'Hitlerian composer'.[4] Richard Strauss, a once heroic figure in world music, now tainted by his lack of heroism.

Can I disconnect myself from the biography of its composer and enjoy *Ein Heldenleben* merely as a piece that Dad loved? Or is it now irrevocably altered in the listening? Such is the debate of our times. I mention my uncertainty to my film-buff friend Anne during a conversation about the furore over Woody Allen's autobiography, which she read and greatly enjoyed. Can we still watch Allen's films with enjoyment, given that he has not been found guilty of any crime? Listen to the music of Michael Jackson? The operas of Wagner? Admire the art of Picasso? What would culture be if wiped of the works of those later judged more harshly – in many cases justifiably – by history?

In the fourth part of *Ein Heldenleben* – 'Des Helden Walstatt' ('The Hero's Battlefield') – the hero's adversaries return with a vengeance, rendered in brass and woodwind, and pitched against the horns, which also represent the hero, the horn being the instrument which Strauss once dubbed 'the yardstick of heroism'.[5] By the fifth part, 'Des Helden Friedenswerke' ('The Hero's Works of Peace'), the hero has prevailed, and we hear a reprise of musical themes from previous songs and tone poems that Strauss had written. The final part – 'Des Helden Weltflucht und Vollendung' ('The Hero's Retirement from the World and Fulfilment') – denotes the sense of peace and accomplishment which characterises the hero's latter days as he looks back on the vicissitudes of his life, the singingly serene solo violin and the muted horns duetting in poignant contentment to the end.

In reply to those critics who found *Ein Heldenleben* arrogant and grandiose, Strauss again denied that the piece was all about him, stating, 'I am not a hero; I haven't got the necessary strength. I prefer to withdraw.'[6] On the April day in 1945 when Hitler died by suicide, Strauss was visited at his Bavarian villa by American soldiers who were keen to requisition it. In 'don't you know who I am?' fashion, Strauss declared, 'I am the composer of *Der Rosenkavalier*,' (his world-famous comic opera whose overture Dad was also fond of), and then sat down at the piano to play some tunes from it.[7] After that, the American soldiers left him alone, this German composer who had survived the Second World War, his home and livelihood still intact, to live and make music for another four years, dying at the age of eighty-five in 1949.

And yet, during the disastrous closing months of the war he wrote an extraordinary piece for strings entitled *Metamorphosen*, a mesmerising and intensely sombre composition. While some have interpreted it as an elegy for Hitler and the Third Reich, others believe it to be a work of mourning for the demise of German culture, and perhaps even Strauss's apology for his erstwhile involvement with the Nazis. I listen to it on a dark day of incessant rain as the coronavirus begins to tighten its grip on the country once more, and this brutal but beautiful music resounds like a lament for this new era of world crisis.

Dad's empirical training meant that there was little room for emotion in his view of the world. We had many discussions about nuclear power: the industry that Dad worked in all his life, overseeing many technological developments. I have a full-page cutting from the *Leicester Mercury* in July 1956, a month before Mum and Dad got married, which profiles the Leicestershire factory where he worked. The article is heroic in tone and in its capitalisation: 'It was at this factory . . . that Sir Frank Whittle and his boffins did most of the pioneer work during the war which led to the production of the first successful aircraft jet engine. AND NOW, THE BACK ROOM BOYS ARE HELPING TO USHER IN THE ATOMIC AGE . . . THEIR PLANS, AIMED AT SECURING THE CONTRACT TO BUILD BRITAIN'S FIRST NUCLEAR POWER STATION ARE NEARLY COMPLETE.' In the bottom right-hand corner of the cutting is a photograph of Dad in a white coat. The caption reads: 'Mr Peter Sanderson handling, with the aid of tongs and rubber gloves, a pellet of uranium due for a temperature check.'

Even after it fell out of favour, Dad remained convinced that nuclear power was the proven solution to our future energy needs. He genuinely couldn't understand why people were so fearful of it, and its fall from grace depressed him. I remember phoning him after the Chernobyl nuclear disaster in 1986 to ask how it had happened and he pointed to a lack of safety features which, he told me, representatives of the British nuclear industry had warned the Soviets about years before. He always declared himself happy to engage in a proper debate with anti-nuclear protestors if they could get their facts right. But in his view, they never did, and neither did almost all newspapers. His adamant and long-held view that the UK should generate as much of its own energy needs as possible looks prescient, however, given the country's continuing dependence on gas imported from overseas, for example.

Dad could also be infuriatingly pedantic, refusing to believe that language evolves, however much I tried to persuade him. The term 'low carbon' was frowned upon because it should, by rights, be 'low carbon dioxide'. 'Green'? 'Sustainable'?

What do those words actually mean? Define your terms! The notion of someone being underprivileged was also suspect: depends what you mean by privilege. So he would have met the term 'white privilege' with complete incomprehension, and I know I would have had a hard time explaining it to him. He liked words to stick to their absolute definition, something that as a writer I found grating. For some reason, the word 'just' was a particular bête noire. 'Just 17'? 'Just £4.99'? Only 17! Only £4.99!

And yet at the heart of this pedantry was a desire for clarity, for transparency, for rigour and for truth. As history tells us, totalitarian regimes specialise in manipulating words and their definitions for nefarious purposes. Dad objected to the frequent modern-day use of the word 'fascist', not because he had any extremist views, but because he considered it a word dangerously weakened by being used out of the context of its original definition (which referred specifically to members of the Italian Fascio d'Azione Rivoluzionaria). If you call someone a 'fascist' nowadays, you should explain exactly what you mean, not assume that it will be clear. And I think that is a moot point: the lazier we are with words, the less understanding we will engender in others.

I remember a conversation when I was a teenager when, seeking to illustrate how words can be manipulated, Dad quoted the use of 'Democratic' in the name of the then 'German Democratic Republic'. We talked some more, and then he said: 'Always be suspicious of a country that doesn't allow people to leave freely. If life is so good there, why would you try and prevent its citizens from telling others so?' It was such an obvious and simple statement, but I have never forgotten it. For when it comes to justice, and human rights, and true democracy, the principles are indeed simple.

I so wish now that I'd been able to talk to Dad about my queasiness concerning Richard Strauss's Nazi associations. Among his books after he died, I found *The Baton and the Jackboot*, a memoir by Berta Geissmar, the Jewish former secretary to Wilhelm Furtwängler, the principal conductor of the Berlin Philharmonic Orchestra. Forced to flee Germany for London in 1935, she knew Strauss, who was an erstwhile friend of her father's, and in her book is highly critical of him for not using his position as president of the Reichsmusikkammer to 'support all of us who were by tradition and merit entrenched within the traditional music culture of the genuine Germany'. 'Had he not played into the hands of the Nazis,' she writes, 'many tragedies in the field of music might have been avoided.' The more I read, the more I grow to despise this man who spuriously wrote a piece of music about the life of a hero but who could not live such a life himself. But Dad, I know, would have questioned my moral superiority. He would have said: Well, what would you have done in his position? If you feared for your loved ones? Can you categorically tell me that, put in the same situation, you would have been the hero that he was not?

I feel exhausted and am not even sure I want to listen to Richard Strauss's music any more, however much Dad loved it. But then I spend one of the first chilly evenings of autumn lying under a blanket on the sofa, listening to the composer's *Vier letzte Lieder* – his *Four Last Songs* – sung by the late Jessye Norman. It's not a piece that Dad ever mentioned, or to my knowledge played, but I've been prompted to listen to it by rereading *Hear Me Out*, in which Armando Iannucci describes hearing this music for the first time as an undergraduate, as it drifted out of a fellow student's open window. 'I'd never heard such unashamed but sincere romanticism before and it had me frozen to the floor,' he writes. Though I'd never heard of the *Four Last Songs* before, I'm now wondering how I could possibly have lived this long without these extraordinary, soul-mining pieces in my life.

Written in the final year of his life, for soprano and orchestra, and inspired, it is said, by his wife Pauline, herself a former professional soprano to whom Strauss had been married for more than fifty years, the songs were not composed as a set but were later placed together by Strauss's publisher. The first three – 'Frühling' ('Spring'), 'Beim Schlafengehen' ('Falling Asleep') and 'September' are settings to poems by Hermann Hesse. The fourth song – 'Im Abendrot' ('At Sunset') – is set to the words of a poem by German Romantic poet Joseph von Eichendorff. A fifth song was unfinished when Strauss died in September 1949. The *Four Last Songs* were premiered at the Royal Albert Hall in London in May 1950 by the Norwegian soprano Kirsten Flagstad, who was also a friend of the composer.

The morning after listening to the *Vier letzte Lieder* for the first time, I drive up to Staffordshire to stay with my friend Caroline. She lives in a big house with staff cottages attached, and that evening, as the light fades, she tells me an eerie story. One of the cottage tenants kept experiencing a mysterious smell of burnt sugar in her kitchen. Being a believer in psychic phenomena, she decided to 'film' the smell on her phone. The resulting footage clearly showed bright lights or 'orbs' darting around the room. A little girl once died in a fire in the house, and the tenant has also – she believes – heard her crying. Caroline and I talk about whether we believe too in ghosts and spirits, whether the dead are still present in some way. As we sit by the fireside, our conversation turns to music, and Caroline starts telling me that it was when her now husband sent her a beautiful piece of music that she began to fall properly in love with him. She reaches for her laptop and calls up the piece without telling me what it is. As the first bars play, a shiver runs through me. It is Richard Strauss's *Four Last Songs* sung by Jessye Norman. It is only a coincidence, of course, but after all we have been talking about, it is a deeply spooky one.

The prevailing theme of the *Four Last Songs* may be death, but they are not tragic pieces. Rather, they are meditations of a crystalline simplicity about what it is to live a contented life and then die a good death. As Clemency Burton-Hill writes in *Year of Wonder*, 'they radiate a mood of serene acceptance, their melodic lines soaring heavenward in a gesture of reconciliation'. The final song – 'Im Abendrot' – portrays an elderly couple, watching the sun set and experiencing the end of their lives in a state of deep serenity in the dusk.

> Hand in hand, we have gone through
> Good times and bad.
> After years of travelling
> We have come to rest in this quiet land
>
> The vale slopes downwards
> The sky is already darkening
> Only two larks still climb dreamily
> Into the haze

>Come, let them whirl away
>Soon it will be time to sleep
>We must not lose our way
>In this secluded place
>
>Oh, how wide and quiet is this peace!
>So deep the red glow of evening
>We are tired of roaming
>Has death now come to greet us?[8]

In *Chopin's Piano*, Paul Kildea places the composition of *Vier letzte Lieder* in the context of the then octogenarian Strauss belonging firmly to the traditions of the late nineteenth century. 'How else to explain ... those impossibly Romantic orchestral songs ... which really had no business being written as late as 1948.' But post-war, he argues, such high culture provided Europe's framework for 'spiritual renewal' in the wake of destruction. New cultural festivals hatched in a spirit of optimism were founded in Britain, including the Edinburgh Festival, and it was a context in which many performers thrived, including Kathleen Ferrier. Kildea believes that at this time, there was an 'instinctive scramble towards important works of the 19th century, which acted almost as moral ballast', with Romanticism in particular providing the material with which to 'paper over nationalist, cultural and political differences between allies and enemies'.

I find this fascinating, particularly in the context of Dad's late 1940s and early 1950s grammar-school education, the wellspring of his abiding love of classical music, a love which continued even as he was making his scientific mark as a backroom boy of the atomic age. This mathematical man, for whom logic, pragmatism and rigour were a way of life, and who was so gifted in his spatial-temporal reasoning skills, remained a devotee all his life of Romantic music, and of pieces like *Ein Heldenleben*. And now I too am beginning to build up my own bank of consolation through music that has such power to provide a conduit for our troubled emotions, at times of crisis in any era.

As Caroline and I listen in silence to Strauss's sublime music, we do not think of the motivations and actions of its composer but only of how it forges in us myriad private emotions, as Jessye Norman's divine voice soars and subsides around us. Like all great art, this wonderful music has the power to transcend the circumstances that give birth to it. And while I imagine there are those who will always have trouble listening to anything Richard Strauss wrote because of who he was, this music, his *Four Last Songs*, brought my friend a beloved husband. And to me, they have brought comfort, because somehow, this music and these words, both simple and deeply spiritual, engender a conviction that Dad is somewhere near at hand, and also at vast, tranquil peace.

In all of us, even in the heroes, there are contradictions. And despite Dad's devotion to the empirical, all his life he was enthralled by things which could not be proven. I guess that is the sign of a true scientist: of someone who is always reaching to explain that which has not yet been explained. In the eulogy I gave at his funeral, I spoke of his love of optics: telescopes, and particular binoculars; an appropriate hobby, I said, for someone who was always trying to see further. Someone who always wanted to see things more clearly.

When I describe Dad as a decent man, a lovely man, I suppose what I mean is this. That he did not have a shred of arrogance. That he was modest and considerate. And courteous to the point of never allowing me to be on the road side of the pavement when we walked together. For a while when I was a young woman this always seemed to me a ridiculously outdated thing to do; as a feminist, I reserved my right to cope manfully with oncoming traffic and the grave danger of being splashed by passing vehicles. But thinking of it now, it is a courtesy that touches me deeply and I miss it.

When I got married, Dad, a reluctant public speaker, made a heartfelt and entertaining father-of-the-bride speech. Only at the end did he turn more solemn as he offered a single piece of advice to the happy couple: be kind. His voice cracking with emotion, he quoted his favourite line from Tennyson: 'Kind hearts are more than coronets.' Traditionally, not a quality much associated with heroes, kindness. But it should be.

Coda

Grief sits by your side on that epic, grinding, post-bereavement journey that you never wanted to go on and wish would end. Am I nearly there yet? Sometimes I think that I've made peace with the truth that nothing can stay the same in life, but then I find myself repeatedly battering myself against that truth. Grief for me is a dull soreness beneath the plaster I've stuck on it, a childhood graze on my knee which makes me wince when I knock it against something.

In early autumn, before the pandemic hits, I drive home from a visit to Mum with a cargo of Dad's old film equipment: his cine projector; and boxed-up reels of cine films. There are also several crates of slides, mostly taken by Mum and dating from the early years of their marriage in the late 1950s, to the late 1980s. They have scarcely been viewed since they returned from processing at Boots long ago. I buy a slide viewer and spend long hours poring over them. Unlike Dad's cine footage and the yellowing images which date from my own first attempts at photography with the little Kodak Instamatic camera I was given for my sixth birthday, the slides have barely faded, the colours as bright as on the day they were taken. They have an immediacy which is both enchanting and heart-wrenching.

Back to life via these gems of Kodachrome come the greens of summers, and my first childhood home: the aspired-to detached house. Built in the 1930s, it had lofty chimneys, a fancy brickwork arch over the front door and leaded-light windows either side. In the front garden rose bushes and a pink hydrangea flourish in front of the bow window of the dining room where Dad used to dispatch his paperwork on a Sunday. And then here, in a photo taken outside the house when I was two months old, is my dad, clasping me tight to his chest as if I am the most precious thing he has ever held. Swaddled tight in a shawl, I seem to be staring off into the distance from under my white hand-knitted bonnet with that abstracted gaze that babies have. But my dad's face seems to say: I will never let you go.

And then I come across another slide of Dad and me, taken nearly four years later. It is the closest I can find to a portrait of myself at the age I was when I first heard Mozart. We are sitting on a grass verge in front of a hedgerow, somewhere near Stamford in Lincolnshire, according to what Dad has written on the cardboard surround. Dad is squatting on his haunches in white shirt, socks, sandals and Ray-Bans. I am dressed in pale blue shorts and a royal blue t-shirt, my fair hair tied back in a ponytail. I guess that it was taken during a lunchtime picnic stop en route to our summer holiday in Sheringham. We are both smiling at the camera but look as if we have been interrupted having a deep conversation.

I look at both these images again and again. And then a few days later I drive two hours north to Leicestershire, and the village where I grew up. It's over two decades since I last visited. When I get there, the crisp and cloudless autumn weather encourages me to walk for miles, retracing the tracks of my early life. I peer through the perimeter fence of my primary school, smirk at the village hall where I had my first kiss at a Scout disco, and hoof round the housing estate where my grandmother used to live. There I look at front-garden walls and smile, remembering how I used to walk the long length of Barry Drive to the shops with my mum as she pushed my brother in his pushchair with one hand, and held onto mine with the other as I stepped up and down onto each low-enough wall, in a trying-to-stay-off-ground game.

When I get to the parade of shops down Cherry Tree Avenue, I sit on a bench and review the wholesale retail changes. A nail bar, and a hairdressing and beauty parlour have replaced Hammonds' the newsagent's where I bought sweets and copies of my favourite comic, *Bunty*. The greengrocer's, whose sharp, fruity smell I can still conjure in an instant has also gone, along with the dress shop called Elegance where Mum bought some of the rare frocks she didn't sew herself.

I discover from a poster tacked to a tree that a new housing estate is to be built on the nearby fields I roamed as a child, mostly alone but sometimes in a gang of the kids from the cul-de-sac beyond where I lived from the age of six. I feel compelled to stand in those fields again, and find I easily remember the route I used to take: down the jitty (local dialect for a narrow passageway), across the brook and up and out onto the fields. It was the quickest way back to my new house from the shops, rather than the longer walk round by Barry Drive, and I had long since grown out of walking on walls. But I would often tarry in those fields, spying on butterflies or picking grasses and shaving off the seed heads with my fingers, while I practised blowing bubbles with the Anglo Bubbly gum I bought in Hammonds' unbeknownst to my mum, a stern guardian against tooth decay.

Swish-swashing through the long grass, I spy a woman walking three small dogs up the hill ahead of me. I approach and speak to her, and ask if it's true about the new houses. It is, and it's a miracle that I have chosen to revisit the fields of my childhood just before they disappear for ever. Then as we chat some more, I realise with a jolt that the woman I have stopped is the mother of my first primary-school best friend, Joanne. It is another small miracle. 'I remember you,' she says. 'You came to one of Joanne's birthday parties in a lovely frock. Someone said: "What a nice felt dress", and quick as a flash you said: "It's not felt, it's velvet."' I feel a bit ashamed of how snippy I must have sounded. But I remember the dress: made by Mum in midnight-blue velvet, high-necked, with tight cuffs and pearl buttons sewn into an inverted triangle design at the throat.

The news of Joanne, who works long hours as a carer in Nottingham and has two grown-up sons, leaves me with a lump in my throat. Still marvelling at the coincidence, I send my best to Joanne, say goodbye to her mother and walk on, across the railway tracks, and up along the cul-de-sac and past our second house. And then on a bit further, I reach Forest Rise and the first house I lived in. The place where I first heard Mozart.

I take a couple of photos, and pace up and down a bit outside. There are two cars in the drive, which surely means someone is in. I hesitate, but then think of the soon-to-vanish fields, and of how quickly change can come. So I walk up the path and ring the bell. An elderly man answers, a concerned look on his face. I explain who I am, and by way of proof hand him a document I have brought with me: my pink Infant Welfare Card, on which my baby weights were recorded, and it has my first-ever address on it, the address that is now his. 'May I please just take a peek into your hall?' I ask. The man remains reserved, but acquiesces. 'Sorry about the mess but my wife is in hospital,' he tells me, motioning for me to step inside.

And there it is. The hall. The stairway. The dining-room door. All as I remember it. Achingly familiar but smaller, and also spooky, as if I've landed in a parallel universe. The hall is now carpeted, but when I mention the parquet the owner says: 'Oh yes, it's still there underneath but we decided it was a bit noisy.' He has softened a little now and invites me in a bit further to view the garden, of which he is clearly proud. The rose beds I remember are no longer there, but at the end of the garden is a tall Bramley apple tree, covered in fruit. 'My mum used to make them into pies,' I tell him.

I am in the house for less than ten minutes, but my short visit has a profound effect on me. The reassurance provided by this confirmation that things were as I remember them is enormous, and on the drive home I feel triumphant and happy. I feed my high by listening not to Mozart, or even to classical music, but to Kacey Musgraves, singing along jauntily about dimestore cowgirls and not being pageant material. But the next day, on returning home from a series of meetings in London, I feel utterly exhausted and for the next week I am frequently in tears.

A few weeks after standing once again in the hallway of my childhood home, it is the sixth anniversary of my dad's death. It's a Saturday and I have my dance class as normal, and then I go food shopping, scrub the shower room, and shuffle some papers and books around my office. I think about listening to Mozart but I get distracted by more household chores and, before I know it, the day has passed.

But Christmas is hard once again. I spend much of the holidays in the kitchen, on the pretext of cooking delicious food, but really I'm hiding away, missing my dad more than I want to say. On Christmas Eve, instead of dutifully listening to the Five Lessons and Carols on the radio while I prep the Christmas feast, I put on a Kate Rusby CD, a charity-shop impulse buy. After weeks of build-up, I've had my fill of Christmas music. But I still want to listen to something traditional and find Rusby's folk harmonies fit the bill, while also chiming with my subversive frame of mind. Thanks to Kathleen Ferrier, I have a new attachment to the seductive cadences and melodies of folk song and before long I am singing along lustily to 'Blooming Heather', Rusby's arrangement of 'Wild Mountain Thyme'.

It sets me thinking about the shifting landscape that is the soundtrack to our lives. For sure, the well-loved pieces that we return again and again, but also the discoveries that we constantly make if music is something that we cannot do without. Dad's principal beef with popular music was, I remind myself, that it changed too often, was too ephemeral, too concerned with novelty. Perhaps he had a point. But despite my listening journey, a journey that has both consoled me and allowed me to do penance for all the times that I failed to make the effort to connect with him, I have no wish to confine my future listening to the same canon as my dad's. It is not who I am. When I muse over my *Desert Island Discs* choices, they are as likely to include 'Born to Run' by Bruce Springsteen – a track which would have made Dad put his fingers in his ears – as Mozart's Piano Concerto No. 22. While I'm hanging on the line, waiting to do a phone interview on BBC Radio Gloucestershire one day, the presenter catches me joyfully yelping 'Oh, what a night!' along to 'December 1963' by the Four Seasons because at that precise moment it sounds to me like the best pop record ever made. Seems so wrong, and yet so right.

So now, as I come to the end of my quest to listen with father, what will Dad's legacy be? He has certainly taught me to listen more attentively and with greater curiosity to pieces that I only skimmed over before. I still feel desolate that I only thought to undertake this journey when my dad was no longer around to share it with me. But it has been far from a one-sided conversation. In fact, listening to the music that he loved has brought me closer to my father than I would ever have thought posthumously possible.

And so, looking ahead into this future without him, there is nothing to stop me continuing with my listening project: after all, Dad has many more CDs in his collection of classical music that I have never heard. I resolve that, slowly and gradually, I will work my way through them. Perhaps I will select a different CD each week and give it – and him – my time. But over the past many months of listening, something has been completed and laid to rest, and this too was the purpose of it all. I've been reading *Dark Salt Clear: Life in a Cornish Fishing Town* by Lamorna Ash, an account of living and working with the fishermen of Newlyn, whose perilous lives are full of the ghosts of those lost at sea. Musing on the dead, Ash quotes Joan Didion when she writes: 'If we are to live outside there comes a point at which we must relinquish the dead, let them go, keep them dead. Let them become the photograph on the table . . . Let go of them in the water.' Must I do this? Yes, perhaps I must.

For the more fortunate among us, the death of someone close to us is an experience we only come to know in middle age. With the sudden death of my brother when I was in my mid-twenties, I knew it earlier than many. Mourning has, I realise, been a part of me for almost as long as I have been an adult. But this process of living in my childhood memories of Dad, of listening to his music, of looking at images of a time when he was alive and younger than I am now, has coincided with that time of crisis that commonly rests at the mid-life fulcrum, that equinox between our past life and our future one.

In her novel *10 Minutes 38 Seconds in This Strange World*, Elif Shafak writes of her deceased heroine: 'Her mother had once told her that childhood was a big, blue wave that lifted you up, carried you forth and, just when you thought it would last forever, vanished from sight.' I realise just how hard I've have been trying to ride that wave again. We routinely use the expression 'middle age', but how often do we really think about the significance of those words which describe this half-way point in our lives where we have to decide which hemisphere of our allotted time will gain ascendency? For half my life, likely more than half my life, I had a father. What will it mean to live out the other half without him? This I am only slowly discovering. And I am starting to wonder whether this is the real journey I must make, one that all this sitting around listening to music has only served to delay. Perhaps it has all been mere indulgence after all. Perhaps it is time to, in that trite phrase, move on.

And then, one day, I hear *Andante festivo* by Jean Sibelius on the radio and I have my answer. Not only do I know it straight away as music by Sibelius, but from the opening bars I also recognise the actual piece. It feels as if I've passed an exam. I turn the music up as loudly as I can and I suddenly feel jubilant and whole. The music streams through me, just as Mozart did that day in the hall. There is me, and there is the music, and for the five minutes or so that it lasts, that is all there is.

But this time I am listening to music that I have found for myself. Dad led me to Sibelius, it's true, but I did the rest. Since I first heard the *Andante festivo*, I have forged a passion for this piece, which featured in a live worldwide radio broadcast on New Year's Day in 1939, in a famously intense rendition, conducted – in his last ever public performance – by Sibelius himself. I love its stately simplicity, the restrained sense of optimism which goes hand in hand with its air of lament, and all the understated emotion that is latent in it.

Over the next few weeks, I listen with newly opened ears to classical music on the radio that I have no previous knowledge of. I enjoy an opera by a composer I've never even heard of: *Halka* by Polish-born Stanisław Moniuszko. I struggle a little with a strange and spooky piece for viola and piano by Benjamin Britten called *Lachrymae*, but then listen with great pleasure to Gustav Holst's *Somerset Rhapsody*, based on three folk tunes. I realise that though I still couldn't analyse it in any precise orchestral sense, I have a very definite penchant for the pastoral English sound you hear in this and pieces like *The Lark Ascending*, and Arnold Bax's *Tintagel*, another particular favourite of Dad's. Listening to Holst – a composer born in Gloucestershire, only miles from where I now live – makes me resolve to cultivate a broader knowledge of his music than just

The Planets, a piece that virtually everyone knows. I have cut loose from Dad's CD collection and embarked on my own voyage of discovery.

I have learned to love classical music. I'm sorry that it took me so long, Dad.

Acknowledgements

Thank you to:

My editor Marissa Constantinou for looking after this story so carefully.

Everyone else at Unbound, especially John Mitchinson, Rina Gill, Sophia Cerullo, Kate Neilan, Anna Simpson, Richard Collins, Kate Quarry, Alex Newby & Amanda Leigh.

My agent Sarah Such, for unfailing encouragement and wise counsel.

Jo Ashworth, for the privilege of including your own story of love and loss and music.

My fellow Gloucestershire writers; the best of support networks. Most especially Jane Bailey, Alice Jolly, Rachel Joyce & Sarah Steele.

My dear and constant friends, Anne Joseph and Caroline Montague for writerly boosting, and generous hospitality.

Christina Stead, my BFF.

David, Alexander & Julia Brookes for everything.

Bibliography

Wolfgang Amadeus Mozart

Blom, Eric, *The Master Musicians: Mozart*, J. M. Dent & Sons Ltd, London, 1935

Campbell, Don, *The Mozart Effect: Tapping the Power of Music to Heal the Body, Strengthen the Mind and Unlock the Creative Spirit,* Avon, New York, 2017

Kym, Min, *Gone: A Violin, A Life Unstrung,* Viking, London, 2017

March, Ivan, Greenfield, Edward and Layton, Robert, *The Penguin Guide to Compact Discs & DVDS: The Key Classical Recordings* (various editions), Penguin, London, 2003 onwards

Radcliffe, Philip, *Mozart Piano Concertos*, Ariel Music, BBC Publications, London, 1978

Rye, Matthew (ed.), *1001 Classical Recordings You Must Hear Before You Die*, Universe, New York, 2007

Steinberg, Michael, *The Concerto: A Listener's Guide*, Oxford University Press Inc., New York, 1998

Suchet, John, *Mozart: The Man Revealed*, Elliot & Thompson, London, 2016

Woodward, Ian and Aitchison, Martin, *Lives of the Great Composers Book 1*, Wills & Hepworth Ltd, Loughborough, 1969

Igor Stravinsky

Baron and Haskell, Alfred Lionel, *Baron at the Ballet,* Collins, London, 1951

Bathurst, Bella, *Sound: Stories of Hearing Lost and Found,* Wellcome Collection, London, 2017

Burton-Hill, Clemency, *Year of Wonder: Classical Music for Every Day,* Headline, London, 2017

Iannucci, Armando, *Hear Me Out: All My Music,* Little, Brown, London, 2017

Oliver, Michael, *20th Century Composers: Igor Stravinsky,* Phaidon, London, 1995

Roe, Sue, *In Montparnasse: The Emergence of Surrealism in Paris, from Duchamp to Dalí,* Penguin Press, London, 2019

Stein, Gertude, *The Autobiography of Alice B Toklas,* Penguin Classics, London, 2001

Stravinsky, Igor, *An Autobiography,* W. W Norton & Company, New York, 1962

Kathleen Ferrier

Ferrier, Winifred, *The Life of Kathleen Ferrier,* Hamish Hamilton, London, 1955

Howard, Maurice, *Kathleen: The Life of Kathleen Ferrier 1912–1953,* Hutchinson, London, 1988

Levitin, Daniel, *This is Your Brain on Music,* Atlantic, London, 2007

Various, *Blow the Wind Southerly: A Celebration of the Centenary of the Birth of Kathleen Ferrier 1912/2012* (book and CD), The Kathleen Ferrier Awards, London, 2012

Johannes Brahms

Boyd, William, *Visions Fugitives* in *Fascination*, Penguin, 2005
Kennedy, Michael and Joyce, and Rutherford-Johnson, Tim, *Oxford Dictionary of Music*, Oxford University Press, Oxford, 2013
Illing, Robert, *A Dictionary of Music*, Penguin, London, 1950
Macdonald, Helen, *H is for Hawk*, Jonathan Cape, London, 2014
Sagan, Françoise & Wiles, Peter (translator), *Aimez-vous Brahms?*, Penguin, London, 1962
Schonberg, Harold C, *The Lives of the Great Composers*, Abacus, London, 1998
Staines, Joe and Clark, Duncan (ed.), *The Rough Guide to Classical Music*, Rough Guides, London, 2005
Vulliamy, Ed, *When Words Fail: A Life With Music, War & Peace*, Granta, London, 2018

Clara and Robert Schumann

Beer, Anna, *Sounds and Sweet Airs: The Forgotten Women of Classical Music*, Oneworld, London, 2016
Riley, Denise, *Time Lived, Without Its Flow*, Picador, London, 2019
Schumann, Robert and Isserlis, Steven, *Robert Schumann's Advice to Young Musicians*, Faber, 2016
Steegman, Monica, *Clara Schumann*, Haus Publishing, London, 2004
Tóibín, Colm, *Brooklyn*, Penguin, London, 2010

Jean Sibelius

Ferguson, Maggie (ed.), *Treasure Palaces: Great Writers Visit Museums*, The Economist, London, 2017
Jansson, Tove and Portch, Elizabeth (translator), *Comet in Moominland*, Puffin Books, London, 1967

Maddocks, Fiona, *Music for Life: 100 Works to Carry You Through*, Faber, London, 2016

Rickards, Guy, *Jean Sibelius*, Phaidon, London, 1997

Rusbridger, Alan, *Play It Again: An Amateur Against the Impossible*, Jonathan Cape, London, 2013

Fryderyk Chopin

Gide, André and Frechtman, Bernard (translator), *Notes on Chopin*, Philosophical Library Inc., New York, 1949

Kildea, Paul, *Chopin's Piano: A Journey Through Romanticism*, Penguin, 2019

Mannix, Kathryn, *With the End in Mind: How to Live and Die Well*, William Collins, 2019

Zamoyski, Adam, *Chopin: Prince of the Romantics*, Harper Press, London, 2011

Richard Strauss

Ashley, Tim, *Richard Strauss*, Phaidon, London, 1999

Geissmar, Berta, *The Baton and the Jackboot: Reflections of Musical Life*, Hamish Hamilton, London, 1944

Goodall, Howard, *The Story of Music*, Chatto & Windus, London, 2013

Sands, Philippe, *East West Street*, Weidenfeld & Nicolson, London, 2016

Coda

Ash, Lamorna, *Dark Salt Clear: Life in a Cornish Fishing Town*, Bloomsbury, London, 2020

Shafak, Elif, *10 Minutes 38 Seconds in This Strange World*, Viking, 2019

Recordings

Wolfgang Amadeus Mozart

Mozart, Wolfgang Amadeus
The Great Piano Concertos – Alfred Brendel
Academy of St Martin in the Fields – Sir Neville Marriner
(Phillips, 1994)

Mozart, Wolfgang Amadeus
Piano Concertos Nos 21 & 22 – Annie Fischer
Philharmonia Orchestra – Wolfgang Sawallisch
(EMI, 2004)

Igor Stravinsky

Stravinsky, Igor
The Rite of Spring/The Firebird
The Columbia Symphony Orchestra – Igor Stravinsky
(Sony, 1997)

Stravinsky, Igor
Petrouchka/The Firebird Suite/Scherzo à la Russe
Cincinnati Symphony Orchestra – Paavo Järvi
(Telarc, 2003)

Kathleen Ferrier

Various
The World of Kathleen Ferrier – Kathleen Ferrier
(Decca, 1990)

Various
Kathleen Ferrier: A Tribute – Kathleen Ferrer
(Decca, 2003)

Bach, Johann Sebastian
Mass in B Minor – Kathleen Ferrier and others
Vienna Symphony – Herbert von Karajan
(Guild GmbH, 2003)

Brahms, Johannes
Four Serious Songs – Kathleen Ferrier
BBC Symphony Orchestra – Sir Malcolm Sargent
(Guild GmbH, 2003)

Mahler, Gustav
Das Lied von der Erde – Kathleen Ferrier
Wiener Philharmoniker – Bruno Walter
(Decca, 2000)

Johannes Brahms

Brahms, Johannes
Symphonies Nos. 1–4
New York Philharmonic – Bruno Walter
(Sony, 2004)

Brahms, Johannes
Serenades 172/Haydn Variations/*Tragic Overture*/*Alto Rhapsody* –
  Janet Baker
London Philharmonic Orchestra/London Symphony Orchestra –
  Sir Adrian Boult
(EMI, 1995)

Clara and Robert Schumann

Schumann, Robert
Fantasie op.17/*Kinderszenen* – Clifford Curzon
(Decca, 2000)

Schumann, Clara and Mendelssohn, Fanny
Piano Trios – Lars Vogt
Atos Trio/London Bridge Trio
(BBC Music Magazine, 2019)

Schumann, Clara
Romance: The Piano Music of Clara Schumann – Isata Kanneh-Mason
Royal Liverpool Philharmonic Orchestra – Holly Mathieson
(Decca, 2019)

Jean Sibelius

Sibelius, Jean
The Symphonies, Nos. 1, 2, and 4/*Finlandia*/*Karelia* Suite
The Symphonies, Nos. 3, 5, 6, & 7/*En Saga*/*Tapiola*
Philharmonia Orchestra – Vladimir Ashkenazy
(Decca, 1997)

Sibelius, Jean
Symphony No. 5/*Finlandia*/*Tapiola*/*Valse Triste*
Berlin Philharmonic – Herbert von Karajan
(Deutsche Grammophon, 1965/7)

Sibelius, Jean
The Complete Symphonies/The Violin Concerto/*Finlandia*/
   Tapiola/*The Swan of Tuonela*
Boston Symphony Orchestra/London Symphony Orchestra – Sir
   Colin Davis
(Philips, 1995)

Fryderyk Chopin

Chopin, Fryderyk
Études, Opus 10, Opus 25 – Murray Perahia
(Sony, 2002)

Richard Strauss

Strauss, Richard
Ein Heldenleben/*Don Juan*/*Till Eulenspiegel*
Philadelphia Orchestra – Eugene Ormandy
Cleveland Orchestra – George Szell
(Sony, 2001)

Notes

1. The Effect of Mozart

1 John Suchet, *Mozart: The Man Revealed,* Elliott & Thompson, London, 2016, p. 210.
2 *Ibid.*, p. 243.
3 *Ibid.*, p. 158.
4 *Amadeus,* screenplay by Peter Schaffer, The Saul Zaentz Company & Orion Pictures, 1984.
5 Vincent P. de Luise, 'What Did Mozart Look Like? A Review of MozartIconography', amusicalvision.blogspot.com/2017/03/what-did-mozart-look-like.html
6 Robert Lee Hotz, 'Study Finds That Mozart Music Makes You Smarter', www.latimes.com/archives/la-xpm-1993-10-14-mn-45497-story.html
7 Frances H. Rauscher et al., 'Music and Spatial Task Performance', www.nature.com/articles/365611a0
8 Will Dowd, 'The Myth of the Mozart Effect', www.proquest.com/docview/225218927?sourcetype=Magazines
9 Kevin Sack, 'Georgia's Governor Seeks Musical Start for Babies', www.nytimes.com/1998/01/15/us/georgia-s-governor-seeks-musical-start-for-babies.html
10 Megan Shoop, 'What Is Spatial-Temporal Reasoning?', www.wisegeek.com/what-is-spatial-temporal-reasoning.htm

11 Matthew Rye (ed.), *1001 Classical Recordings You Must Hear Before You Die*, Universe, New York, 2007, p. 167.
12 Suchet, *Mozart: The Man Revealed*, p. ix.
13 Allan Kozinn, 'Annie Fischer, Pianist, Was 81; Noted for Insight and Musicality', www.nytimes.com/1995/04/13/obituaries/annie-fischer-pianist-was-81-noted-for-insight-and-musicality.html?mcubz=0
14 Konrad Wolff quoted by David Ewen (ed.) in *The Complete Book of Classical Music*, Robert Hale, London, 1989, p. 214.

2. The Rite of Stravinsky

1 Michael Oliver, *20th Century Composers: Igor Stravinsky*, Phaidon, London, 1995, p. 11.
2 Igor Stravinsky, *An Autobiography*, WW Norton & Company, New York, 1962, p. 7.
3 *Ibid.*, p. 26.
4 *Ibid.*, p. 27.
5 *Ibid.*, p. 29.
6 Oliver, *20th Century Composers: Igor Stravinsky*, p. 52.
7 Stravinsky, *An Autobiography*, p. 31.
8 'Fantasia', www.rottentomatoes.com/m/fantasia
9 Deems Taylor, from narration to 'The Rite of Spring' in *Fantasia*, Walt Disney Animation Studios, United States, 1941.
10 Stravinsky, *An Autobiography*, p.31
11 'Notes on Stravinsky's *The Rite of Spring*', fuocoso.wordpress.com/2014/07/01/notes-on-stravinskys-the-rite-of-spring/
12 Stravinsky, *An Autobiography*, p. 40.
13 *Ibid.*, p. 41.
14 Sue Roe, *In Montparnasse: Picasso, Matisse and Modernism in Paris, 1900–1910*, Fig Tree, London, 2014, p. 14.

15 *Ibid.*, p. 14.
16 Stravinsky, *An Autobiography*, p.47.
17 *Ibid.*, p. 34.
18 *Ibid.*, p. 48.
19 Video of the Mariinsky Ballet performance of 2013, celebrating the 100-year anniversary of *Le Sacre du Printemps*, www.youtube.com/watch?v=u7835eiU8iM
20 Tom Service, '*The Rite of Spring*: "The work of a madman"', www.theguardian.com/music/2013/feb/12/rite-of-spring-stravinsky
21 'Stravinsky: *The Rite of Spring*', *All in a Chord*, www.bbc.co.uk/programmes/b088973x
22 *Ibid.*
23 *Ibid.*
24 *Ibid.*
25 'Stravinsky: *The Rite of Spring* (CD review)', Classical Candor, classicalcandor.blogspot.com/2013/05/stravinsky-rite-of-spring-cd-review.html
26 'Igor Stravinsky: An "Inirentor of Music" Whose Works Created a Revolution', www.nytimes.com/1971/04/07/archives/igor-stravinsky-an-inventor-of-music-whose-works-created-a.html
27 *Ibid.*
28 'Stravinsky in South Africa', www.bbc.co.uk/programmes/p058zhsn
29 Service, '*The Rite of Spring*', www.theguardian.com/music/2013/feb/12/rite-of-spring-stravinsky
30 Stravinsky, *An Autobiography*, p. 53.
31 *Ibid.*, p. 163.

3. The Feelings of Ferrier

1 'Blow the Wind Southerly', traditional song from Northumberland, Roud Folk Song Index, archives.vwml.org/songs/RoudFS/S138338

2 Rupert Christiansen, 'Where have all the contraltos gone?', www.telegraph.co.uk/culture/music/classicalmusic/7309084/Where-have-all-the-contraltos-gone.html#

3 Maurice Leonard, *Kathleen: The Life of Kathleen Ferrier 1912–1953*, Hutchinson, London, 1988, p. 30.

4 *Ibid.*, p. 55.

5 Ian Jack, 'Klever Kaff' in *Granta 76: Music*, Granta, London, 2001, p. 91.

6 Leonard, *Kathleen*, p. 19.

7 Rupert Christiansen in *Blow the Wind Southerly (book & CD)*, The Kathleen Ferrier Awards, 2012, pp.18–19.

8 Paul Strang in *Blow the Wind Southerly*, The Kathleen Ferrier Awards, 2012, p. 3.

9 Leonard, *Kathleen*, p. 80.

10 Kazuma Mori and Makoto Iwanaga, 'Two types of peak emotional responses to music: The psychophysiology of chills and tears', www.nature.com/articles/srep46063

11 Kathleen Ferrier speaking, www.youtube.com/watch?v=aq3cnT7PzNQ

12 Graham Spicer, 'Kathleen Ferrier: on the 70th anniversary of her death, eminent friends remember her', www.gramilano.com/2023/10/kathleen-ferrier-memoirs/

13 Leonard, *Kathleen*, p. 99.

14 Jack, 'Klever Kaff', p. 98.

15 Jack, 'Klever Kaff', p. 109.

16 Leonard, *Kathleen*, p. 113.

17 *Ibid.*, p. 181.
18 *Ibid.*, p. 195.
19 *Blow the Wind Southerly* (CD).
20 Leonard, *Kathleen*, p. 246.
21 *Blow the Wind Southerly*, p. 18.
22 Jack, 'Klever Kaff', p. 98.
23 *Blow the Wind Southerly*, p. 7.
24 *Ibid.*, p. 19.
25 Anno Hellenbroich, 'Johannes Brahms' "Four Serious Songs" – An Introduction', archive.schillerinstitute.com/fid_02-06/032_brahms.html
26 Jack, 'Klever Kaff', p. 105.
27 *Ibid.*, p. 110.
28 *Blow the Wind Southerly*, p. 17.

4. The Love of Brahms

1 Joe Staines and Duncan Clark (ed.), *The Rough Guide to Classical Music*, Rough Guides, London, 2005, p. 94.
2 Harold C. Schonberg, *The Lives of the Great Composers*, Abacus, London, 1998, p. 336.
3 John Cleese and Connie Booth, 'A Touch of Class', *Fawlty Towers*, first aired 19 September 1975 by BBC Two, London.
4 Clemency Burton-Hill, *Year of Wonder*, Headline, London, 2017, p. 113.

5. The Serendipities of Schumann

1 Harold C. Schonberg, *The Lives of the Great Composers*, Abacus, London, 1998, p. 180.
2 *Ibid.*, p. 181.
3 Ray Minshull, sleeve notes, *Schumann Kinderszenen*, Decca, 2000.

4 'Clifford Curzon', Naxos, www.naxos.com/Bio/Person/Clifford_Curzon/7004
5 Colm Tóibín, *Brooklyn*, screenplay by Nick Hornby, Lionsgate Films, 2015.
6 Janice Galloway, 'Clara' in *Granta 76: Music*, Granta, London, 2001, p. 227.
7 Anna Beer, *Sounds and Sweet Airs*, Oneworld, London, 2016, p. 201–11.
8 *Ibid.*, p. 214.
9 Colleen Wheelahan, 'From the Repertoire List of Clara Schumann', 91classical.org/post/from-the-repertoire-list-of-clara-schumann/
10 Monica Steegmann, *Clara Schumann*, Haus Publishing, London, 2004, p. 50.
11 *Ibid.*, p. 51.
12 *Ibid.*, p. 51.
13 Robert Schumann and Steven Isserlis, *Robert Schumann's Advice to Young Musicians*, Faber, London, 2016, p. 46.
14 *Ibid.*, p. 19.

6. The Swan Songs of Sibelius

1 '01. First symphony op. 39 (1899–1900)', sibelius.fi/en/the-music/orchestral-works/symphonies-1-7/first-symphony-op-39-1899-1900/
2 Christopher Nupen, *Jean Sibelius: The Early Years*, Allegro Films, 1984, remastered 2006.
3 Guy Rickards, *Jean Sibelius*, Phaidon, London, 2008, p. 134.
4 Christopher Nupen, *Jean Sibelius: Maturity & Silence*, Allegro Films, 1984, remastered 2006.
5 *Ibid.*

6 Rickards, *Jean Sibelius*, p. 79.
7 Nupen, *Jean Sibelius: The Early Years*.
8 'Where Sibelius Fell Silent' by Julian Barnes, in Maggie Fergusson (ed.), *Treasure Palaces: Great Writers Visit Great Museums*, The Economist Books, London, 2017, p. 145.
9 'Aino Sibelius (1871–1969)', sibelius.fi/en/ainola/the-occupants-of-ainola/aino-sibelius/
10 'A child's death, and international breakthrough, 1900-1902', sibelius.fi/en/the-man/a-childs-death-and-international-breakthrough-1900-1902/
11 Rickards, *Jean Sibelius*, p. 114.
12 Nupen, *Jean Sibelius: Maturity & Silence*.
13 *Ibid.*
14 *Ibid.*
15 *Ibid.*
16 Rickards, *Jean Sibelius*, p. 191.

7. The Consolations of Chopin

1 Paul Kildea, *Chopin's Piano: A Journey Through Romanticism*, Penguin, London, 2019, p. 51.
2 Julian Harris and André Lévêque, *Basic Conversational French*, *Daily Express* Language Courses, London, 1962, p. 23.
3 'Song without Words No. 2 in F-sharp minor, Opus 67', Classical Connect, www.classicalconnect.com/Piano_Music/Mendelssohn/Song_without_Words/1448
4 Kildea, *Chopin's Piano*, p. 111.
5 David Ewen (ed.), *The Complete Book of Classical Music*, Robert Hale, London, 1989, p. 504.
6 'Quiz: Are you logical or emotional, based on your taste in music?', Classic FM, www.classicfm.com/lifestyle/quizzes/quiz-logical-emotional-taste-in-music/

7 'Classical pianist and conductor Murray Perahia', NPR, www.npr.org/2002/09/27/1150719/classical-pianist-and-conductor-murray-perahia

8. The Soul of Strauss

1 Tim Ashley, *Richard Strauss*, Phaidon, London, 1999, p. 163.
2 *Ibid.*, p. 164.
3 Philippe Sands, 'Why did Richard Strauss write music for a Nazi war criminal?', www.theguardian.com/music/2014/may/23/richard-strauss-composer-classical-music-nazi-war-criminal
4 'Richard Strauss', Music and the Holocaust, holocaustmusic.ort.org/politics-and-propaganda/third-reich/strauss-richard/
5 Ashley, *Richard Strauss*, p. 69.
6 *Ibid.*, p. 71.
7 *Ibid.*, p. 200.
8 Joseph von Eichendorff, 'Im Abendrot' from *Frühling und Liebe in Gedichte,* Simion, Berlin, 1841. Translated from the German by the author.

Unbound is a publisher which champions bold, unexpected books.

We give readers the opportunity to support books directly, so our authors are empowered to take creative risks and write the books they really want to write. We help readers to discover new writing they won't find anywhere else.

We are building a community in which authors engage directly with people who love what they do. It's a place where readers and writers can connect with and support one another, enjoy unique experiences and benefits, and make books that matter.

This book is in your hands because readers made it possible. Everyone who pledged their support is listed below. Join them by visiting unbound.com and supporting a book today.

Raphael Abrahams
Caitlin Allen
Helen Andrews
Bernard Angell
Christine Asbury
Sarah Aspinall
Helena Attlee
Anna Bailey
Jane Bailey
Richard Baker
Alison Barrow

Alison Baxter
Sarah Beal
Genevieve Benest
Vicky Bennett
Michael Bhaskar
Nick Blackburn
Elaine Blatchford
Louise Brice
David Brookes
Mark Brookes
Caroline Brown

Lauren Brown
Fiona Brownlee
Nancy Campbell
Keggie Carew
Alicia Carey
Caroline Carpenter
Jane Churchill
Hugh Comerford
Peter Conradi
James Cook
Jude Cook
Amanda Craig
Vybarr Cregan-Reid
Andrea Darby
Fiona Davidson
Caitlin Davies
Rachael de Moravia
Jenny Dee
Jane Duffy
Lily Dunn
Owen Eastwood
Sarah Edghill
Jean Egbunike
Susan Elkin
Camilla Elworthy
Katie Fforde
Nathan Filer
Angela Findlay
Molly Flatt
Susan Fletcher
Alison Flood

Lucas Fothergill
Emma Gannon
Jamila Gavin
Julia Gilbert
Tom Gillingwater
Melanie Golding
Peter Grayson
John Greening
Mark Guest
Tessa Harris
Grace Harrison
Caroline Harrowby
Conroy Harrowby
Christine Headley
Charlotte Heathcote
Vernon Hendy
Paul Henry
Helene Hewett
Liam Hinkley
Mary Hulford
Jo James
Katie Jarvis
Cindy Jefferies
Dinah Jefferies
Denton John
Liz Johnson
Margaret Jones
Mark Jones
Nicolette Jones
Philip Jones
Christine Jordan

Anne Joseph
Rachel Joyce
Jackie Kabler
Jonathan Kennedy
Ruth Killick
Kathryn King
Stephen Kinsella
Alexis Kirschbaum
Emily Koch
Roman Krznaric
Pierre L'Allier
Patrick Limb
Rowan Limb
Little Toller Books
Elizabeth Loudon
Isabel Losada
Charlotte Lyster
Anne MacAskill
Helen Macdonald
Iain MacGregor
Katherine MacInnes
Clare Mackintosh
Ira Mathur
Katherine May
Stephen May
Beth McHattie
Paul McLaughlin
Katharine McMahon
Diane Mezzanotte
Lisa Milton
John Mitchinson

Jonathan Mogford
Bel Mooney
Georgina Moore
Ann Morgan
Eve Morgan-Lace
Polly Morland
Georgina Morley
Steve Morley
Tony Morris
JLM Morton
Mummy - Miles & Edward
Helen H Murray
Tiffany Murray
Dave Mutton
Shannon Newton
Fiona Noble
Alice O'Keeffe
Sheila O'Reilly
Nikki Owen
Sabrina Pace-Humphreys
Benedicte Page
Laura Parker
Penny Parkes
Christina Patterson
AJ Pearce
Hannah Persaud
Nicki Pettitt
Lizzie Pickering for Laura Parker
Jennifer Powell
Paul Powell

Victoria Powell
Alex Preston
Katharine Quarmby
Katie Read
Jini Reddy
Cathy Rentzenbrink
Patricia Reyburn
Amanda Reynolds
David Reynolds
John Richardson
Mandy Robotham
Katie Roden
Meg Sanders
Margaret Sanderson
Bill Scott-Kerr
Svenja Segchelhoorn
Anita Sethi
Tanya Shadrick
Dominique Shead
Katri Skala
Louise Slater
Dr Ann Kennedy Smith
Charmian Spencer
Christina Stead
Sarah Steele
Sue Wilson Stephens
Gillian Stern
Fiona Stewart

Nina Stibbe
Nicholas Sumner
Bev Thomas
Ian Thomas-Bignami
Tom Tivnan
Maggie Tolman
Carole Tonkinson
Svitlana Trevor
James Upsher
Mira Upsher
Maria Vassilopoulos
Gaia Vince
Susanna Wadeson
Lucy Ward
Rachel Ward
Jenna Warren
Rachel Webster
Marie-France Weiner
Tony Whelpton
Tony White
Rachel & Toby Whitty
Louise Willder
Anna Wilson
Rebecca Wolman
Heloise Wood
Jon Woolcott
Debbie Young
Doug Young

In Memoriam

This book was also supported in memory of the following people.

Arthur Anthony Asbury
Vernon Hendy
Professor Christopher Johnson (1958-2017)
Irvine Loudon
Bernard McLaughlin
Hermannes Segchelhoorn